Learning Cocoa

Learning Cocoa

Apple Computer, Inc.

O'REILLY®

Beijing · Cambridge · Farnham · Köln · Paris · Sebastopol · Taipei · Tokyo

Learning Cocoa
by Apple Computer, Inc.

Copyright © 2001 O'Reilly & Associates, Inc. All rights reserved.
Printed in the United States of America.

Published by O'Reilly & Associates, Inc., 101 Morris Street, Sebastopol, CA 95472.

Editor: Troy Mott

Production Editor: Ann Schirmer

Cover Designer: Emma Colby

Printing History:

May 2001: First Edition.

ISBN: 0-596-00160-6
[M]   [6/01]

Table of Contents

Preface

When you begin any enterprise, you must find a starting point. You set out from that starting point and acquire a basic vocabulary, a notion of boundaries and techniques, and a sense of how things fit together and what is possible. For those who want to learn how to create Cocoa applications, this book provides such a starting point.

This book eases your way into the experience of Cocoa programming. It encourages you to play, explore, and "kick the tires." When you finish this book, you will be much better prepared to take on serious application development with Cocoa. Working through this book will not only make Apple's development environment less mysterious, but also will make it an environment you'll want to program in.

Extensive programming experience is not required to complete the examples in this book, though some experience with the C programming language is helpful. The code for each example is included in the text so you can simply type it in, and you can access the examples at the site listed in the URLs that follow. If you're already familiar with an object-oriented programming language like Java or Smalltalk, you'll quickly feel right at home with Objective-C, used throughout this book.

No prior experience programming on Mac OS X is necessary to complete the tutorials in this book. You may at some point want to explore the wealth of developer documentation that Apple includes with Mac OS X. In /Developer/Documentation, you'll find detailed information on the Mac OS X system architecture, developer tools, release notes, and so on. Most Cocoa programming documentation is located in /Developer/Documentation/Cocoa, where you'll find information about programming using the Objective-C language, along with Cocoa API reference documentation, including specifications of classes, protocols, functions, types, and constants. You can access this documention using Apple Help. Go to Developer Help Center, then choose Cocoa.

The programming examples in this book can be found on the Apple web site at:

http://developer.apple.com/techpubs/macosx/Cocoa/CocoaTopics.html

And on the O'Reilly site at:

http://www.oreilly.com/catalog/learncocoa

Although the aim is primarily to educate, this book is also intended—for those interested in programming—to be fun.

Organization of This Book

Learning Cocoa is structured in three parts.

Part I, Cocoa Overview

Cocoa Overview introduces the Cocoa frameworks and describes the high-level features they provide application programmers. It also includes a brief introduction to object-oriented programming, the Objective-C language, and the development tools used in Cocoa programming.

Chapter 1, *Introduction to Cocoa*, explains the history of Cocoa, places it in the context of the Mac OS X programming environment, and introduces the frameworks and classes that make up the Cocoa API.

Chapter 2, *Object-Oriented Programming*, makes clear the benefits of OOP practices as compared to procedural programming. It also provides an introduction to the terminology and core concepts that you must understand to effectively use the Cocoa frameworks that are introduced in Chapter 1.

Chapter 3, *Objective-C Primer*, covers the basics of the Objective-C programming language.

Chapter 4, *Development Tools*, begins by introducing Project Builder and Interface Builder, the primary tools used in Cocoa development. It then goes on to describe the wide array of tools and utilities available to assist in building, debugging, and performance tuning applications on Mac OS X.

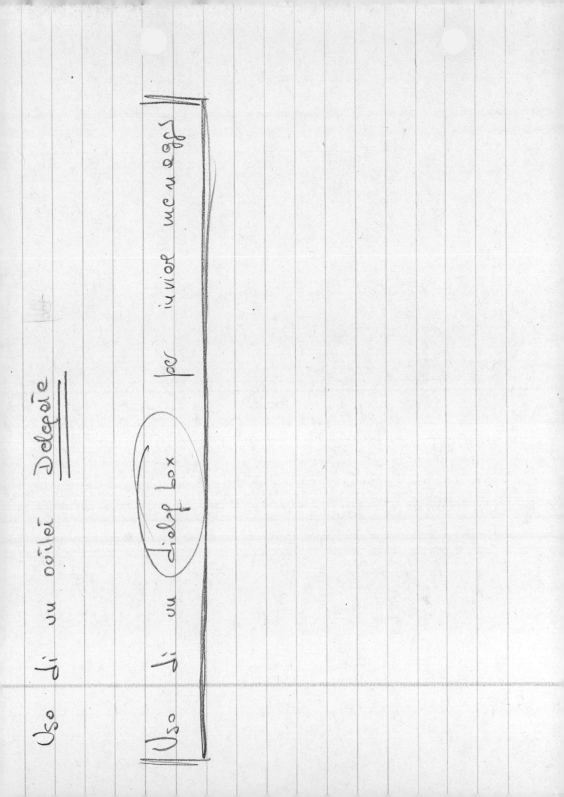

Part II, Single-Window Applications

Single-Window Applications begins with some simple tutorials to help you become familiar with the basic elements of Cocoa programming. It then proceeds to guide you through the creation of a series of increasingly complex example applications. The techniques and concepts you learn in one tutorial lay the foundation for the more advanced techniques and concepts in the next.

Chapter 5, *Hello World*, is a short tutorial that shows you how to use the Mac OS X development environment to create a traditional Hello World application for Cocoa.

Chapter 6, *Essential Cocoa Paradigms*, uses a series of minitutorials to introduce the most fundamental design patterns used in constructing Cocoa applications.

Chapter 7, *Currency Converter Tutorial*, shows how to build a simple application from beginning to end, giving you an opportunity to experience the complete work flow typical of Cocoa application development. You'll also learn to use a common object-oriented design paradigm called Model-View-Controller.

Chapter 8, *Event Handling*, focuses on events—both user and program generated—and how, as a programmer, you intercept, handle, and coordinate them in Cocoa.

Chapter 9, *Data Functionality*, uses a simple tutorial application to introduce table views—user interface objects that display data as rows and columns. In the second part of the chapter, you'll extend the application so that it can save its data to persistent storage.

Chapter 10, *Travel Advisor Tutorial*, completes Part II of the book with a large tutorial that gives you an opportunity to combine all of the techniques that you have learned so far in a single application. Travel Advisor is a forms-based application used to maintain travel-related information associated with various countries to which the user travels.

Part III, Multiple-Window Applications

Multiple-Window Applications uses an extended tutorial (interwoven with key conceptual material) that shows you how to build a complex document-based application with Cocoa's multiple-document architecture. You'll design and code an application called To Do that allows you to go to specific dates on a calendar and enter a list of appointments or tasks for a particular day.

Chapter 11, *Cocoa's Multiple-Document Architecture*, describes Cocoa's remarkable architecture that drastically simplifies the work developers must do to implement a multidocument application.

Chapter 12, *To Do: Basics*, walks you through the design and initial creation of the To Do application using Cocoa's multiple-document architecture.

Chapter 13, *To Do: Extended*, takes you through the process of adding advanced features to the application you created in Chapter 12. You'll add a Mac OS X Info window for setting various to-do item attributes such as alarms and due date rescheduling.

Chapter 14, *To Do: Finishing Touches*, wraps up the To Do application by adding some final polish. You'll prepare the application for deployment by turning on compiler optimization, adding application and document icons, and configuring build settings to include things like version information and an application signature.

Appendix A, *Drawing in Cocoa*, provides an introduction to drawing using the Cocoa and Core Graphics (Quartz) APIs.

Conventions Used in This Book

The following typographical conventions are used in this book:

Italic is used for introducing new terms and to indicate URLs.

`Constant width` is used to indicate command-line computer output and code examples, as well as filenames, data types, directories and pathnames, functions, constants, variables, and flow-control statements like `repeat`.

`Constant-width bold` is used to indicate user input.

How to Contact Us

We have tested and verified the information in this book to the best of our ability, but you may find that features have changed (or even that we have made mistakes!). Please let us know about any errors you find, as well as your suggestions for future editions, by writing to:

O'Reilly & Associates, Inc.
101 Morris Street
Sebastopol, CA 95472
(800) 998-9938 (in the United States or Canada)
(707) 829-0515 (international/local)
(707) 829-0104 (fax)

You can also send us messages electronically. To be put on the mailing list or request a catalog, send email to:

info@oreilly.com

To ask technical questions or comment on the book, send email to:

bookquestions@oreilly.com

The web site for *Learning Cocoa* lists examples, errata, and plans for future editions. You can access this page at:

http://www.oreilly.com/catalog/learncocoa

For more information about this book and others, see the O'Reilly web site:

http://www.oreilly.com

I

Cocoa Overview

1

Introduction to Cocoa

Cocoa is an extensive library of reusable software components used for building applications that run on Mac OS X. You can think of Cocoa as a large set of application building blocks that you can use "off the shelf" or adapt for your specific needs. This chapter gives you a high-level overview of those building blocks, shows you how they are organized, and explains the features they provide.

Cocoa poses a learning curve for newcomers, but once you learn to use it, application development will suddenly seem far easier and more fun. Because the Cocoa frameworks give you so much fundamental application functionality "for free," you can spend your time and creative energy building new technology, not reinventing the wheel.

Cocoa has actually been around a long time— almost as long as the Macintosh itself. That's because it is to a large extent based on OpenStep, which as NeXTSTEP was introduced in 1987. OpenStep evolved through many releases, was adopted by many companies as their development and deployment environment of choice, and received glowing reviews in the press. It was, and continues to be, solid technology, based on a design that was years ahead of anything else in the market and it has been perfected year after year.

Let's take a closer look at Cocoa's features and frameworks to give you a better idea of how to use Cocoa to create various applications. Figure 1-1 shows the general structure of the Mac OS X system software.

Cocoa is one of the principal application environments for Mac OS X. Cocoa's advanced object-oriented APIs allow you to develop applications written in Java and Objective-C. Cocoa is an integrated set of shared object libraries, or *frameworks*, plus a runtime system and development environment that does three principal things:

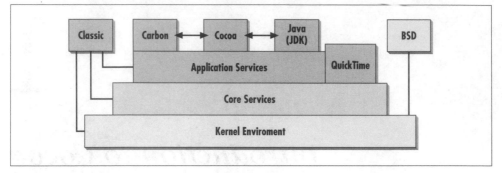

Figure 1-1. Cocoa is part of Mac OS X's system software

- Insulates programs from the internal workings of the core operating system, mediating access to system resources and preventing programs from trashing one another's address space

- Provides all infrastructure that programs typically need

- Brings the benefits of object orientation to program development

You can think of Cocoa as a layer of objects that acts as mediator and facilitator between programs and the core operating system. The stability, performance, and reliability of these programs therefore depend on the underlying core operating system having these characteristics.

Cocoa Features

This section describes some of the high-level features available to you when you develop using Cocoa.

Imaging and Printing Model

The imaging and printing model for Mac OS X is Adobe's Portable Document Format (PDF). Unlike in previous versions of the Mac OS, the same mechanism is used to view and print what appears on the screen. You no longer have to duplicate code to send output both to the screen and to PostScript-based devices. The best of Apple's graphics technologies, including ColorSync and QuickDraw GX typography, is being brought to core graphics.

Multimedia

Cocoa applications can take advantage of some of the most powerful technologies available—QuickTime and OpenGL.

QuickTime

Mac OS X comes packaged with the latest version of QuickTime. QuickTime is a powerful multimedia technology used for manipulating, enhancing, and storing video, sound, animation, graphics, text, music, and even 360-degree virtual reality.

QuickTime streaming allows users to view live and video-on-demand movies using the industry-standard protocols RTP (Real-Time Transport Protocol) and RTSP (Real-Time Streaming Protocol). Users can view streaming live broadcasts, previously recorded movies, or a mixture of both. Broadcasts can be either unicast (one-to-one) or multicast (one-to-many).

OpenGL

Mac OS X includes Apple's highly optimized implementation of OpenGL as the system API and library for three-dimensional (3D) graphics. OpenGL is an industry-wide standard for developing portable 3D graphics applications. OpenGL is one of the most widely adopted graphics API standards today, which makes code written to OpenGL highly portable. It is specifically designed for games, animation, CAD/CAM, medical imaging, and other applications that need a rich, robust framework for visualizing shapes in two and three dimensions. Mac OS X's version of OpenGL produces consistently high-quality graphical images at a high level of performance.

OpenGL offers a broad and powerful set of imaging functions, including texture mapping, hidden surface removal, alpha blending (transparency), antialiasing, pixel operations, viewing and modeling transformations, atmospheric effects (fog, smoke, and haze), and other special effects. Each OpenGL command directs a drawing action or causes special effects, and developers can create lists of these commands for repetitive effects. Although OpenGL is largely independent of the windowing characteristics of each operating system, special "glue" routines are implemented to enable OpenGL to work in an operating system's windowing environment.

Internet

Apple intends for Mac OS X to be a major technological force on the Internet. The development platform features APIs for Internet-based mail, messaging, directories, and security services. Cocoa also offers built-in HTML rendering capabilities.

Localization and Internationalization

You can easily localize Cocoa applications largely because of a well-designed localization architecture and Unicode support, both built into the frameworks. In this architecture, user interface elements are kept separate from the executable. It's therefore possible to have a single code base that is qualified for various locales. You can even have multiple localizations bundled with one application, greatly reducing the overall footprint of an application in its various localizations. Your localization bundles can be added to or removed from an existing application easily, making new localizations distributable through updaters.

Because Cocoa uses Unicode 2.0 as its native character set, applications can easily handle all of the world's living languages. The prevalence of Unicode also eliminates many character-encoding hassles. To help you handle non-Unicode text, Cocoa also provides APIs to help you translate between Unicode and other major character sets in use today.

Apple's development environment supports localization in several important ways. It gives you an easy way to identify which files are to be localized (and for which language). It also enables you to create a series of archivable user interfaces, each designed for a particular locale.

Text and Fonts

Cocoa offers a powerful set of text services that can be readily adapted by text-intensive applications requiring high performance. These services, which can support text buffers as large as the virtual memory space, include kerning, ligatures, tab formatting, and rulers. The text system also supports embedded graphics and other inline attachments.

Cocoa supports a variety of font formats, including Type 1 PostScript, Type 3 PostScript, Type 42 PostScript, and TrueType (including the typographic capabilities of TrueType GX). The goal for Mac OS X is an open font architecture that makes it easy for users to work with any font format they want.

Component Technologies

One of the key advantages of Cocoa as a development environment is the capability to develop programs quickly and easily by assembling reusable components. With the proper programming tools and a little work, you can build Cocoa components that can be packaged and distributed for use by others. Applications are an obvious example of this component technology, but there are others. With Cocoa and Apple's development tools, you can create:

- Frameworks that other developers can use to create programs by writing code based on the framework APIs

- Bundles containing executable code and associated resources that programs can load dynamically

- Palettes containing custom user interface objects that other developers can drag and drop into their own user interfaces using Mac OS X development tools

With Cocoa's component architecture, you can easily create and distribute extensions and plug-ins for applications.

The Cocoa Frameworks

Cocoa has two object-oriented frameworks: Foundation (`Foundation.framework`) and Application Kit (`AppKit.framework`), as shown in Figure 1-2.

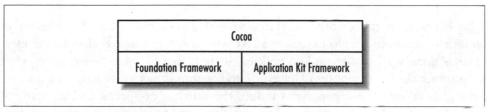

Figure 1-2. The Cocoa frameworks

The classes in Foundation provide objects and functionality that are the basis, or "foundation," of Cocoa. The classes in Application Kit furnish the objects and behavior that your users see in the user interface, such as windows and buttons, and handle their mouse clicks and key presses. The Application Kit depends directly on Foundation.

Foundation

The Foundation framework defines a base layer of Objective-C classes. Besides providing a set of useful primitive object classes, it introduces several paradigms that define functionality not covered by the Objective-C language (detailed in Chapter 3, *Objective-C Primer*). The Foundation Framework is designed with these goals in mind:

- Provide a set of basic utility classes.

- Make software development easier by introducing consistent conventions for paradigms such as memory management.

- Support Unicode strings, object persistence, and file management.

The Foundation framework includes the root object class, classes representing basic data types such as strings and byte arrays, collection classes for storing other objects, classes representing system information like dates and classes representing communication ports. Figure 1-3 shows the features provided by Foundation.

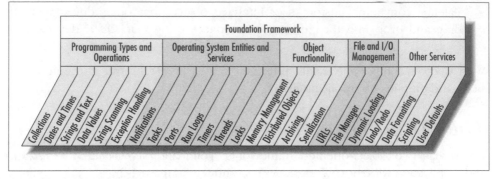

Figure 1-3. The Foundation framework's features

The Foundation framework introduces several paradigms to avoid confusion in common situations and to introduce a level of consistency across class hierarchies. This is done with some standard policies, such as that for object ownership (who is responsible for disposing of objects), and with abstract classes that enumerate over collections. These paradigms reduce the number of special and exceptional cases in API and allow you to code more efficiently by reusing the same mechanisms with various kinds of objects.

The following sections cover some of the highlights of the Foundation framework.

Programming types and operations

Cocoa's Foundation framework provides many basic data types, including strings, arrays, dictionaries, and numbers. Foundation furnishes several classes whose purpose is to hold other objects—the collection classes. You'll learn more about these data types throughout the chapters in this book.

Foundation also provides functions for byte swapping, as well as classes for parsing and exception handling.

Collections.   Collections allow you to organize and retrieve your data in a logical manner. These collection classes are very useful, as they can store and locate their contents through a number of mechanisms:

* Arrays store and retrieve objects in an ordered fashion through zero-based indexing.

* Dictionaries store and retrieve objects quickly using key-value pairs. For example, the key "TextColor" may be associated with a color object representing red.

- Sets are unordered collections of distinct elements.

- Counted sets are sets that can contain duplicate (nondistinct) elements; these duplicates are tracked through a counter. Use sets when the speed of membership testing is important.

Collection objects provide a valuable way to store data. When you store (or archive) a collection object in the file system, its constituent objects are also stored.

The collection classes come in two versions: mutable and immutable. The mutable versions of these classes allow you to add and remove objects programmatically after the collection object is created; the immutable versions do not.

Cocoa collections are all dynamically growable.

The collection classes are discussed in greater detail in Chapter 6, *Essential Cocoa Paradigms*.

Dates and times. Date and time classes offer methods for calculating temporal differences, for displaying dates and times in any desired format, and for adjusting dates and times based on location.

Strings and text. String objects represent character strings. Almost all text in an application—from labels to spreadsheet entries to word-processing documents— uses strings. Specifically, NSStrings (or string objects) supplant that familiar C programming data type, `char *`. String objects contain Unicode characters rather than the narrow range of characters afforded by the ASCII character set. Hence, they can represent words in Chinese, Arabic, and many other languages.

The string classes provide an API to create both mutable and immutable strings and to perform string operations such as substring searching, string comparison, and concatenation.

Data and values. Data objects are object-oriented wrappers for byte buffers. Data objects let simple allocated buffers (that is, data with no embedded pointers) take on the behavior of Foundation objects. Data objects are typically used for data storage and are also useful in applications in which data contained in data objects can be copied or moved between applications.

Data objects can wrap data of any size. When the data size is more than a few memory pages, virtual memory management is used. A data object can also wrap existing data, regardless of how the data was allocated. The object contains no information about the data itself (such as its type); the responsibility for deciding how to use the data lies with the client. For typed data, there are value objects.

A value object is a simple container for a single data item. It can hold any of the scalar types, such as integers, floats, and characters, as well as pointers, structures, and object addresses. The purpose of these objects is to allow items of such data types to be added to collections, which require their elements to be objects.

String scanning.   String scanning interprets and converts the characters of a string into number and string values. The scanner progresses through the characters of the string from beginning to end as you request items from it.

While scanning, you can change the scan location to rescan a portion of the string after an error or to skip ahead a certain number of characters. You can also configure a scanner to skip a set of characters or to consider or ignore case.

Exception handling.   An exception is a special condition that interrupts the normal flow of program execution. Each application can interrupt the program for different reasons. For example, one application might interpret saving a file in a directory that's write-protected as an exception. In this sense, the exception is equivalent to an error. Foundation provides the functionality to implement exception handling and obtain information about an exception.

Operating system entities and services

Foundation provides you with classes to access core operating system functionality, such as locks, threads, and timers. These services all work together to create a robust environment for your application to run in.

Notifications. The notification-related classes implement a system for broadcasting notifications of changes within an application. Any object can specify and post a notification, and any other object can register itself as an observer of that notification. Notifications are discussed in greater detail in Chapter 8, *Event Handling.*

Threads.   A thread controls a thread of execution. You use a thread when you want to have a method run in its own thread of execution or if you need to terminate or delay the current thread.

A thread is an executable unit. A task is made up of one or more threads. Each thread has its own execution stack and is capable of independent input/output. All threads share the virtual memory address space and communication rights of their task. When a thread is started, it is detached from its initiating thread. The new thread runs independently. That is, the initiating thread does not know the new thread's state. Different threads can run on different CPUs on multiprocessor systems, even if both threads are running inside the same task.

Locks. A lock is used to coordinate the operation of multiple threads of execution within the same application. A lock can be used to mediate access to an application's global data or to protect a critical section of code, allowing it to run atomically—meaning that, at any given time, only one of the threads can access the protected resource.

Tasks. Using tasks, your program can run another program as a subprocess and monitor that program's execution. A task creates a separate executable entity; it differs from a thread in that it does not share memory space with the process that creates it.

Ports. A port represents a communication channel to or from another port, which typically resides in a different thread or task. The distributed objects system uses ports to send messages back and forth between threads or tasks.

Run loops. The run loop is the programmatic interface to objects managing input sources. A run loop processes input for sources such as mouse and keyboard events from the window system, ports, timers, and other connections.

Because of Foundation, your application doesn't need to either create or explicitly manage run loops. Each thread has a run loop automatically created for it. Each process begins with a default thread and therefore has a default run loop. Application Kit handles running the main thread's run loop, but other threads' run loops must be run manually.

Timers. You use timers to send a message to an object at specific intervals. For example, you could create a timer to tell a window to update itself after a certain time interval. Timers are discussed further in Chapter 13, *To Do: Extended*.

Object functionality

Foundation provides the functionality to manage your objects—from creating and destroying them to saving them and sharing them in a distributed environment.

Memory management. Memory management ensures that objects are properly deallocated when they're no longer needed. This mechanism, which depends on general conformance to a policy of object ownership, automatically tracks objects that are marked for release and deallocates them at the close of the current run loop. Understanding memory management is important in creating successful Cocoa applications and is discussed in greater detail in Chapter 6.

Distributed objects. Distributed objects is an interprocess messaging solution. This mechanism enables a Cocoa application to make one or more of its objects available to other applications.

Serialization and archiving. Serializers make it possible to represent the data an object contains in an architecture-independent format, allowing sharing of data across applications. Coders take this process a step further by storing class information along with the data, thereby enabling archiving and distribution.

Archiving stores encoded objects and other data in files. Distribution is the transmission of encoded object data between different processes, threads, or even machines.

You'll use archiving later in Chapter 9, *Data Functionality*.

File and I/O management

File system and I/O functionality includes URL handling, file management, and dynamic loading of code and localized resources.

URL handling. URLs and the resources they reference are accessible using Foundation. Foundation understands URLs as specified in RFCs 1808 and 1738.

URLs can be used to refer to files and are, in fact, the preferred way to do so. Cocoa objects that can read or write data from or to a file can usually accept a URL in addition to a pathname as the file reference.

Other services

The Foundation framework also provides the ability to manage user preferences, the undo and redo of actions, and data formatting. Cocoa applications can also be made responsive to AppleScript commands.

Application Kit

The Application Kit is a framework containing all objects you need to implement your graphical, event-driven user interface: windows, panels, buttons, menus, scrollers, and text fields, among others. The Application Kit handles all the details for you as it efficiently draws on the screen, communicates with hardware devices and screen buffers, clears areas of the screen before drawing, and clips views. Figure 1-4 shows the Application Kit's conceptual class hierarchy.

The more than one hundred classes in the Application Kit may seem daunting at first. However, most Application Kit classes are support classes that you use indirectly. The sections that follow briefly cover Application Kit's architectural highlights.

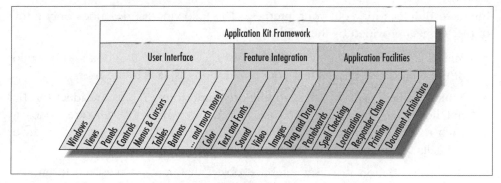

Figure 1-4. The Application Kit framework's features

User interface

Your user interface is how the user interacts with your application. You can create and manage the windows, dialog boxes, menus, pop-up lists, and other controls provided by Application Kit. You'll be using many user interface elements in the tutorials later in the book.

Windows. The two principal functions of a window are to provide an area in which views can be placed and to accept and distribute (to the appropriate views) events the user causes through actions with the mouse and keyboard.

You typically set up windows using Interface Builder, which allows you to position them, set up many of their visual and behavioral attributes, and lay out views in them. The programmatic work you do with windows more often involves bringing them on and off the screen; changing dynamic attributes, such as the window's title; and monitoring certain window actions, such as closing, zooming, and resizing.

Views. A view is an abstract representation for all objects displayed in a window. Views provide the structure for drawing, printing, and handling events. Views are arranged within a window in a nested hierarchy of subviews.

Panels. Panels are a type of window that you use to display transient, global, or pressing information. For example, you would use a panel rather than a window to display error messages or to query the user for a response to remarkable or unusual circumstances. The Application Kit implements some common panels for you, such as the Save, Open, and Print panels, used to save, open, and print documents. Using these panels gives the user a consistent look and feel across applications for common operations.

Controls. Cocoa provides a common set of user interface objects such as buttons, sliders, and browsers that you can manipulate graphically to control some aspect of your application. Just what a particular item does is up to you. You typically use

Interface Builder to lay out your interface. The following list describes only a few of the widgets provided by the Application Kit:

- **Menus and cursors**. The menu and cursor classes define the look and behavior of the menus and cursors that your application displays to the user.

- **Tables**. Tables display data in row and column form. Tables are ideal for, but not limited to, displaying database records, in which a row corresponds to each record and columns contain record attributes. The user can edit individual cells and rearrange the columns.

- **Buttons**. A button is a user interface object that sends a message to another object when clicked. You can create a single button, such as a push button, or a group of related buttons, such as a group of switches or radio buttons.

In addition to these widgets, Cocoa provides sheets, sliders, drawers, and toolbars, to name just a few.

Feature integration

The Application Kit gives your applications ways to integrate and manage colors, fonts, and printing (even providing the dialog boxes for these features).

Text and fonts.   Text fields implement a simple editable text field, and a text view provides more comprehensive editing features for larger text bodies. A Font panel allows users to customize fonts appearing in their text views.

Images.   Images encapsulate graphics data, allowing you to easily and efficiently access images stored in files on the disk and displayed on the screen. You do not need to know how to draw images of different formats because Cocoa handles this for you.

Color.   Color is supported by a variety of classes representing colors and color views. There is a rich set of color formats and representations, including custom ones. Cocoa color classes automatically handle different color spaces. The color support classes define and present panels and views that allow the user to select and apply colors. For example, the user can drag colors from the Color panel to any color well. You can also extend the standard Color panel.

Facilities

The Application Kit also provides a number of other facilities that allow you to create a robust application taking advantage of all the features your users expect from an application on Mac OS X.

Document architecture. Document-based applications, e.g., word processing and spreadsheet applications, are some of the more common types of applications developed today. Word processors and spreadsheet applications are two well-known examples of document-based applications.

Various Application Kit classes provide an architecture for document-based applications that simplifies the work you must do to implement the features listed in the previous section. These classes divide and orchestrate the work of creating, saving, opening, and managing the documents of an application. The document architecture is discussed in more detail in Chapter 11, *Cocoa's Multiple-Document Architecture.*

Responder chain. A responder chain is an ordered list of objects that respond to user events. When the user clicks the mouse or presses a key, an event is generated and the Application Kit searches in a specific order for an object that can "respond" to it. Understanding the flow of control in your application is discussed in Chapter 8.

Sharing data with other applications. The pasteboard is a repository for data that's copied from your application, and it makes this data available to any application that cares to use it. The pasteboard implements the familiar cut-copy-paste and drag-and-drop operations.

Drag and drop. With very little programming on your part, objects can be dragged and dropped anywhere. The Application Kit handles all the details of tracking the mouse and displaying the dragged image.

Printing. The printing classes work together to provide the means for printing the information that your application displays in its windows and views. You can also create a PDF representation of a view.

Accessing the file system. File wrappers correspond to files or directories on disk. A file wrapper holds the contents of the file in memory so that it can be displayed, changed, or transmitted to another application. It also provides an icon for dragging the file or representing it as an attachment. A file manager can be used to access and enumerate file and directory contents. The Open and Save panels also provide a convenient and familiar user interface to the file system.

Spellchecking. A spell server lets you define a spellchecking service and provide it to other applications. To connect your application to a spellchecking service, you use a spellchecker. Cocoa's text system provides automatic spellchecker integration.

Localization.   If an application is to be used in more than one part of the world, its resources may need to be customized, or "localized," for language, country, or cultural region. For example, an application may need to have separate Japanese, English, French, and German versions of character strings, icons, user interface definitions, or context help. Resource files specific to a particular language are grouped together in a subdirectory of the bundle directory (the directories with the `.lproj` extension). The localized resources that are appropriate to the user's preferences are then dynamically loaded into your application when it is launched.

2

Object-Oriented Programming

For some Mac OS developers, the most striking adjustment they'll make when they start developing Cocoa programs is not the tool set: it is the shift in mind-set that is required to take full advantage of object-oriented programming (OOP). Instead of thinking in terms of procedures and data, you have to think in terms of objects—discrete programmatic units containing their own data as well as procedures that act on that data.

You can't get far in Cocoa development without a grasp of the basic concepts of object-oriented programming. For those new to this approach to programming, it might seem strange at first glance, but a common reaction after learning a bit more is, "Yes, of course." This chapter presents an overview of object-oriented programming from the particular perspective of Objective-C. For additional background on OOP and Objective-C, see *Inside Cocoa: Object-Oriented Programming and the Objective-C Language* in /Developer/Documentation/Cocoa.

Learning how to program with objects takes some initial effort, but in a very short time, object-oriented programming begins to seem natural, elegant, and powerful. And, with the rich functionality of the Cocoa frameworks to tap, application development becomes easier—you get a huge number of application features "for free." Programming with objects, especially Cocoa objects, increases your productivity by freeing you from many repetitive coding tasks. You have more time to accomplish what is truly creative.

The Advantages of Object-Oriented Programming

Object orientation is the software equivalent of the Industrial Revolution. In the same way that modern factories assemble products out of prefabricated components rather than manufacture every product from scratch, object orientation allows programmers to build complex software by reusing software components called *objects*. Specifically, objects lead to several measurable advantages:

- **Greater reliability**. By breaking complex software projects into small, self-contained, and modular objects, object orientation ensures that changes to one part of a software project will not adversely affect other portions of the software. Being small, each of these objects is a well-tested module of code, so the overall reliability of the software increases.

- **Easier maintainability**. Since objects are modular and usually small (in terms of the overall code size of a project), bugs in code are easier to locate. Developers can also change the implementation of an object without causing havoc in other parts of an application.

- **Greater productivity through reuse**. One of the principal benefits of object orientation is reuse. One object can be integrated into many applications. You can also create new, specialized objects by inheriting functionality from an existing class and then adding new code to modify or extend that class's behavior. This technique reduces coding and promotes greater reliability because the new class implements only the behavior or logic specific to your application. It obtains basic functionality from Cocoa framework objects.

Object-oriented programming delivers its greatest benefits to large and complex programs. But its advantages can also be demonstrated using a very simple example.

With procedural programming techniques, the application is directly responsible for data manipulation. One problem with this is illustrated in Figure 2-1. It shows a data structure consisting of a count variable and a data pointer. Since the application directly manipulates the data, it has the opportunity to introduce inconsistencies. Here, it has added an item to the data but has forgotten to increment the count; the count variable says there are still only two data elements when in fact there are three. The structure has become inconsistent and unreliable.

Another problem with procedural programming techniques is that all parts of the application must have intimate knowledge about the structure of the data. If the allocation of data elements is changed from a statically allocated array to a dynamically allocated linked list, it would affect every part of the application that accesses, adds, or deletes elements from the list.

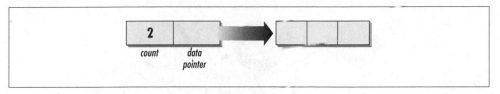

Figure 2-1. Data manipulation in procedural programs

With the procedural approach, the network of interaction between procedures and data becomes increasingly complex as an application grows. A simple change in data structure can affect many procedures and lines of code, and potentially many different source files—a nightmare for those who must maintain and enhance applications. Procedural programming also leads to nasty, hard-to-find bugs in which one function inadvertently changes data that another function relies on.

With an object-oriented programming paradigm, the application as a whole doesn't manipulate the data structure directly; rather, that task is entrusted to a particular object. Since the application doesn't access the data directly, it can't introduce inconsistencies. This feature of OOP is illustrated in Figure 2-2.

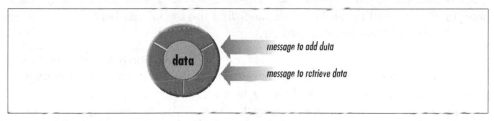

Figure 2-2. Data manipulation in an object-oriented program

Note that it's possible to change the implementation of the object without breaking other parts of the application. For example, the data storage method could be changed to optimize performance. If the object responds to the same messages, other parts of the application are unaffected by internal implementation details.

Programming with Objects

Object-oriented programming is more than just another way of organizing data and functions. It permits software engineers to conceive and construct solutions to complex programs using a model that resembles—much more so than traditional programs—the way we organize the world around us. The object-oriented model for program structure simplifies problem resolution by clarifying roles and relationships.

You can think of an object-oriented program as a network of objects with well-defined behavior and characteristics, objects that interact through messages, as depicted in Figure 2-3.

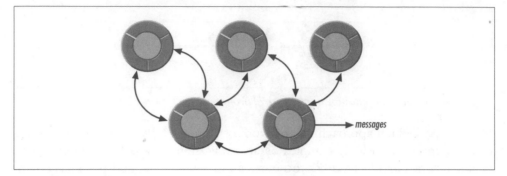

Figure 2-3. The object network in an object-oriented application

Different objects in the network play different roles. Some correspond to graphical elements in the user interface. In an application, each window is represented by a separate object, as is each button, menu item, or display of text.

Applications also assign to objects functionality that isn't directly apparent in the interface, giving each object a different area of responsibility. Some of these objects might perform very specific computational tasks, while others might manage the display and transfer of data, mediating the interaction between user interface objects and computational objects.

Once you've defined your objects, creating a program is largely a matter of "hooking up" these objects, creating the connections that objects will use to communicate with one another. The task is to fit your pieces with the pieces that are already provided by the Cocoa frameworks. As you'll realize after awhile, much of the task of writing object-oriented programs is simply implementing methods that respond to system-generated messages.

Fundamental Object-Oriented Concepts

There are only a handful of key concepts that you need to understand to grasp the essence of object-oriented programming. This section presents those key concepts along with Objective-C implementation details, where appropriate.

Objects

An object is a self-contained programmatic unit that combines data and the procedures that operate on that data. An object's data is kept in *instance variables*. The functions that affect or make use of the data in an object's instance variables are known as *methods*.

Like objects in the physical world, objects in a program have identifying characteristics and behavior. Often, programmatic objects are modeled on real objects. For example, an object such as a button has an analogue in the buttons on control devices, such as stereo equipment and telephones. A button object includes the data and code to generate an appearance on the screen that simulates a "real" button and to respond in a familiar way to user actions.

Encapsulation

Just as procedures compartmentalize code, objects compartmentalize both code and data. This results in data encapsulation, effectively surrounding data with the procedures for manipulating that data. Figure 2-4 shows this relationship between an object's data and its methods.

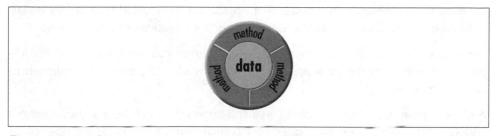

Figure 2-4. An object

Though it might look a bit like a jelly doughnut or a slashed tire, this symbol illustrates data encapsulation, the essential characteristic of objects. Other objects or external code cannot access the encapsulated data directly, but must send messages to the object requesting its data.

Typically, an object is regarded as a *black box*, meaning that a program never directly accesses an object's variables. Indeed, a program shouldn't even need to know what variables an object has in order to perform its functions. Instead, the program accesses the object only through its methods. In a sense, the methods surround the data, not only shielding an object's instance variables but mediating access to them.

Objects are the basic building blocks of object-oriented applications. By representing a responsibility in the problem domain, each object encapsulates a particular area of functionality that the program needs. The object's methods provide the interface to this functionality. For example, an object representing a database record both stores data and provides well-defined ways to access that data.

Using this modularity, object-oriented programs can be divided into distinct objects for specific data and specific tasks. Programming teams can easily parcel out areas of responsibility among individual members, agreeing on interfaces to the distinct objects while implementing data structures and code in the most efficient way for their specific area of functionality.

Classes

Some of the objects networked together in an application are of different kinds, and some may be of the same kind. Objects of the same kind belong to the same class. A *class* is a programmatic entity that creates instances of itself—objects. A class defines the structure and interface of its instances and specifies their behavior.

When you want a new kind of object, you define a new class. You can think of a class definition as a type definition for a kind of object. It specifies the data structure that all objects belonging to the class will have and the methods they will use to respond to messages. Any number of objects can be created from a single class definition. In this sense, a class is like a factory for a particular kind of object.

In terms of lines of code, an object-oriented program consists mainly of class definitions. The objects the program uses to do its work are created at runtime from class definitions.

A class is more than just an object "factory," however; it can be assigned methods and (in some object-oriented languages) contain variables, just as an object can. Unlike an instance variable, a class variable is not created each time a new instance of the class is created. There is only one copy of the variable for the entire class, no matter how many instances exist. Class methods are typically used to allow a variety of options for creating instances.

Methods and Messages

Methods are procedures implemented by a class for its objects (or, in the case of class methods, to provide functionality not tied to a particular instance). Methods can be public or private; public methods are declared in the class's header file, while private methods appear only in the class's implementation file.

Messages are the mechanism by which an object invokes methods. A message requests an object to perform some functionality or to return a value. In Objective-C, a message expression is enclosed in square brackets, as shown in Figure 2-5.

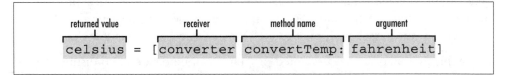

Figure 2-5. Objective-C message expressions

In Figure 2-5, converter is the *receiver*, the object that receives the message. Everything to the right of the receiver is the message itself; it consists of a method name and any arguments the method requires. The message received by `converter` tells it to convert a temperature from Fahrenheit to Celsius and return that value. In this example the conversion result is returned from `converter` and stored in the variable name `celsius`.

In Objective-C, every message argument is identified with a label. Arguments follow colon-terminated keywords, which are considered part of the method name. One argument per keyword is allowed. If a method has more than one argument—as NSString's `rangeOfString:options:` method does, for example—the name is broken apart to accept the arguments:

```
range = [string rangeOfString:@"Cocoa" options:NSLiteralSearch];
```

See Figure 2-6 for a breakdown.

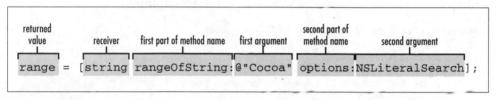

Figure 2-6. Objective-C message expression with multiple arguments

Often, but not always, messages return values to the sender of the message. Returned values must be received in a variable of an appropriate type. In the preceding example, the variable range must be of type NSRange. Messages that return values can be nested. By enclosing one message expression within another, you can use a returned value as an argument or as a receiver without having to declare a variable for it.

The following code fragment nests two other messages, each of which returns a value used as an argument. The innermost message expression is resolved first, then the next nested message expression is resolved, then the third message is sent and a value is returned and stored in `newString`:

```
newString = [stringOne stringByAppendingString:
        [substringFromRange:[stringTwo rangeOfString:
        @"Cocoa" options:NSAnchoredSearch]]];
```

Polymorphism and Dynamic Binding

Although the purpose of a message is to invoke a method, a message isn't the same as a function call. An object "knows about" only those methods that were defined for it or that it inherits. It can't confuse its methods with another object's methods, even if the methods are named identically.

Each object is a self-contained unit, with its own *namespace*—an area of the program where a symbol is uniquely recognized by name. Just as local variables within a C function are isolated from other parts of a program, so too are the variables and methods of an object. Thus if two different kinds of objects have the same names for their methods, both objects could receive the same message, but each would respond to it differently. The ability of one message to cause different behavior in different receivers is referred to as *polymorphism.*

The advantage polymorphism brings to application developers is significant. It helps improve program flexibility while maintaining code simplicity. With polymorphism, you can write code that might have an effect on a variety of objects without having to know at the time you write the code what objects they might be. Example 2-1 and Example 2-2 contrast two possible implementations of a general-purpose routine that displays different types of geometrical objects. The first example is written in C, which doesn't support polymorphism.

Example 2-1. Display Function Without Polymorphism

```
void displayShape(Shape ob)
{
    // Figure out what kind of shape we have.
    switch (ob->type) {
        case SQUARE:
            // Display a square.
            displaySquare(ob);
            break;
        case TRIANGLE:
            // Display a triangle.
            displayTriangle(ob);
            break;
        default:
            printf("Unknown Shape");
    }
}
```

In Example 2-1 you can see that each kind of shape must have a special case in the code. Adding a new shape object to the program would require modifying the display routine. Now compare this example with Example 2-2, written in Objective-C, which does support polymorphism.

Example 2-2. Display Function with Polymorphism

```
- (void) displayShape:(Shape *)ob
{
    // Send the display message to the shape object.
    [ob display];
}
```

Using polymorphism, as shown in Example 2-2, the displayShape: routine doesn't have to know what kind of object is being handled. In Objective-C (and other object-oriented languages), you can send the display message to any object that implements a display method, and the object will draw itself in its own way.

These examples also highlight the role of inheritance in polymorphism: a subclass often implements an identically named method (that is, overrides the method) of its superclass to achieve more specialized behavior.

Dynamic binding is perhaps even more useful than polymorphism. It means both the object receiving a message and the message that an object receives can be set within your program as it runs. This is particularly important in a graphical, user-driven environment, in which one user command—say, Copy or Paste—may apply to any number of user interface objects.

Using dynamic binding, a runtime process finds the method implementation appropriate for the receiver of the message; it then invokes this implementation and passes it the receiver's data structure. This mechanism makes it easier to structure programs that respond to selections and actions chosen by users at runtime.

For example, either or both parts of a message expression—the receiver and the method name—can be variables whose values are determined by user actions. A simple message expression can deliver a Cut, Copy, or Paste menu command to whatever object controls the current selection. Dynamic binding even enables applications to deal with new kinds of objects—ones that were not envisioned when the application itself was built.

Polymorphism and dynamic binding depend on two other features: dynamic typing and introspection. The Objective-C language allows you to identify objects generically with the data type of id. This type defines a pointer to an object and its data structure (that is, instance variables), which, by inheritance from the root class NSObject, include a pointer to the object's class. What this means is that you don't have to type objects strictly by class in your code: the class for the object can be determined at runtime through introspection.

Introspection means that an object, even one typed as id, can reveal its class and divulge other characteristics at runtime. Several introspection methods allow you to ascertain the inheritance relationships of an object, the methods to which it responds, and the protocols to which it conforms.

Inheritance

Inheritance is one of the most powerful aspects of object-oriented programming. Just as people inherit traits from their forebears, instances of a class inherit attributes and behavior from that class's "ancestors." An object's total complement of instance variables and methods derives not only from the class that creates it, but also from all the classes that class inherits from.

Because of inheritance, an Objective-C class definition doesn't have to specify every method and variable. If there's a class that does almost everything you want, but you need some additional features, you can define a new class that inherits from the existing class. The new class is called a *subclass* of the original class; the class it inherits from, its *superclass*.

Creating a new class is often a matter of specialization. Since the new class inherits all its superclass's behavior, you don't need to reimplement the things that work as you want them to. The subclass merely extends the inherited behavior by adding new methods and any variables needed to support the additional methods. All the methods and variables defined for—or inherited by—the superclass are inherited by the subclass. A subclass can also alter superclass behavior by overriding an inherited method, reimplementing the method to achieve a behavior different from the superclass's implementation. See Figure 2-7.

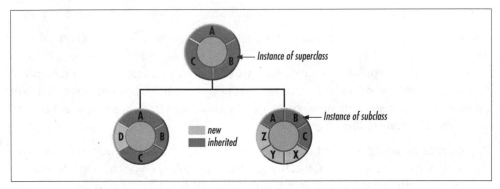

Figure 2-7. Inheritance

A class can have any number of subclasses, but only one superclass. This means that classes are arranged in a branching hierarchy, with one class at the top—the root class—that has no superclass. A representative portion of the Cocoa class hierarcy is shown in Figure 2-8.

NSObject is the root class of this hierarchy, as it is of most Objective-C class hierarchies. From NSObject, other classes inherit the basic functionality that makes messaging work, enables objects to work together, and otherwise invests objects with the ability to behave as objects. The root class also creates a framework for the creation, initialization, deallocation, introspection, and storage of objects.

As noted earlier, you often create a subclass of another class because that superclass provides most, but not all, the behavior you require. But a subclass can have its own unique purpose that does not build on the role of an existing class. To define a new class that doesn't need to inherit any special behavior other than the default behavior of objects, you make it a subclass of the NSObject class. Subclasses of NSObject, because of their general-purpose nature as objects, are very common in Cocoa applications. They often perform computational or application-specific functions.

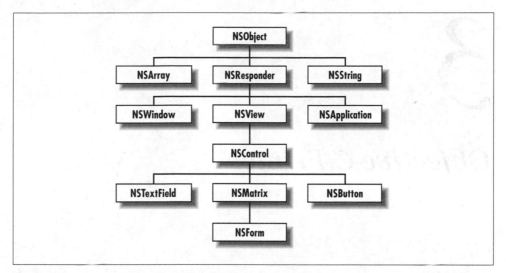

Figure 2-8. The root class in Objective-C

Inheritance makes it easy to bundle functionality common to a group of classes into a single class definition. For example, every object that draws on the screen—whether it draws an image of a button, a slider, a text display, or a graph of points—must keep track of which window it draws in and where in the window it draws. It must also know when it's appropriate to draw and when to respond to a user action. The code that handles all these details is part of a single class definition (the NSView class in the Application Kit). The specific work of drawing a button, a slider, or a text display can then be entrusted to a subclass.

This bundling of functionality both simplifies the organization of the code that needs to be written for an application and makes it easier to define objects that do complicated things. Each subclass need implement only the things it does differently from its superclass; there's no need to reimplement anything that has already been done.

What's more, hierarchical design assures more robust code. By building on a widely used, well-tested class such as NSView, a subclass inherits a proven foundation of functionality. Because the new code for a subclass is limited to implementing unique behavior, it's easier to test and debug that code.

Any class can be the superclass for a new subclass. Thus inheritance makes every class—those provided by Cocoa, those you create, and those offered by third-party vendors—easily extensible.

3

Objective-C Primer

The Objective-C language is a superset of ANSI C with special syntax and runtime extensions that make object-oriented programming possible. Objective-C syntax is uncomplicated, but powerful in its simplicity. You can mix standard C with Objective-C code. Programmers familiar with C and object-oriented programming techniques often find themselves right at home with Objective-C in a matter of days.

This chapter is divided into two main sections. The first section is a basic language summary listing all additions to the language. The second section summarizes some of the most frequently used aspects of the language.

See *Inside Cocoa: Object-Oriented Programming and the Objective-C Language* in `/Developer/Documentation/Cocoa` for complete details.

Language Summary

Objective-C adds a small number of constructs to the C language and defines a handful of conventions used to effectively interact with the runtime system.

Messages

Message expressions are enclosed in square brackets:

```
[receiver message]
```

The receiver can be:

• A variable or expression that evaluates to an object (including the variable `self`)

- A class name (indicating the class object)
- `super` (indicating an alternative search for the method implementation)

The message is the name of a method plus any arguments passed to it.

Defined Types

The principal types used in Objective-C are defined in the header file `objc/objc.h`:

Type	Definition
id	An object (a pointer to its data structure)
Class	A class object (a pointer to the class data structure)
SEL	A selector, a compiler-assigned code that identifies a method name
IMP	A pointer to a method implementation that returns an id
BOOL	A Boolean value, either YES or NO

`id` can be used to type any kind of object, class, or instance. In addition, class names can be used as type names to statically type instances of a class. A statically typed instance is declared to be a pointer to an instance of its class or to an instance of any class it inherits from.

The `objc.h` header file also defines these useful terms:

Type	Definition
nil	A null object pointer, (id)0
Nil	A null class pointer, (Class)0

Preprocessor Directives

The preprocessor understands these new notations:

Notation	Definition
#import	Imports a header file. This directive is identical to #include, except that it won't include the same file more than once.
//	Begins a comment that continues to the end of the line.

Compiler Directives

Directives to the compiler begin with @. The following directives are used to declare and define classes, categories, and protocols:

Directive	Definition
@interface	Begins the declaration of a class or category interface
@implementation	Begins the definition of a class or category
@protocol	Begins the declaration of a formal protocol
@end	Ends the declaration/definition of a class, category, or protocol

The following mutually exclusive directives specify the visibility of instance variables:

Directive	Definition
@private	Limits the scope of an instance variable to the class that declares it
@protected	Limits the instance variable scope to declaring and inheriting classes
@public	Removes restrictions on the scope of instance variables

The default is @protected.

In addition, there are directives for these particular purposes:

Directive	Definition
@class	Declares the names of classes defined elsewhere.
@selector(*method*)	Returns the compiled selector that identifies *method*.
@protocol(*name*)	Returns the *name* protocol (an instance of the Protocol class). (@protocol is also valid without (*name*) for forward declarations.)
@encode(*spec*)	Yields a character string that encodes the type structure of *spec*.
@defs(*classname*)	Yields the internal data structure of *classname* instances.

Classes

A new class is declared with the @interface directive. The interface file for its superclass must be imported:

```
#import "ItsSuperclass.h"

@interface ClassName : ItsSuperclass < protocol list >
{
    instance variable declarations
}
method declarations
@end
```

Everything but the compiler directives and class name is optional. If the colon and superclass name are omitted, the class is declared to be a new root class. If any protocols are listed, the header files where they're declared must also be imported.

A file containing a class definition imports its own interface:

```
#import "ClassName.h"

@implementation ClassName
method definitions
@end
```

Categories

You can add methods to a class by declaring them in an interface file under a category name and defining them in an implementation file under the same name. The category name indicates that the methods are additions to a class declared elsewhere, not a new class.

A category can be an alternative to a subclass. Rather than define a subclass to extend an existing class, through a category you can add methods to the class directly. For example, you could add categories to NSArray and other Cocoa classes. As in the case of a subclass, you don't need source code for the class you're extending.

The methods the category adds become part of the class type. For example, methods added to the NSArray class in a category will be among the methods the compiler will expect an NSArray instance to have in its repertoire. Methods added to the NSArray class in a subclass would not be included in the NSArray type. (This matters only for statically typed objects, since static typing is the only way the compiler can know an object's class.)

Category methods can do anything that methods defined in the class proper can do. At runtime, there's no difference. The methods the category adds to the class are inherited by all the class's subclasses, just like other methods.

A category is declared in much the same way as a class. The interface file that declares the class must be imported:

```
#import "ClassName.h"

@interface ClassName ( CategoryName ) < protocol list >
method declarations
@end
```

The protocol list and method declarations are optional. If any protocols are listed, the header files where they're declared must also be imported.

Like a class definition, a file containing a category definition imports its own interface:

```
#import "CategoryName.h"

@implementation ClassName ( CategoryName )
method definitions
@end
```

Protocols

Class and category interfaces declare methods that are associated with a particular class—mainly methods that the class implements. Informal and formal protocols, on the other hand, declare methods not associated with a class, but which any class, and perhaps many classes, might implement.

A *protocol* is simply a list of method declarations, unattached to a class definition. For example, these methods that report user actions on the mouse could be gathered into a protocol:

```
-(void)mouseDown:(NSEvent *)theEvent;
-(void)mouseDragged:(NSEvent *)theEvent;
-(void)mouseUp:(NSEvent *)theEvent;
```

Any class that wanted to respond to mouse events could adopt the protocol and implement its methods.

Protocols free method declarations from dependency on the class hierarchy, so they can be used in ways that classes and categories cannot. Protocols list methods that are (or may be) implemented somewhere, but the identity of the class that implements them is not of interest. What is of interest is whether or not a particular class conforms to the protocol—whether it has implementations of the methods the protocol declares. Thus objects can be grouped into types not just on the basis of similarities due to the fact that they inherit from the same class but also on the basis of their similarity in conforming to the same protocol. Classes in unrelated branches of the inheritance hierarchy might be typed alike because they conform to the same protocol.

Protocols can play a significant role in object-oriented design, especially when a project is divided among many implementors or incorporates objects developed in other projects. Cocoa software uses them heavily to support interprocess communication through Objective-C messages.

However, an Objective-C program doesn't need to use protocols. Unlike class definitions and message expressions, they're optional. Some Cocoa frameworks use them; some don't. It all depends on the task at hand.

Formal protocols are declared using the @protocol directive:

```
@protocol ProtocolName
< protocol list >
method declarations
@end
```

The list of incorporated protocols and the method declarations are optional. The protocol must import the header files that declare any protocols it incorporates.

Within source code, protocols are referred to using the similar @protocol() directive, where the parentheses enclose the protocol name.

Protocol names listed within angle brackets < . . . > are used to do three different things:

- In a protocol declaration, to incorporate other protocols (as shown before)

- In a class or category declaration, to formally adopt the protocol (as shown under the section "Classes" and the section "Categories")

- In a type specification, to limit the type to objects that conform to the protocol

Within protocol declarations, these type qualifiers support remote messaging:

Type Qualifier	Definition
oneway	The method is for asynchronous messages and has no valid return value.
in	The argument passes information to the remote receiver.
out	The argument gets information returned by reference.
inout	The argument both passes information and gets information.
bycopy	A copy of the object, not a proxy, should be passed or returned.
byref	A reference to the object, not a copy, should be passed or returned.

Method Declarations

The following conventions are used in method declarations:

- A + precedes declarations of class methods.

- A – precedes declarations of instance methods.

- Arguments are declared after colons (:). Typically, a label describing the argument precedes the colon. Both labels and colons are considered part of the method name.

- Argument and return types are declared using the C syntax for typecasting.

- The default return and argument type for methods is id, not int as it is for functions. (However, the modifier unsigned when used without a following type always means unsigned int.)

Method Implementations

Each method implementation is passed two hidden arguments:

- The receiving object (self)
- The selector for the method (_cmd)

Within the implementation, both self and super refer to the receiving object. super replaces self as the receiver of a message to indicate that only methods inherited by the implementation should be performed in response to the message.

Methods with no other valid return typically return void.

Naming Conventions

The names of files that contain Objective-C source code have a .m extension. Files that declare class and category interfaces or that declare protocols have the .h extension typical of header files.

Class, category, and protocol names generally begin with an uppercase letter; the names of methods and instance variables typically begin with a lowercase letter. The names of variables that hold instances usually also begin with lowercase letters.

In Objective-C, identical names that serve different purposes don't clash. Within a class, names can assigned freely:

- A class can declare methods with the same names as methods in other classes.
- A class can declare instance variables with the same names as variables in other classes.
- An instance method can have the same name as a class method.
- A method can have the same name as an instance variable.

Likewise, protocols and categories of the same class have protected namespaces:

- A protocol can have the same name as a class, a category, or anything else.
- A category of one class can have the same name as a category of another class.

However, class names are in the same namespace as global variables and defined types. A program can't have a global variable with the same name as a class.

Objective-C in Action

This section touches upon the more frequently used aspects of the Objective-C language, using code snippets where appropriate to illustrate how the language constructs are actually used in the context of an application. Don't worry if you don't completely understand every detail in every section. Objective-C is easy to pick up by example, and you'll have plenty of time to absorb it as you work through the tutorials in the later chapters.

Declarations

Objects can be declared statically or dynamically. Statically typed objects are declared as a pointer to a class:

```
NSString *mystring;
```

Static typing results in better compile-time type checking and makes code easier to understand. Note that in the previous example, `mystring` doesn't have to be an instance of NSString; it could also be an instance of any class that inherits from NSString.

Dynamically typed objects are declared as `id`:

```
id myObject;
```

Since the class of dynamically typed objects is resolved at runtime, you can refer to them in your code without knowledge of their class membership. Type objects in this way if they are likely to be involved in polymorphism and dynamic binding.

Declarations of instance methods begin with a minus sign (-); a space after the minus sign is optional:

```
- (NSString *)countryName;
```

Put the type of value returned by a method in parentheses between the minus sign (or plus sign) and the beginning of the method name. Methods that return nothing should have a return type of `void`.

Method argument types are in parentheses and go between the argument's keyword and the argument itself:

```
- (id)initWithName:(NSString *)name andType:(int)type;
```

Be sure to terminate all declarations with a semicolon.

By default, the scope of an instance variable is protected, making that variable directly accessible only to objects of the class that declares it or of a subclass of that class. To make an instance variable private (accessible only within the declaring class), insert the @private directive before the declaration.

Messages and Method Implementations

Message expressions consist of a variable identifying the receiving object followed by the name of the method you want to invoke. In Objective-C, the expression is enclosed in square brackets:

```
[anObject doSomethingWithArg:anArgument];
```

As in standard C, terminate statements with a semicolon.

Messages often result in values being returned from the invoked method; you must have a variable of the proper type to receive this value on the left side of an assignment (or, as in C, you can ignore the return value entirely):

```
int result = [anObj calcTotal];
```

You can nest message expressions inside other message expressions. This example gets the window of an NSForm object and makes the returned NSWindow object the receiver of another message:

```
[[form window] makeKeyAndOrderFront:self];
```

A method is structured like a function. After the full declaration of the method comes the body of the implementing code enclosed by braces.

Use nil to specify a null object; this is analogous to a null pointer. Note that some Cocoa methods do not accept nil as an argument.

A method can usefully refer to two implicit identifiers: self and super. These identifiers are used by an object to reference itself. When an object sends a message to itself, the use of these identifiers affects the search for a method implementation. The keyword self starts the search in the sender's class; super starts the search in the sender's superclass. For example:

```
[self redraw];
```

causes the object's own redraw method to be invoked.

In general, super is used only when overriding a method in the superclass so that a subclass can implement new behavior but still perform whatever tasks are required by the superclass. For example:

```
- (id)init {
    [super init];
    [self setDate: [NSCalendarDate date]];
    return self;
}
```

causes the init method of the superclass to be invoked before the object performs its subclass-specific initializations.

In methods you can directly access the instance variables of your class's instances. However, accessor methods are recommended instead of direct access, except in cases in which performance is of paramount importance.

Defining a Class

You define classes in two parts: one part declares the instance variables and the interface (principally the methods that can be invoked by messages sent to objects belonging to the class), and the other part actually implements those methods. The interface is public. The implementation is private and can change without affecting the interface or the way the class is used.

The basic procedure for defining a class is covered in Chapter 7, *Currency Converter Tutorial*. However, here is a supplemental list of conventions and other points to remember when you define a class:

- The public interface for a class is usually declared in a header file (with a .h extension), the name of which is the name of the class. This header file can be imported into any program that makes use of the class.

- The code implementing a class is usually in a file taking the name of the class and having an extension of .m. This code must be present—in the form of a framework, a dynamic shared library, a static library, or the implementation file itself—when the project containing the class is compiled.

- Method declarations and implementations must begin with a minus sign (-) or a plus sign (+). A hyphen indicates that these methods are used by instances of the class; a plus sign precedes methods that the class object itself uses.

- Method definitions are much like function definitions. Note that methods not only respond to messages, they often initiate messages of their own—just as one function might call another.

- In a method implementation you can refer directly to an object's instance variables, as long as that object belongs to the class the method is defined in. There's no extra syntax for accessing variables or passing the object's data structure. The language keeps all that hidden.

- A method can also refer to the receiving object as self. This variable makes it possible for an object, in its method definitions, to send messages to itself.

Overriding a Method

A subclass can not only add new methods to the ones it inherits, it can also replace an inherited method with a new implementation. No special syntax is required; all you do is reimplement the method.

Overriding methods doesn't alter the set of messages that an object can receive; it alters the method implementations that will be used to respond to those messages. As mentioned earlier, this ability of each class to implement its own version of a method is referred to as *polymorphism*. Overriding a method in a particular class does not in any way affect the behavior of that method in the superclass.

It's also possible to extend an inherited method, rather than replace it outright. To do this, you override the method but invoke the superclass's same method in the new implementation. This invocation occurs with a message to super, which is a special receiver in the Objective-C language. The term super indicates that an inherited method should be performed, rather than one defined in the current class.

Object Creation

One of the primary functions of a class is to create new objects of the type the class defines. For example, the NSButton class creates new NSButton objects, and the NSArray class creates new NSArrays. Objects are created at runtime in a two-step process that first allocates memory for the instance variables of the new object and then initializes those variables. An init message is generally coupled with an alloc or allocWithZone: message in the same line of code; the receiver for the alloc message is a class:

```
TheClass *newObject = [[TheClass alloc] init];
```

The alloc method dynamically allocates memory for a new instance of the receiving class and returns the new object. The receiver for the init message is the new object that was dynamically allocated by alloc. An object isn't ready to be used until it has been initialized. An object should be initialized only once. The version of the init method defined in the NSObject class does no initialization; it simply returns self.

After being allocated and initialized, a new object is a fully functional member of its class with its own set of variables—newObject can receive messages, store values in its instance variables, and so on. If you need more objects, create them in the same way from the same class definition.

Subclass versions of the init method should return the new object (self) after it has been successfully initialized. If it can't be initialized, the method should release the object and return nil. In some cases, an init method might release the new object and return a substitute. Programs should therefore always use the object returned by init, and not necessarily the one returned by alloc or allocWith-Zone:, in subsequent code.

Every class must guarantee that the init method either returns a fully functional instance of the class or raises an exception. Subclass versions of init need to incorporate the initialization code for the classes they inherit from, through a message to super:

```
- init
{
    if (self = [super init]) {
    /* class-specific initialization goes here */
    }
    return self;
}
```

Note that the message to super precedes the initialization code added in the method. This ensures that initialization proceeds in the order of inheritance.

Designated Initializers

Subclasses often define init . . . methods with additional arguments to allow specific values to be set. The more arguments a method has, the more freedom it gives you to determine the character of initialized objects. Classes often have a set of init . . . methods, each with a different number of arguments. For example:

```
- init;
- initArg:(int)tag;
- initArg:(int)tag arg:(struct info *)data;
```

The convention is that at least one of these methods, usually the one with the most arguments, includes a message to super to incorporate the initialization of classes higher up the hierarchy. This method is called the *designated initializer* for the class. The other `init . . .` methods defined in the class directly or indirectly invoke the designated initializer through messages to `self`. In this way, all `init . . .` methods are chained together. For example:

```
- init
{
    return [self initArg:-1];
}

- initArg:(int)tag
{
    return [self initArg:tag arg:NULL];
}

- initArg:(int)tag arg:(struct info *)data
{
    [super init. . .];
    /* class-specific initialization goes here */
}
```

In this example, the `initArg:arg:` method is the designated initializer for the class. If a subclass does any initialization of its own, it must define its own designated initializer. This method should begin by sending a message to super to perform the designated initializer of its superclass.

Suppose, for example, that the three methods illustrated previously are defined in the B class. The C class, a subclass of B, might have this designated initializer:

```
- initArg:(int)tag arg:(struct info *)data arg:anObject
{
    [super initArg:tag arg:data];
    /* class-specific initialization goes here */
}
```

If inherited `init . . .` methods are to successfully initialize instances of the subclass, they must all be made to (directly or indirectly) invoke the new designated initializer. To accomplish this, the subclass is obliged to override only the designated initializer of the superclass. For example, in addition to its designated initializer, the C class would also implement this method:

```
- initArg:(int)tag arg:(struct info *)data
{
    return [self initArg:tag arg:data arg:nil];
}
```

This ensures that all three methods inherited from the B class also work for instances of the C class. Often the designated initializer of the subclass overrides the designated initializer of the superclass. If so, the subclass need implement only the one `init . . .` method.

These conventions maintain a direct chain of `init`... links and ensure that the new method and all inherited `init`... methods return usable, initialized objects. They also prevent the possibility of an infinite loop wherein a subclass method sends a message (to `super`) to perform a superclass method, which in turn sends a message (to `self`) to perform the subclass method.

The `init` method is the designated initializer for the NSObject class. Subclasses that do their own initialization should override it, as described earlier.

4

Development Tools

Apple has a powerful, integrated, cross-platform development environment for Cocoa on Mac OS X. It consists of a suite of applications and tools that deliver maximum productivity from the frameworks, subsystems, libraries, components, and other resources of Mac OS X.

In developing applications with Cocoa, you have a choice of programming languages. You can write programs, in whole or in part, in C, C++, Java, or Objective-C. You can subclass Cocoa classes in Java and mix "pure" Java and Cocoa objects in your code. Note that you cannot access the Cocoa APIs from C++.

In addition to the material provided in this chapter, you can find reference documentation covering the compiler, the debugger, and other tools located in `/Developer/Documentation/DeveloperTools`.

Project Builder

Project Builder is an application that manages software-development projects and orchestrates and streamlines the development process. Project Builder's key features include:

- A project browser
- A full-featured code editor
- Language-savvy symbol recognition
- Sophisticated project search capabilities
- Header file and documentation access

- Built-in integration with the CVS source-control management system
- Build customization
- A graphical source-level debugger

Project Builder's main window is shown in Figure 4-1.

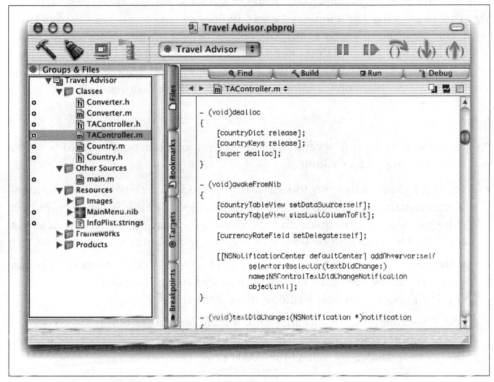

Figure 4-1. The Project Builder main window

Feature Highlights

When you write code with Project Builder you have a set of "workbench" tools at your disposal.

Delimiter checking

If you double-click a brace (left or right), the code between the braces (including the delimiters) is highlighted. Similarly, you can double-click a square bracket in a message expression to locate the matching bracket and double-click a parenthesis character to select the enclosing code. If there is no matching delimiter, Project Builder emits a warning beep.

Emacs key bindings

Emacs is a popular editor for writing code on Unix platforms. You can use the most common Emacs commands in Project Builder's code editor. For example, there are the commands page forward (Control-V), word forward (Meta-F), delete word (Meta-D), kill forward (Control-K), and yank from kill ring (Control-Y). Some Emacs commands may conflict with some of the standard Macintosh key bindings. You can modify the key bindings Project Builder's code editor uses to substitute other command keys—such as the Option key or Shift-Control—for Emacs' Control or Meta keys. Option (Meta) key bindings are not enabled by default on Mac OS X because the Option key is used to generate special characters. Consult Project Builder's documention for information on using these features.

Find

Project Builder gives you several ways to get information on Cocoa APIs when you're developing an application.

- The Find pane allows you to search for definitions of classes, methods, functions, constants, and other symbols in your project. Since it is based on project indexing, searching is quick and thorough and leads directly to the relevant code. Searches can also be textual or regular-expression based.

- If the results of a search using Project Find include Cocoa symbols, you can easily get related reference documentation that describes that symbol by clicking on the book icon next to the result of interest.

- You can browse the header files and documentation related to Cocoa frameworks within Project Builder. The Application Kit and Foundation frameworks always are included by default for Cocoa projects.

Flexible build system

Project Builder contains a very flexible build system, allowing you to build applications using either the application's GUI or a command line. Project Builder facilitates the creation of different types of projects (such as palettes, frameworks, and bundles, in addition to applications). Consult Project Builder's online help system—availiable from the Help menu—for additional information on using these features.

Interface Builder

Interface Builder makes it easy to create application interfaces. You just drag an object from a palette and drop it on the graphical user interface you're creating (Figure 4-2). You can then set attributes of these objects through an Info window and connect them to other objects in your application so they can send messages to one another. Interface Builder also assists in the definition of custom classes and allows you to test an interface without having to compile a line of code.

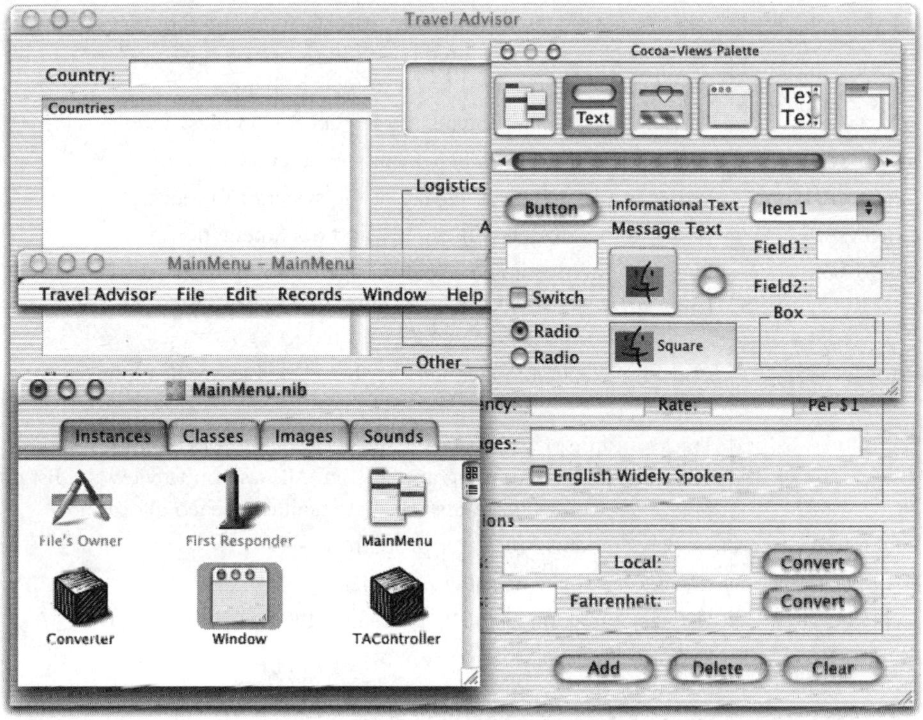

Figure 4-2. Interface Builder

Interface Builder's standard palettes hold an assortment of Application Kit objects. Other palettes can include Cocoa objects from other frameworks, third-party objects, and custom-compiled objects. You can also store noncompiled configurations of objects on dynamic palettes. Interface Builder archives and restores elements of a user interface (including connections) as objects—it doesn't "hardwire" them into the interface.

Other Development Tools

In addition to Project Builder and Interface Builder, there are other applications you can use in the Cocoa development process. Development tools featuring a graphical user interface are listed in Table 4-1. Except where noted, these applications are installed in /Developer/Applications.

Table 4-1. Development Tools

Name	Description
FileMerge	Visually compares the contents of two files or two directories. You can use FileMerge, for example, to determine the differences between versions of the same source code file or between two project directories. You can also use it to merge changes.
icns Browser	Displays the entire contents of Mac OS X icon files.
IconComposer	Creates Mac OS X icon files from source art.
IORegistryExplorer	Provides a hierarchical display of the system I/O registry.
JavaBrowser	Displays the Java class hierarchy and documentation.
MallocDebug	Measures the dynamic-memory usage of applications, finds memory leaks, analyzes all allocated memory in an application, and measures the memory allocated since a given time.
MRJAppBuilder	Converts executable Java into double-clickable applications for Mac OS X.
ObjectAlloc	Tracks and displays all object allocations (both Cocoa and Core Foundation) for a running application. Allows you to view the list of objects as well as the call stack that resulted in each allocation.
OpenGL Info	Displays OpenGL renderer properties.
PackageMaker	Creates Mac OS X installer packages.
PEFViewer	Displays the contents of PEF (Preferred Executable Format) executables.
Pixie	Magnifies the screen area under the cursor, allowing you to see the exact pixels comprising any onscreen object. Magnification is adjustable from 1 to 12 times normal.
PropertyListEditor	Opens, displays, and/or modifies the contents of a property list (`.plist`) file.
QuartzDebug	Displays a list of all windows known to the system. Allows you to turn on a Quartz debugging mode that flashes yellow over areas of the screen as they are updated by the window server.
Sampler	Analyzes performance characteristics of your application by sampling the call stack of your program over a user-specified period of time.

Useful Command-Line Tools

Apple has created or modified several command-line tools for compilation, debugging, performance analysis, and so on. Table 4-2 lists some of the more useful tools. You can get further information by using the manpages system. The tools are all located in the `/usr/bin` directory.

Table 4-2. Command-Line Development Tools

Name	Description
cc	Compiles C, Objective-C, and C++ source code files.
gdb	Is a source-level symbolic debugger for C, extended by Apple to support Objective-C and C++.
gnumake	Builds the product(s) of a programming project based on dependency information.
as	Assembles; translates assembly code into object code.
defaults	Reads, writes, searches, and deletes user defaults. The defaults system records user preferences that persist when the application isn't running. When users specify defaults in an application's Preferences panel, NSUserDefaults methods are used to write the defaults.
nibtool	Reads the contents of an Interface Builder nib file. Prints classes, the hierarchy, objects, connections, and localizable strings.
libtool	Creates static or dynamic libraries from specified object bin files for one or multiple architectures.
otool	Displays specified parts of object files or libraries.
nm	Displays the symbol table, in whole or in part, of the specified object file or files.
fixPrecomps	Creates or refreshes a precompiled header file for each of the major frameworks.
strip	Removes or modifies the symbol table attached to assembled and linked output.

Although the Mac OS X development environment includes many of the tools discussed in this chapter, the tutorials in this book focus almost exclusively on the use of Project Builder and Interface Builder. Some tools, such as the compiler and the linker, are usually invoked indirectly through Project Builder. Most other tools are not strictly necessary for building Cocoa applications. However, the debugging and performance analysis tools ObjectAlloc, QuartzDebug, and Sampler are extremely useful for understanding the details of an application's inner workings. Feel free to experiment with them at any point in the tutorial-building process.

II

Single-Window Applications

5

Hello World

This chapter fulfills the obligation of all self-respecting tutorials to include a Hello World program. The chapter's tutorial shows you how to use the Project Builder application described in Chapter 4, *Development Tools*, to create a project that builds a Hello World program for Cocoa. Hello World represents the simplest possible working program that does something detectable (like printing a string to the screen). A working Hello World program verifies that your development environment is functioning properly.

Creating the Project

The simplest type of Cocoa program is called a Foundation tool. Because this type of program uses only the Foundation framework, it has no graphical user interface (GUI). A Cocoa program that has no GUI is called a *tool*, to clearly distinguish it from a Cocoa program that does have a GUI, which is called an *application*. Unlike Cocoa applications that use the Application Kit Framework (detailed in Chapter 1, *Introduction to Cocoa*), Foundation tools can be run only from within Project Builder and from the command line.

Foundation tools are a great way to quickly create very powerful command-line applications for use in the Mac OS X BSD environment. A Foundation tool is very similar to a standard C program but, because it links with the Foundation framework, it has access to all the power of the Foundation classes in addition to the standard Objective-C constructs.

In this section you'll be led through the steps necessary to create a very simple foundation tool that prints the string "Hello World!"

Open Project Builder

Before you can start building applications with Project Builder, you need to launch the application:

1. Find Project Builder in /Developer/Applications.

2. Double-click the icon.

The first time you start Project Builder, you'll be presented with an Assistant to set up your application preferences:

1. Click Next on the Assistant's welcome page.

2. Choose your build products location and click Next. The first page of the Assistant asks where you'd prefer to keep the build products (an executable or library, for example) and intermediate build files (object files, for instance). The default is to keep both in the build directory of the current project, but you can choose whatever directory you wish.

3. Choose your editing preference and click Finish. The second and final Assistant page asks whether you prefer to open new text files in separate windows or to open them in Project Builder's single-window code editor.

Choose the New Project Command

When Project Builder is first launched, only its menu bar appears. To create a project, choose New Project from the File menu. Project Builder will then display the New Project Assistant, shown in Figure 5-1), which will take you through a few simple steps to create a new project.

Select Project Type

Though this book focuses on building Cocoa applications, Project Builder can be used for other types of projects, ranging from Carbon and Java applications to Mac OS X kernel extensions and frameworks. The Assistant lets you choose a project template so you'll have a useful working starting point for your application:

1. Select Foundation Tool from the list of templates and click Next. The New Project Assistant gives you an opportunity to name your new project and choose a location in the file system in which to save it. See Figure 5-2.

2. Type **Hello World** in the Name field.

3. If you don't want to use the default project location (your home directory), click the Set button and use the file-system browser to navigate to the directory where you want your project to be saved

4. Click Finish.

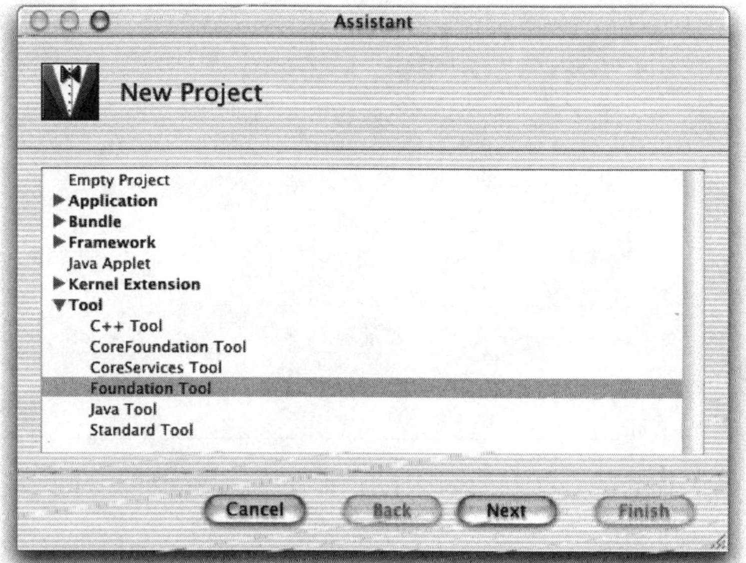

Figure 5-1. Project Builder's New Project Assistant

The Main Window

When you are done, Project Builder displays the main project window. See Figure 5-3.

The main project window contains all the tools you need for application development. From this central location, you can:

- View, edit, and organize your source files
- Invoke the build system
- Modify debugger settings, set breakpoints, and step through code
- Modify project settings
- Search your source files as well as the system headers
- Invoke Help Viewer to access documentation

Figure 5-2. Naming a Project Builder project

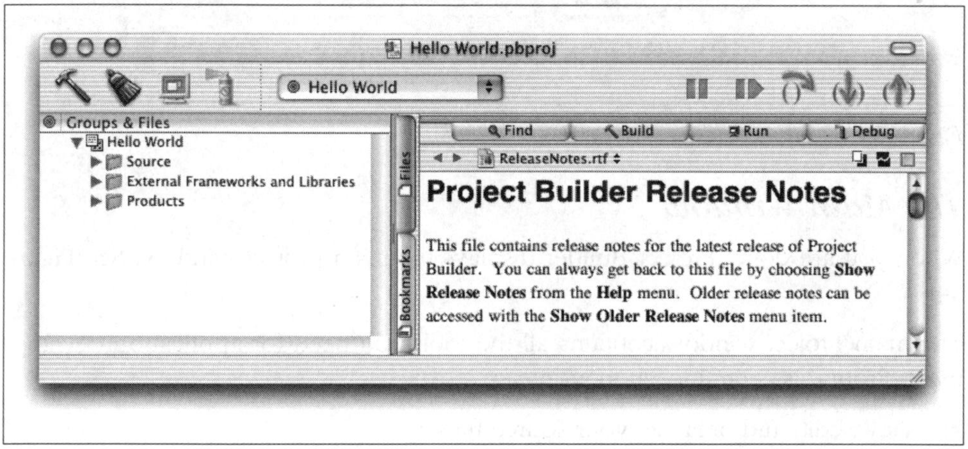

Figure 5-3. Hello World main window

Build the Application

1. In the Groups & Files list of Project Builder's main window, click the disclosure triangle to the left of the Source group.

2. Click main.m. You will see the contents of the file in the code editor, as shown in Figure 5-4.

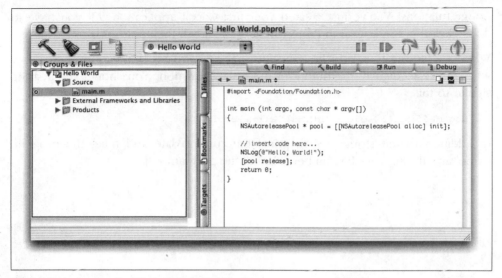

Figure 5-4. Project Builder's Groups & Files list

The `main.m` implementation file contains the entry point for the application. The Foundation Tool project template provides a standard `main` function for you that prints "Hello World" to Project Builder's Run pane. Don't worry about the function of the NSAutoreleasePool right now; it will be covered in the next chapter.

```
int main (int argc, const char *argv[]) {
    NSAutoreleasePool * pool = [[NSAutoreleasePool alloc] init];

    // insert code here
    NSLog(@"Hello, World!");

    [pool release];
    return 0;
}
```

3. The `NSLog` function works very much like `printf` in the C language. The difference is that `NSLog` takes an NSString object instead of a C string. Apple's Objective-C compiler includes the `@""` directive, which creates an NSString object using the characters between the quotation marks.

4. Click the Build button in the main window.

Now the build process begins. Project Builder's Build pane opens to reveal detailed information about the build as it progresses. When Project Builder finishes—and encounters no errors along the way—it displays Build Succeeded in the lower-left corner of the project window.

Congratulations! You've just created your first Cocoa application. All you have to do is click the Run button in Project Builder to launch the application.

When the application launches, the Run pane of Project Builder's main window will enlarge to display the output of the NSLog function. You should see a string similar to this:

```
Nov 10 15:56:12 Hello World[256] Hello, World!
```

In addition to the string, NSLog prints the current date and time, the program name, and the process ID number (PID) of the program.

6

Essential Cocoa Paradigms

In this chapter you will explore a handful of programming topics that represent the fundamental building blocks of a Cocoa application. First, you'll learn how to use Cocoa's collection classes, a set of objects whose purpose is to hold other objects. Next, you'll explore the basics of building graphical user interfaces in Cocoa. You'll learn to use Interface Builder and discover how this powerful tool interacts with Project Builder and the Cocoa frameworks to allow you to very quickly prototype and build applications. Last, you'll delve into the intricacies of object ownership and disposal in Cocoa, ensuring that your applications use resources efficiently.

These topics have been singled out for special attention because they are central to the design of the Cocoa frameworks, and the architectural perspectives involved are likely to be unfamiliar to developers new to the subtleties of object-oriented programming. Exploring these design patterns will help steep you in the mindset of Cocoa's creators, as well as illustrate some of the powerful design approaches available with a language as dynamic as Objective-C. Understanding the principles involved will help you use the Cocoa tools and frameworks more effectively, providing the experience you need to work with them instead of against them.

Cocoa's Collection Classes

Several classes in Cocoa's Foundation framework create objects whose purpose is to hold other objects (literally, references to objects); these classes are called *collection classes*. The two most commonly used collection classes are NSArray and NSDictionary. NSArray stores and retrieves objects in an ordered fashion through zero-based indexing. Dictionaries store and retrieve objects using key-value pairs. These collection classes, shown in Figure 6-1, are extremely useful in Cocoa application development.

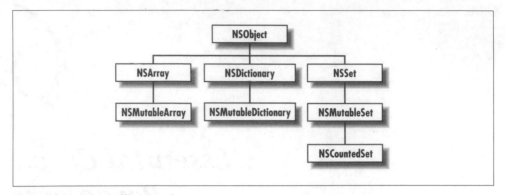

Figure 6-1. Cocoa collection classes

Collection classes come in two forms, mutable and immutable. The immutable versions of these classes (NSArray and NSDictionary, for example) allow you to add items when the collection is created but no further changes are allowed. The mutable versions (NSMutableArray, NSMutableDictionary) allow you to add and remove objects programmatically after the collection object is created.

All collection objects enable you to access a contained value that satisfies a particular external property. This property, generally referred to as a *key*, varies according to the organizing scheme enforced by the type of collection. For example, the key for an array is an integer that specifies position within the collection; however, a dictionary—for which the term key has more of a conventional meaning—permits any arbitrary value to act as the key for retrieving a contained value.

In addition to storage and retrieval using keys, much of the power of collection classes lies in their ability to manipulate the objects they contain. The collection classes implement methods for performing a variety of functions on the objects they contain. Not every collection object can perform every function, but in general, collection objects can:

- Derive their initial contents from files and URLs as well as other collections of objects

- Add, remove, locate, and sort their contents

- Compare their contents with other collection objects

- Enumerate over their contents

- Send a message to their contents

- Store their contents to a file on disk and later retrieve it (with the help of NSArchiver/NSUnarchiver)

Because you will use collection objects frequently when building Cocoa applications, it's important to get a basic feel for how they work. Exploring the collection classes will also provide an opportunity to exercise your Objective-C and Project Builder skills.

Working with NSArray

In this section you will modify the Hello World application from Chapter 5, *Hello World*, so that it instantiates and exercises an instance of the NSMutableArray class:

1. Open the Hello World project if it is not already open.

2. Open `main.m` and add a declaration for an NSMutableArray just after the declaration of the autorelease pool and before the call to NSLog:

   ```
   NSMutableArray *myArray;
   ```

3. Add the code to create a new array:

   ```
   myArray = [[NSMutableArray alloc] init];
   ```

4. Add code to print the contents of the array object. In this call to NSLog, the `%@` is replaced by the object. The `%@` works exactly as it would in a `printf` call; `%@` is the escape for an object value, in this case, an NSString. Note that NSLog automatically sends the `description` message to the array so that information about the array's contents will be printed:

   ```
   NSLog(@"Array description: %@ items.\n", myArray);
   ```

5. Add code to release the array. This statement tells the runtime that we are finished with the array so it can be safely deallocated:

   ```
   [myArray release];
   ```

Your main function should look exactly like that in Example 6-1.

Example 6-1. Creating a Mutable Array

```
int main (int argc, const char *argv[])
{
    NSAutoreleasePool * pool = [[NSAutoreleasePool alloc] init];
    NSMutableArray *myArray;

    NSLog(@"Hello World: This is a Foundation Tool.\n");

    myArray = [[NSMutableArray alloc] init];

    NSLog(@"Array description: %@ items.\n", myArray);

    [myArray release];
    [pool release];
    return 0;
}
```

Build and run the application. You should see a new string in the Run pane similar to this:

```
Nov 10 15:56:12 HelloWorld[256] Array description: () items.
```

Right now, the array is empty, but when you add items, their descriptions will appear between the parentheses.

Spend a few minutes playing with NSMutableArray. Here are some suggestions:

- Add a string. Note that arrays retain but do not copy their member objects. See the section "Build and debug the application" later in this chapter for more information.

  ```
  [myArray addObject: @"Here's a string!"];
  ```

- Find out how many items are in the array:

  ```
  int itemCount;
  itemCount = [myArray count];
  ```

- Get an object from the array:

  ```
  NSString *myString;
  myString = [myArray objectAtIndex: 0];
  ```

- Insert an object:

  ```
  [myArray insertObject: @"Hello2" atIndex: 0];
  ```

- Swap items:

  ```
  [myArray exchangeObjectAtIndex: 0 withObjectAtIndex: 1];
  ```

Consult the class specifications for NSArray and NSMutableArray in /Developer/Documentation/Cocoa for comprehensive documentation on all of the methods for this container class.

Working with NSDictionary

A dictionary—an object of the NSDictionary or NSMutableDictionary class—is a hashing-based collection whose keys for accessing its values are arbitrary, program-defined pieces of data. Although the key is usually a string (an NSString object), it can be any object—with certain caveats: the object used as a key must conform to the NSCopying protocol and respond to the isEqual: message). The keys of dictionaries are unlike the keys of the other collection objects in that, conceptually, they are also contained by the collection along with the values. Dictionaries are primarily useful for holding and organizing data that can be labeled, such as values extracted from text fields in the user interface.

In Cocoa, a dictionary differs from an array in that the key used to access a particular value in the dictionary remains the same as values are added to or removed from the dictionary—until a value associated with a particular key is replaced or removed. In an array, the key (the index) that is used to retrieve a particular value can change over time as values are inserted into or deleted from the array. Also, unlike an array, a dictionary does not put its values in any order. To enable later retrieval of a value, the key of the key-value pair should be constant (or be treated as constant); if the key changes after being used to put a value in the dictionary, the value might not be retrievable. The keys of a dictionary form a set; in other words, keys are guaranteed to be unique in a dictionary.

Working with dictionaries

In this section you will again modify the Hello World application so that it instantiates and exercises an instance of the NSMutableDictionary class:

1. Open the Hello World project if it is not already open, and bring up `main.m` for editing.

2. Add a declaration for a local variable of type NSMutableDictionary.

   ```
   NSMutableDictionary *myDict;
   ```

3. Add the code to create a new dictionary:

   ```
   myDict = [[NSMutableDictionary alloc] init];
   ```

4. Add code to print the contents of the dictionary object:

   ```
   NSLog(@"Dict description: %@ items.\n", myDict);
   ```

5. Add code to release the dictionary:

   ```
   [myDict release];
   ```

Spend a few minutes playing with NSMutableDictionary. Here are some suggestions:

- Add a key-value pair:

  ```
  [myDict setObject:@"stringOne" forKey:@"keyOne"];
  ```

- Get an object from the dictionary using its key:

  ```
  myString = [myDict objectForKey:@"keyOne"];
  ```

- Add several different key-value pairs to the dictionary and then get an array of all the keys. Use a loop to print them all out:

```
keyArray = [myDict allKeys];
for (index = 0; index < [keyArray count]; index++)
    NSLog(@"Dictionary key at index %i is: %@.\n", index,
        [keyArray objectAtIndex: index]);
```

Consult the class specifications for NSDictionary and NSMutableDictionary for comprehensive documentation on all methods for this container class.

Create Graphical User Interfaces in Cocoa

In this section you'll see how Cocoa and Interface Builder combine to simplify and accelerate the process of constructing applications with a graphical user interface. You'll learn about:

- **Windows**. A window is an area on the screen (usually, but not always, rectangular) in which an application displays things such as controls, fields, text, and graphics.

- **Nib files**. Nib files are files created by Interface Builder that contain windows as well as other user interface objects.

- **Outlets**. Outlets are special instance variables created by Interface Builder that allow objects to send messages to one another.

Finally, you'll apply what you've learned by creating a Cocoa application that displays a window with a single text field containing the current date and time.

Windows in Cocoa

A window in Cocoa looks very similar to windows in other user environments such as Microsoft Windows or Mac OS 9. A window can be moved around the screen, and windows can be stacked on top of one another like pieces of paper. A typical Cocoa window has a titlebar, a content area, and several control objects.

NSWindow and the window server

Many user interface objects other than the standard window are windows. Menus, pop-up menus, and scrolling lists are primarily windows, as are dialog boxes, alerts, Info windows, and tool palettes, to name a few. In fact, anything drawn on the screen must appear in a window. End users, however, may not recognize or refer to them as "windows."

Two interacting systems create and manage Cocoa windows. On the one hand, a window is created by the window server. The window server is a process that uses the internal window management portion of Quartz (the low-level drawing system) to draw, resize, hide, and move windows using Quartz graphics primitives. As depicted in Figure 6-2, the window server also detects user events (such as mouse clicks) and forwards them to applications.

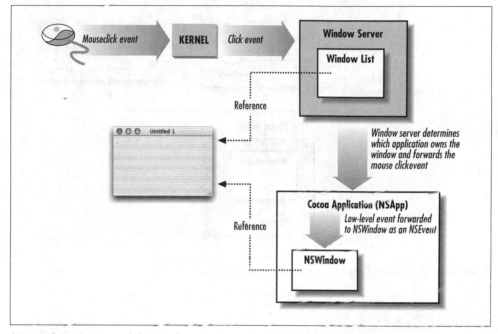

Figure 6-2. Cocoa and the window server

The window that the window server creates is paired with an object supplied by the Application Kit—an instance of the NSWindow class. Each physical window in a Cocoa program is managed by an instance of NSWindow (or subclass). When you create an NSWindow object, the window server creates the physical window that the NSWindow object manages. The window server references the window by its window number, and the NSWindow by its own identifier (see Figure 6-3.)

Application, window, and view

In a running Cocoa application, NSWindow objects occupy a middle position between an instance of NSApplication and the views of the application. (A *view* is an object that can draw itself and detect user events.) The NSApplication object keeps a list of its windows and tracks the current status of each. Each NSWindow, on the other hand, manages a hierarchy of views in addition to its window, as shown in Figure 6-4.

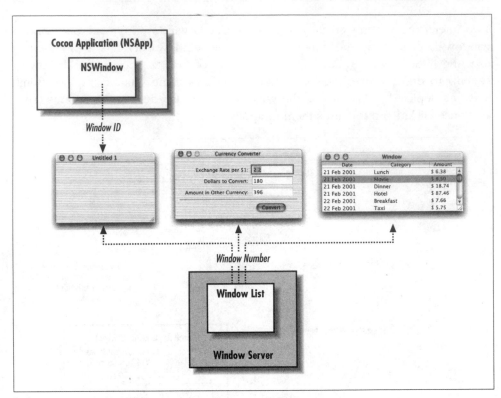

Figure 6-3. NSWindow objects and window server windows

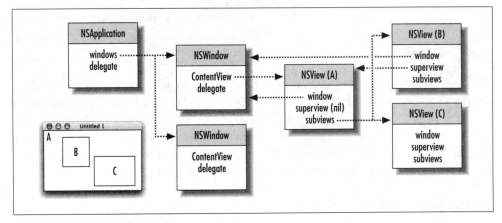

Figure 6-4. The view hierarchy

At the top of this hierarchy is the Content view, which fits just within the window's content rectangle. The Content view encloses all other views (its subviews), which come below it in the hierarchy. The NSWindow distributes events to views in the hierarchy and regulates coordinate transformations among them.

Another rectangle, the frame rectangle, defines the outer boundary of the window and includes the titlebar and the window's controls. Cocoa uses the lower-left corner of the frame rectangle to define the window's location relative to the screen's coordinate system and to establish the base coordinate system for the views of the window. This is different from Carbon and Classic applications, which use the upper-left corner as the origin of the coordinate system. Views draw themselves in coordinate systems transformed from (and relative to) this base coordinate system.

Key and main windows

Windows have numerous characteristics. They can be onscreen or offscreen. Onscreen windows are layered on the screen in tiers managed by the window server. Onscreen windows also can carry a status: key or main.

The key window responds to key presses for an application and are the primary recipient of messages from menus and dialog boxes. Usually a window is made key when the user clicks it. Each application can have only one key window at a time.

An application has one main window at any given time, which can often have key status as well. The main window is the principal focus of user actions for an application. Often user actions in a modal key window (typically a dialog box such as the Font dialog box or an Info window) have a direct effect on the main window.

Nib Files

A nib file is an archive of object instances generated by Interface Builder. Unlike the product of many user interface building systems, a nib file is not generated code; it is a true object that has been specially encoded and stored on disk. The objects in the nib file are created and manipulated using Interface Builder's graphical tools.

Nib files typically package a group of related user interface objects and supporting resources, along with information about how the objects are related—both to one another and to other objects in your application. Every application with a graphical user interface has at least one nib file that is loaded automatically when the application is launched. The main nib file typically contains the application menu, while auxiliary nib files contain the application windows with their associated user interface objects. An important advantage of splitting an application's interface into several nib files is that portions of the user interface may be loaded only when needed.

A nib file contains one or more of the following:

- **Archived objects**. These objects are also known in object-oriented terminology as "flattened" or "serialized" objects, meaning that the object has been encoded in such a way that it can be saved to disk (or transmitted over a network connection) and later restored in memory. Archived objects contain information such as their size, location, and position in the object hierarchy. At the top of the hierarchy of archived objects is the file's owner object, a proxy object that points to the actual object that owns the nib file (typically the one that loaded the nib file from disk).

- **Class references**. Interface Builder can store the details of Cocoa objects and objects that you make into a palette, but it does not know how to archive instances of your custom classes, since it doesn't have access to the code. For these classes, Interface Builder stores a proxy object to which it attaches class information.

- **Connection information**. Interface Builder creates special connector objects to store information about how objects within the object hierarchy are interconnected. When you save the document, connector objects are archived in the nib file along with the objects they connect.

Outlets

An outlet is an instance variable that contains a reference to another object. An object can communicate with other objects in an application by sending messages to them through outlets, as shown in Figure 6-5.

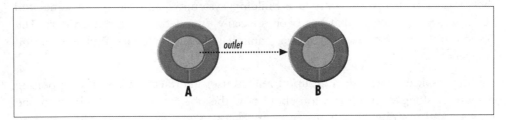

Figure 6-5. Using an outlet to send a message

An outlet can reference any object in an application: user interface objects such as text fields and buttons, windows and dialog boxes, instances of custom classes, and even the application object itself. What distinguishes outlets from other instance variables is their relationship to Interface Builder.

Interface Builder can "recognize" an outlet declaration in a header file, allowing you to set its value by drawing connection lines between objects. Specifying these relationships between objects in Interface Builder saves you from having to write initialization code by hand. There are ways other than outlets to reference objects in an application, but outlets and Interface Builder's facility for initializing them are a great convenience.

Create a Cocoa Application Project

In this section you'll use Interface Builder and Project Builder to create a simple Cocoa application. When it is run, the application displays a single window containing a text field and uses an outlet to display the current date and time in that text field.

1. If Project Builder is not already running, launch it.

2. Choose the New Project command. Project Builder will display the New Project Assistant, as shown in Figure 6-6.

Figure 6-6. New Project Assistant

3. Select Cocoa Application from the list of project templates and click Next. Much like the Foundation Tool template you used in the Hello World example, the Cocoa Application template provides a starting point for applications with a GUI. It includes a default nib file containing a window and standard menu bar.

4. Type **Nib Files** in the Project Name field and click Finish.

Notice that Project Builder uses hierarchical groups to organize a project. The default groups for a Cocoa application are:

- **Classes**. This group is empty at first, but it will be used to hold the implementation (.m) and header (.h) files for your project's classes.

- **Other sources**. This group contains main.m, the main function that loads the initial set of resources and runs the application. (You shouldn't have to modify this file.)

- **Resources**. This group contains the nib files (.nib) and other resources that specify the application's user interface.

- **Frameworks**. This group contains references to the frameworks (which are similar to libraries) that the application imports to gain access to system services.

- **Products**. This group contains the results of project builds and is automatically populated with references to the products created by each target in the project.

These groups are very flexible in that they do not necessarily reflect either the on-disk layout of the project or the manner in which the build system handles the files. The default groups created for you by the templates can be used as they are, or rearranged however you like.

Open the Main Nib File

In order to begin constructing a user interface, you must open the application's main nib file in Interface Builder.

1. In the Finder, locate and open the Nib Files.pbproj that you created earlier.

2. Double-click MainMenu.nib in the Resources group of the Groups & Files list of Project Builder's main window. This will launch Interface Builder (if it is not already running) and open the nib file.

A default menu bar and window titled Window will appear when Interface Builder opens the nib file, as shown in Figure 6-7.

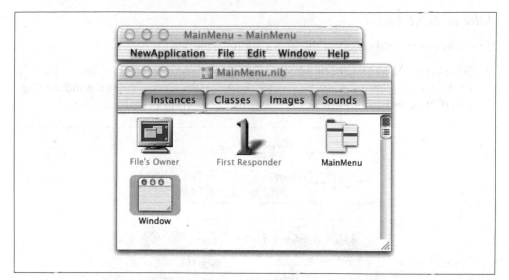

Figure 6-7. A new Cocoa application's default menu bar and nib file

Move and Resize the Window

Interface Builder stores all kinds of information about user interface objects in nib files. For example, you can set both the size and initial location of an application's main window by simply resizing and moving the window in Interface Builder:

1. Move the window near the upper-left corner of the screen by dragging its titlebar.

2. Make the window smaller using the resize control at the bottom-right corner of the window, as shown in Figure 6-8.

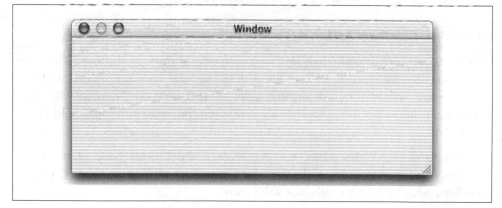

Figure 6-8. Cocoa window with resize control

Add a Text Field

Now add a text field object to the application's window.

1. Select the Views palette by clicking the second button from the left at the top of the Cocoa objects window. If you don't see the Cocoa palette window (Figure 6-9), select Palettes from the Tools menu to bring it forward.

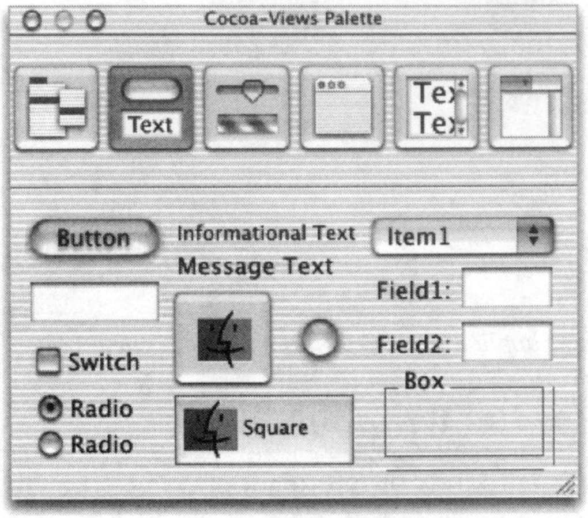

Figure 6-9. Interface Builder's Views Palette

2. Drag a text field object onto the window. You'll find it beneath the Button object on the left side of the Views palette.

3. Resize the text field to make it wider by grabbing the right handle and dragging toward the right, as shown in Figure 6-10.

Create a Custom Subclass

Object-oriented applications frequently contain one or more *controller* classes that are responsible for reacting to user input from the user interface objects and performing some activity (often delegating tasks to other objects). The controller class in this application will be responsible for sending the text to the text field object for display.

In order to define a new class, you must go to the Classes pane of the Main-Menu.nib window. Once there, the first thing you do is choose the superclass, the class from which your new subclass will inherit.

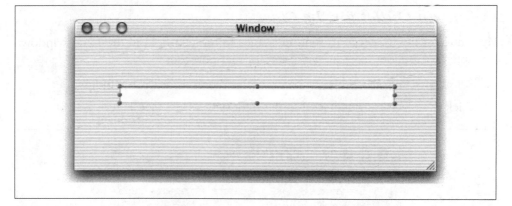

Figure 6-10. Resizing a text field

1. Select the Classes pane by clicking the Classes tab in the `MainMenu.nib` window.

2. Your new subclass will not need to inherit any complex behavior, so select NSObject from the list of classes (it's at the very top of the list, as shown in Figure 6-11). NSObject will provide it with everything necessary to function as a Cocoa object.

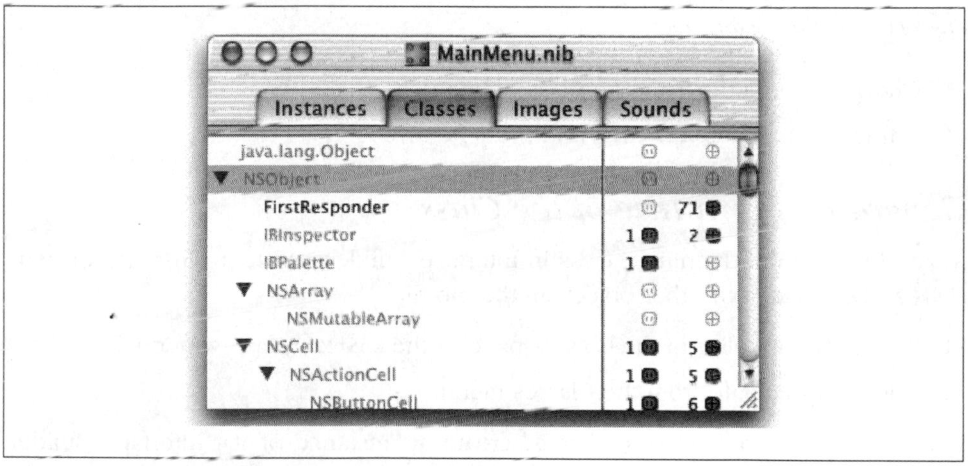

Figure 6-11. Subclassing NSObject

3. Choose Subclass from the Classes menu.

4. Type **MyController** to replace the text MyObject and press Return.

Now your class is established in the hierarchy of classes within the nib file.

Define an Outlet for the Class

MyController needs a way to send messages to the text field in the main window. Use Interface Builder to create an outlet for that purpose:

1. Select MyController in the Classes pane of the MainMenu.nib window.

2. Click the electrical outlet icon to the right of the class (see Figure 6-12).

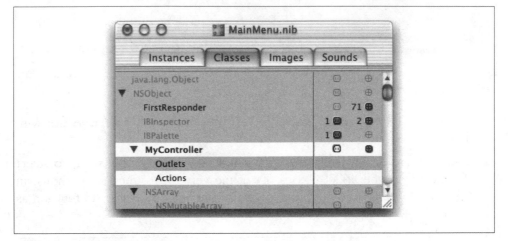

Figure 6-12. Adding an outlet

3. Choose Add Outlet from the Classes menu.

4. Name this outlet **textField** and press Return.

Generate an Instance of the Class

As the final step of defining a class in Interface Builder, create an instance of your class and connect it to other objects in the nib file:

1. Select MyController in the Classes pane of the MainMenu.nib window.

2. Choose Instantiate from the Classes menu.

When you instantiate a class (that is, create an instance of it), Interface Builder switches to the Instances pane (shown in Figure 6-13) and highlights the new instance, which is named after the class.

In fact, the Instantiate command does not generate a true instance of MyController. It creates a proxy object used within Interface Builder for defining connections to other objects in the nib file. When the application is launched and the nib file's contents are unarchived, the runtime system creates a true instance of MyController and uses the proxy object to establish connections to other objects in the nib file.

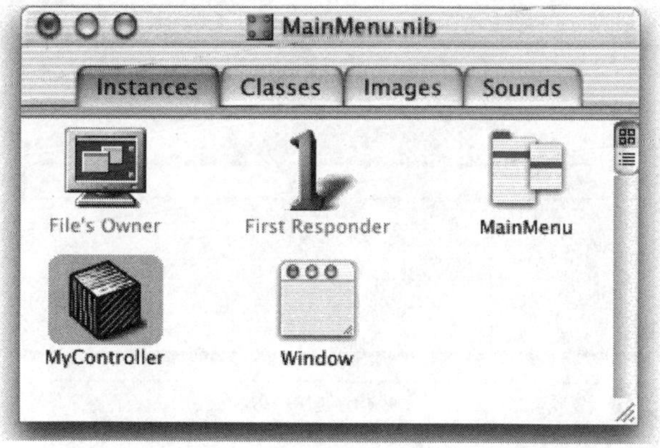

Figure 6-13. Interface Builder's Instances pane

Connect the Custom Class to the Interface

Now that you have created a proxy instance of MyController, you can use it to declare a connection between it and the text field you created earlier:

1. In the Instances pane of the MainMenu.nib window, Control-drag a connection line from the MyController instance to the text field. When the text field is outlined (Figure 6-14), release the mouse button.

2. Interface Builder brings up the Connections pane of the Custom Object Info window shown in Figure 6-15.

3. Click the Connect button.

4. Save the nib file (Command-S).

Now that you have created this connection, when the nib file is loaded at application launch time, the runtime system will know that you want MyController's textField outlet (remember, an outlet is just an instance variable) to be initialized to refer to the text field object in the window.

Generate the Source Files

Interface Builder generates source code files from the (partial) class definitions you've made. These files are skeletal, in the sense that they contain little more than essential Objective-C directives and the class definition information. You'll usually need to supplement these files with your own code. Note that, unlike some interface construction tools, the files generated by Interface Builder do not contain the code to create the interface you laid out; all of that information is stored in object archives in the nib file.

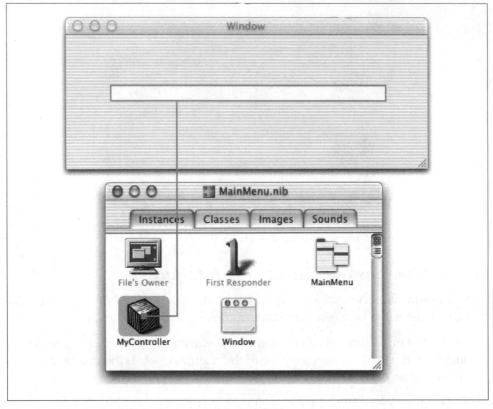

Figure 6-14. Connecting the instance to the text field

1. Go to the Classes pane of the nib file window.

2. Select the MyController class.

3. Choose Create Files from the Classes menu.

Interface Builder then displays the dialog box shown in Figure 6-16.

1. Verify that the checkboxes in the Create column next to the .h and .m files are selected.

2. Verify that the checkbox next to Nib Files is selected.

3. Click the Choose button.

Now we leave Interface Builder for the Nib Files application. You'll complete the application using Project Builder.

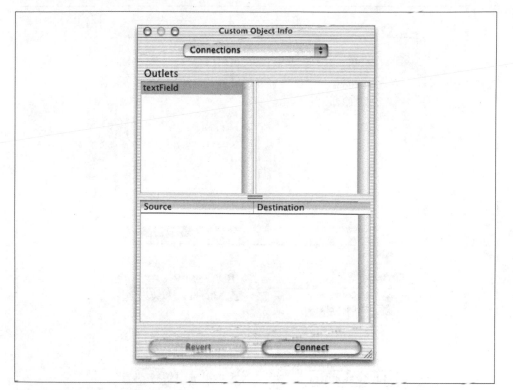

Figure 6-15. Custom Object Info window

Examine a Header File in Project Builder

When Interface Builder adds the source files to the Nib Files project, Project Builder does its best to figure out which group the new files belong in by examining the existing groups. Project Builder will add the source files to the group that contains other source files or at the top level, if no other source files are in the project. Project Builder's groups are simply arbitrary organizational containers, so you can arrange files however you wish. However, because these files are the interface and implementation for a class, it makes sense to put them in the Classes group.

1. Activate Project Builder's main window.

2. Drag MyController.h and MyController.m into the Classes group.

Clicking a file's name in the list will cause its contents to be displayed in the code editor on the right side of Project Builder's main window.

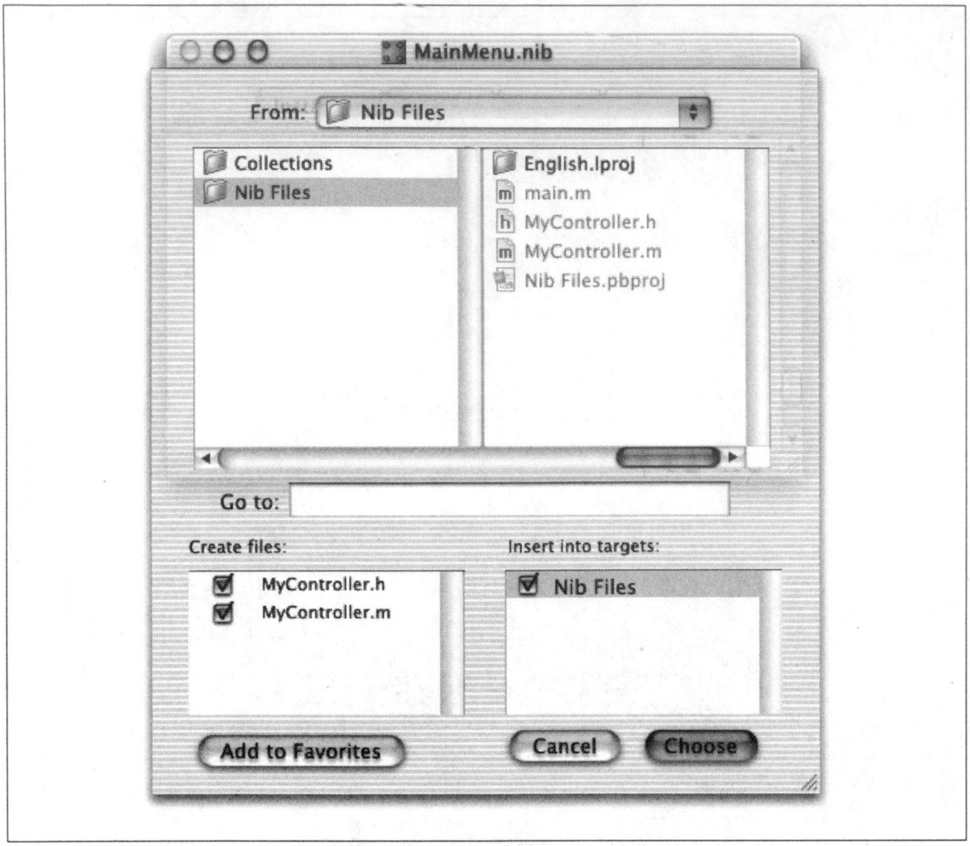

Figure 6-16. The Create Files dialog box

Statically Type the Outlet

By default, outlet declarations are dynamically typed using the id keyword. You can use id as the type for any object, meaning that the class of the object is determined at runtime. When you don't need a dynamically typed object, you can—and should—statically type it as a pointer to an object. It takes a little extra time, but it is good programming practice. Static typing also allows the compiler to perform type checking, potentially saving you debugging time later.

Generic outlets are declared as:

```
IBOutlet id variableName;
```

Change the declaration in:

```
MyController.h
```

to read:

```
IBOutlet NSTextField *textField;
```

Implement MyController's awakeFromNib Method

When an application is launched, the NSApplicationMain function loads the main nib file. After a nib file has been completely unpacked and its objects connected, the runtime system sends the awakeFromNib message to all objects that were derived from information in the nib file, signaling that the loading process is complete. All object's outlets are guaranteed to be initialized when awakeFromNib is called. This gives the objects in the nib file an opportunity to do any extra setup that they require before the user or the rest of the application attempts to interact with them.

In this example, you will use MyController's awakeFromNib method to print a message to the text field in the application's main window.

Declare the awakeFromNib method in MyController.h:

1. Select MyController.h from the Classes group in the Groups & Files list in Project Builder's main window.

2. Insert the declaration between the instance variable declarations and the @end statement:

```
@interface MyController : NSObject
{
    IBOutlet NSTextField *textField;
}
- (void)awakeFromNib;
@end
```

Method implementations go in MyController.m, between @implementation <class name> and @end. This is where you will add the code for MyController's awakeFromNib method:

1. Select MyController.m from the Classes group in Project Builder's main window.

2. Insert the code for awakeFromNib:

```
@implementation MyController
- (void)awakeFromNib
{
    [textField setObjectValue:[NSCalendarDate date]];
}
@end
```

The `awakeFromNib` method implementation simply sends the current date and time to the text field for display.

Build, Debug, and Run Nib Files

By clicking the Build button in Project Builder, you invoke the build process, coordinating the compilation and linking procedure that results in an executable file. It also performs other tasks needed to build an application.

The build process invokes the compiler, passing it the source code files of the project. Compilation of these files (Objective-C, C++, and standard C) produces machine-readable object files for the architecture or architectures specified for the build.

In the linking phase of the build, the build tool executes the linker, passing it the libraries and frameworks to link against the object files. Frameworks and libraries contain precompiled code that can be used by any application. Linking integrates the code in libraries, frameworks, and object files to produce the application executable file.

During the build process, nib files, sound, images, and other resources are copied from the project to the appropriate localized or nonlocalized locations in the application package. An application package is a directory that contains the application executable and the resources needed by that executable. This directory appears as a single file in the Finder that can be double-clicked to launch the application.

Build the project

When you click the Build button, the build process begins. When Project Builder finishes—and encounters no errors along the way—it displays Build Succeeded in the lower-left corner of the main window.

1. Save source code files and any changes to the project.

2. Click the Build button in the main window.

Debug the project

Of course, rare is the project that is flawless from the start. Project Builder is likely to catch some errors when you first build your project. To see the error-locating features of Project Builder, introduce a trivial mistake into the code:

1. Delete a semicolon in the code, creating an error.

2. Click the Build button in the main window.

1. Creare la clone come sottoclasse di NSObject
2. Creare le outlets (o le actions)
3. Trascinare la clone
4. Connettere le outlets (o le actions)
5. CREARE , FILE per la clone ———> Classe menu
   _____

=> consider le di chiarazioni id delle
demi in dichiarazioni sintetiche

(invece di: IBOutlet id TextField
IBOutlet NSTextField * TextField)

3. Click the error-notification line that appears in the build error browser.

4. Fix the error.

5. Rebuild the project.

One aspect of developing and debugging Cocoa applications that differs substantially from other environments is the role Interface Builder plays in the process. Because so much of the runtime behavior of applications is determined by connections you create in Interface Builder, you must remember to check not only your code for problems, but the nib files as well.

For example, if you run the Nib Files application and nothing happens, it could be that there is nothing at all wrong with your code; it may be that you just didn't connect the objects properly in Interface Builder. So remember, when something goes wrong, first think about the nature of the problem and decide if it makes sense to look in Interface Builder or at your code for the source of the problem.

Run the application

Click the Run button in Project Builder to launch the application.

If you want, you can locate the application in the Finder (in the build subdirectory of the Nib Files project, unless you changed the default location), double-click it, and try it out. In either case, you should see something very similar to Figure 6-17.

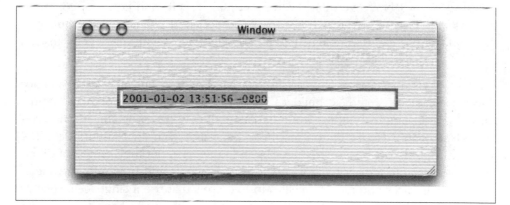

Figure 6-17. Nib files final output

Controls, Cells, and Formatters

Controls and cells lie behind the appearance and behavior of most user interface objects in Cocoa, including buttons, text fields, sliders, and browsers. Although they are quite different types of objects, they interact closely.

Controls enable users to signal their intentions to an application and thus control what is happening. Cells are rectangular areas embedded within a control. Some controls can hold multiple cells as a way to partition their surfaces into active areas. Cells can draw their own contents either as text or image (and sometimes as both), and they can respond individually to user actions. Figure 6-18 shows the relationship between controls and cells.

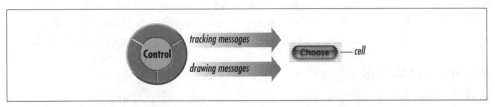

Figure 6-18. Controls and cells

Controls act as managers of their cells, telling them when and where to draw and notifying them when a user event (mouse click or keystroke) occurs in their areas. This division of labor, given the relative "weight" of cells and controls, conserves memory and provides a great boost to application performance. For example, a matrix of buttons can be implemented as a single control with many cells, instead of a set of individual controls.

A control does not have to have a cell associated with it, but most user interface objects available on Interface Builder's standard palettes are cell-control combinations. Even a simple button—from Interface Builder or programmatically created—is a control (an NSButton instance) associated with an NSButtonCell. The cells in a control such as a matrix must be the same size, but they can be of different classes. More complex controls, such as table views and browsers, can incorporate various sizes and types of cells. Most controls that use a single cell, such as NSButton, provide convenience methods so you don't usually have to deal with the contained cell directly.

Cells and Formatters

When one thinks of the contents of cells, it's natural to consider only text (NSString) and images (NSImage). The content seems to be whatever is displayed. However, cells can hold other kinds of objects, such as dates (NSDate), numbers (NSNumber), and custom objects (say, phone number objects).

One way to make your application's user interface more attractive is to format the contents of fields that display currencies and other numeric data. Fields can have fixed decimal digits, limit numbers to specific ranges, have currency symbols, and show negative values in a special color.

Formatters are objects that translate the values of certain objects to specific onscreen representations; formatters also convert a formatted string on a user interface into the represented object. For example, Figure 6-19 shows how a date formatter translates the contents of an NSDate object into a specific string for display.

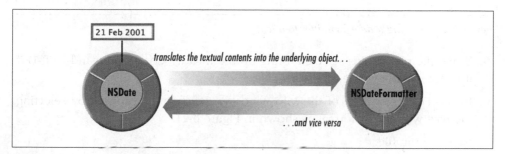

Figure 6-19. A date formatter

You can create, set, and modify formatter objects programmatically or by using Interface Builder. And you can create your own special formatter objects (that format phone numbers, for example) and add them to your own palette.

Formatter objects handle the textual representation of the objects associated with cells and translate what is typed into a cell into the underlying object. You can attach a formatter object to a cell in Interface Builder or use NSCell's setFormatter: method to programmatically associate a formatter with a cell.

A Formatted Cell Example

In this example you will modify the project you created in the previous section (nib files) so that the text cell formats the date before display. Interface Builder provides two formatter objects on its standard palettes, one for formatting dates and the other for formatting numbers. You'll use the first of these.

1. Open the Nib Files project.

2. Double click the MainMenu.nib file to open it in Interface Builder.

3. Select the Data Views Palette in the palette window.

4. Drag a date formatter object to the text field, as shown in Figure 6-20.

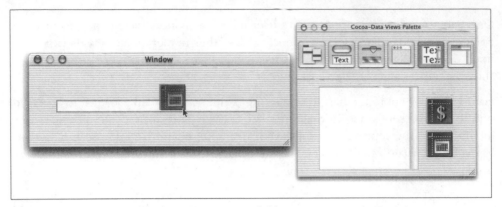

Figure 6-20. Adding a date formatter to a text field

5. While the text field is selected, bring up the Info window (Command-Shift-I) if it is not already visible.

6. In the Formatter pane of the Info window, specify a date format by selecting the row with the %c format as shown in Figure 6-21.

7. Save the nib file.

8. Build and run the project. You should see something very much like Figure 6-22.

Target/Action

The target/action pattern is part of the mechanism by which user interface controls respond to user actions, enabling users to communicate their intentions to an application. The target/action pattern specifies a one-to-one relationship between two objects; the control (more specifically, the control's cell) and its target. When a user clicks a user interface control, the control sends an action message to the target object as depicted in Figure 6-23.

The target/action relationship is typically defined using Interface Builder, in which you select a target object for a control, along with the specific action message that will be sent to the target. Target/action relationships can also be set (or modified) while an application is running.

Target/Action Example

The following steps take you through the process of building a simple example application that uses the target/action pattern. In this example, clicking a button in the main window causes the date and time to be updated in a text field.

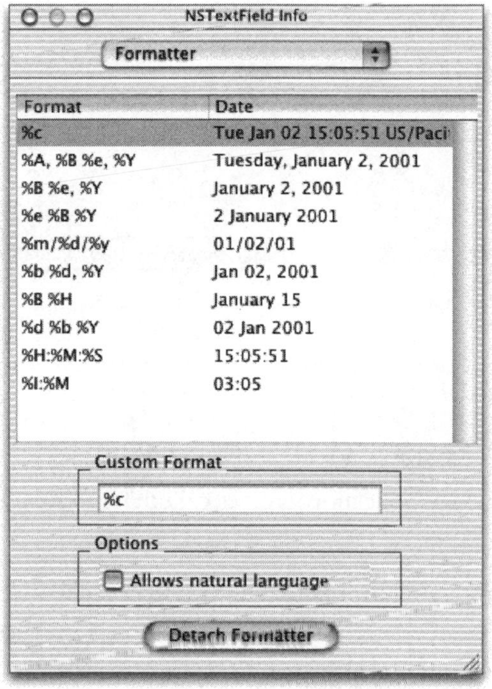

Figure 6-21. Configuring a date formatter

Figure 6-22. Nib files application using a date formatter

Create the project and user interface

Since the first example provided detailed instructions on creating projects using Project Builder, this example generally does not repeat those instructions. If you forget how to do a step, refer back to the Nib Files project in the section "Create Graphical User Interfaces in Cocoa" to refresh your recollection.

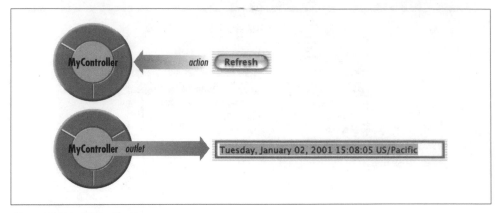

Figure 6-23. Target/action

1. Start Project Builder, if it is not already running.

2. Create a new Cocoa application project called TargetAction.

3. Open the main nib file.

4. Drag a text field onto the main window and make it about four times the default width.

5. Drag a button onto the main window

6. Double-click the button and rename the button by typing **Refresh**.

When you're finished, you should have a window that looks something like Figure 6-24.

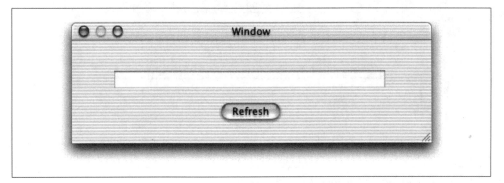

Figure 6-24. Target/action application interface

Create the controller class

Here you'll subclass NSObject to create a controller class for the application.

1. Click the Classes tab of the `MainMenu.nib` window.

2. Select NSObject from the list of classes.

3. Press Return to create a new subclass and type **MyController** to replace the text MyObject.

Define the outlets of the class

The controller class needs an outlet for the text field so it can send messages to the text field.

1. Select MyController in the Classes pane.

2. Click the electrical outlet icon to the right of the class.

3. Press Return to create a new outlet.

4. Name this outlet **textField** and press Return.

Define an action for the class

You will define one action method for MyController called `refresh:`. When the user clicks the Refresh button, a `refresh:` message is sent to the target object, an instance of MyController. Action refers both to a message sent to an object when the user manipulates a control object and to the method that is invoked.

1. Click Actions under MyConverter in the Classes pane shown in Figure 6-25.

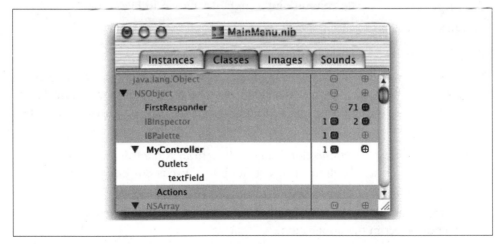

Figure 6-25. Defining an action

2. Press Return to create a new action, and type the name of the method, **refresh**. IB adds the : for you.

Generate an instance of the class

Now you must create a proxy instance of the controller class so you can make connections between the controller object and UI objects.

1. Click MyController in the Classes list to select it.

2. Choose Instantiate from the Classes menu. The instance will appear in the Instances pane.

Connect the interface controls to the class's actions

For MyController to receive an action message from the button in the user interface, you must connect the button to MyController. The button object keeps a reference to its target using an outlet—not surprisingly, the outlet is named target.

You can view (and complete) target/action connections in the Connections Info window in Interface Builder. The upper-right column of the Connections Info window lists all action methods defined by the class of the target object and known by Interface Builder.

1. Control-drag a connection from the Refresh button to the MyController instance in the MainMenu.nib window. When the instance is outlined, release the mouse button, as shown in Figure 6-26.

2. In the Connections pane, make sure target in the Outlets column is selected.

3. Select refresh: in the column on the right, as shown in Figure 6-27.

4. Click the Connect button.

5. Save the main nib file.

Developers new to Cocoa sometimes get confused when making action and outlet connections in Interface Builder. In general, you need only follow a simple rule to know which way to draw a connection line. Draw the connection in the direction that messages will flow:

- To make an action connection, draw a line from a control object in the user interface, such as a button or a text field, to the custom instance that should receive the action message.

- To make an outlet connection, draw a line from the custom instance to another object in the application.

The difference between target/action and outlet connections is depicted in Figure 6-28.

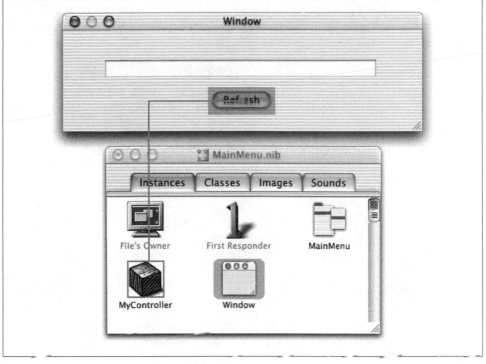

Figure 6-26. Connecting a button to un object instance

Another way to clarify connections is to consider who needs to find whom. With outlets, the custom object needs to find some other object, so the connection is from the custom object to the other object. With actions, the control object needs to find the custom object, so the connection is from the control object.

Connect the custom class to the interface

So that you can tell when the refresh: action method is invoked, the application must provide some kind of feedback. For this example, clicking the Refresh button will print the current date and time.

Connect MyController to the text field in the main window as you did in the section "Create Graphical User Interfaces in Cocoa." The refresh: method will use this outlet to send text to the text field.

1. In the Instances pane of the nib file window, Control-drag a connection line from the MyController instance to the text field. When the instance is outlined, release the mouse button.

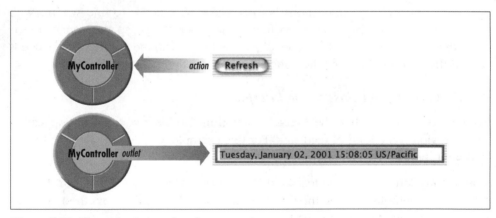

Figure 6-27. Connecting the target to its action

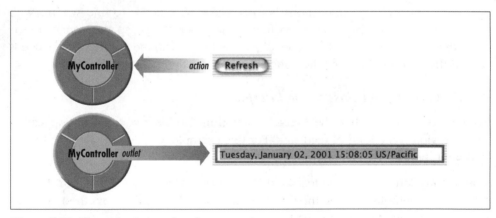

Figure 6-28. Target/action and outlet connections

2. Interface Builder brings up the Connections pane of the Info window. Select the outlet `textField`.

3. Click the Connect button.

Generate the source files

At this point you've finished declaring MyController's outlets, actions, and connections, so it's time to create the source files for the class and add them to the Project Builder project.

1. Go to the Classes pane of the nib file window.

2. Select the MyController class.

3. Choose Create Files in the Classes menu.

4. Verify that the checkboxes in the Create column next to the `.h` and `.m` files are selected.

5. Verify that the checkbox next to the TargetAction target is selected.

6. Click the Choose button.

7. Save the nib file.

Now we leave Interface Builder for this application. You'll complete the application using Project Builder.

Implement MyController's action method

Fill in the implementation of MyController's `refresh:` method.

1. In Project Builder, move `MyController.h` and `MyController.m` into the Classes group.

2. Select `MyController.m` and insert the code for `refresh:` as shown:

```
@implementation MyController
- (IBAction)refresh:(id)sender
{
    [textField setObjectValue:[NSCalendarDate date]];
}
@end
```

The method simply sends the current date and time to the text field so it is updated every time you click the Refresh button.

Build and debug the application

To smooth the task of debugging, Project Builder puts a graphical user interface over the GNU debugger, GDB. To help familiarize you with the debugger, use it now to set a breakpoint on the `refresh:` method.

1. Click MyController.m in Project Builder's Groups & Files list.

2. Locate the refresh: method in the Text pane.

3. Set a breakpoint by clicking in the column to the left of the code listing. See Figure 6-29

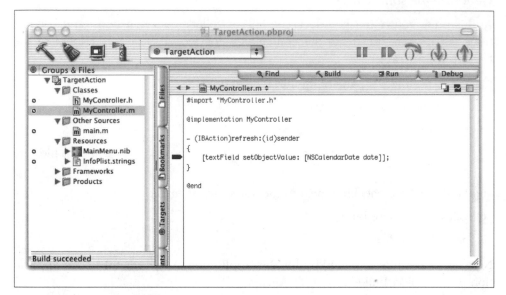

Figure 6-29. Setting a breakpoint

4. Click on the Build button to build the project.

5. Run the debugger by clicking the Debug button, or press Command-R.

6. When the application launches, click the Refresh button in its window.

7. When you click Refresh, the debugger will activate, stop at the breakpoint, and allow you to examine the call stack and the value of local variables.

To perform complex debugging tasks, you can use the GDB console. Click the Console tab at the top righthand corner of the window to expose the Console. When you click in the Console window and press Return, the (gdb) prompt appears. There are many GDB commands that you can type at this prompt that are not represented in the user interface. For online information on these commands, enter **help** at the prompt.

Object Ownership, Retention, and Disposal

The problem of object ownership and disposal is a natural concern in object-oriented programming. When an object is created and passed around among various "consumer" objects in an application, which object is responsible for disposing of it? And when? If the object is not deallocated when it is no longer needed, memory leaks. If the object is deallocated too soon, problems may occur in other objects that assume its existence, and the application may crash.

The Foundation framework introduces a mechanism and a policy that helps to ensure that objects are deallocated when—and only when—they are no longer needed.

The policy is quite simple: you are responsible for disposing of all objects that you own. You own objects that you create, either by allocating or copying them. You also own (or share ownership in) objects that you retain. The flip side of this rule is that you should never release an object that you have not retained or created.

Object Initialization and Deallocation

In Cocoa you usually create an object by allocating it (`alloc`) and then initializing it (`init` or a variant). For example:

```
NSArray *myArray = [[NSArray alloc] init];
```

When an array's `init` method is invoked, the method implementation initializes its instance variables to default values and completes other startup tasks. Similarly, when an object is deallocated, its `dealloc` method is invoked, giving it the opportunity to release objects it has created, free allocated memory, and so on.

But now another question arises. If the owner of an object must release the object within its programmatic scope, how can it give that object to other objects? The short answer is: the `autorelease` method, which marks the receiver for later release, enabling it to live beyond the scope of the owning object so that other objects can use it.

The `autorelease` method must be understood in a larger context of the autorelease mechanism for object deallocation. Through this programmatic mechanism, you implement the policy of object ownership and disposal.

Reference Counting

Each object in Cocoa has an associated reference count. When you allocate or copy an object, its reference count is set at 1. You send `release` to an object to decrement its reference count. When the reference count reaches 0, NSObject invokes the object's `dealloc` method, after which the object is destroyed. However, successive consumers of the object can delay its destruction by sending it `retain`, which increments the reference count. You retain objects to ensure that they won't be deallocated until you're done with them.

Autorelease Pools

Each application puts in place at least one autorelease pool (for the event cycle) and can have many more. An autorelease pool tracks objects marked for eventual release and releases them at the appropriate time. You put an object in the pool by sending the object an `autorelease` message. In the case of an application's event cycle, when code finishes executing and control returns to the application object (typically at the end of the cycle), the application object sends `release` to the autorelease pool, and the pool releases each object it contains. If afterward the reference count of an object in the pool is 0, the object is deallocated. Figure 6-30 illustrates the process.

1. `myObj` creates an object:

       anObj = [[MyClass alloc] init];

2. `myObj` returns the object to `yourObj`, autoreleased. This puts the object in the autorelease pool; that is, the autorelease pool starts tracking the object:

       return [anObj autorelease];

3. `yourObj` retains the object. The `retain` message increments the reference count to 2 (both `myObj` and `yourObj` now have references to `anObj`):

       [anObj retain];

4. At the end of the event cycle, the autorelease pool sends `release` to all of its objects, thereby decrementing their reference counts. Objects with reference counts of 0 are deallocated. Since `anObj` previously had a reference count of 2, when the autorelease pool sends a `release` message to it, `anObj` still has a reference count of 1, so it is not deallocated.

5. When `yourObj` no longer needs `anObj`, it sends `autorelease` to `anObj`, putting it into an autorelease pool again. At the end of the event cycle, the autorelease pool once again sends `release` to its objects; since the reference count of `anObj` is now 0, it's deallocated.

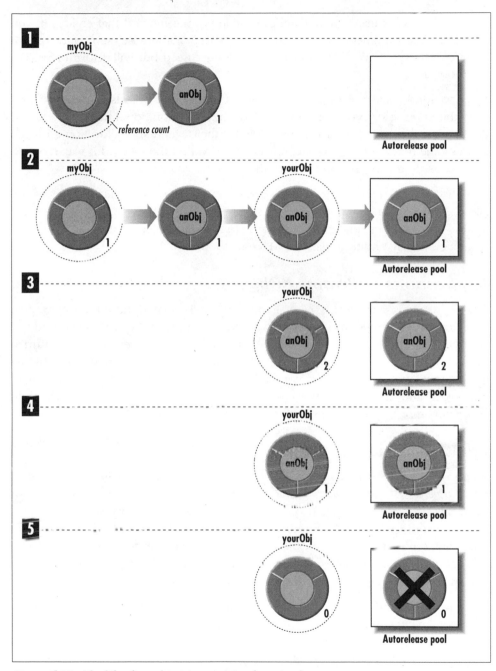

Figure 6-30. The life of an object in an autorelease pool

When an object is used solely within the scope of the method that creates it, you can deallocate it immediately by sending it `release`. Otherwise, send `autorelease` to all objects you have created that you no longer need but will return or pass to other objects.

You shouldn't release objects that you receive from other objects (unless you precede the `release` or `autorelease` with a `retain`). You don't own these objects and can assume that their owner is responsible for their eventual deallocation. You can also assume that a received object remains valid within the method it was received in. That method can also safely return the object to its invoker.

You should send `release` or `autorelease` to an object only as many times as are allowed by its creation (one) plus the number of `retain` messages you have sent it. You should never send `free` or `dealloc` to a Cocoa object (with one exception: when you are overriding a class's `dealloc` method).

Implications of Retained Objects

When you retain an object, you're sharing it with its owner and other objects that have retained it. While this might be what you want, it can lead to some undesirable consequences. If you had retained an object's instance variable (returned from an accessor method) and the owner is released, the object referred to by the instance may well be invalid. If you had retained an instance variable of the owning object, and that instance variable refers to a mutable object that is later modified, your code could be referencing something it does not expect.

Copying Versus Retaining

When deciding whether to retain or copy objects, it helps to categorize them as *value objects* or *entity objects*. Value objects are objects such as NSNumbers or NSStrings that encapsulate a discrete, limited set of data. Entity objects, such as NSViews and NSWindows, tend to be larger objects that manage and coordinate subordinate objects. For value objects, use `copy` when you want your own snapshot of the object (the object must conform to the NSCopying protocol); use `retain` when you intend to share the object. Always retain entity objects.

For more information on the subtleties of copying objects in Cocoa, see the reference documentation for the NSCopying protocol.

Reference Counting in Accessors

Accessor methods are used to get and set an object's instance variables. The declaration for an accessor method that returns a value is, by convention, the name of the instance variable preceded by the type of the returned value in parentheses. An accessor method that sets the value of an instance variable begins with `set`, followed by the name of the instance variable (initial letter capitalized). The set method's argument takes the type of the instance variable and the method itself returns void.

If you don't want to allow an instance variable's value to be changed by any object other than one of your class, don't provide a set method for the instance variable. If you do provide a set method, make sure objects of your own class use it when specifying a value for the instance variables. This has important implications for subclasses of your class.

In accessor methods that set value-object instance variables, you usually (but not always) want to make your own copy of the object and not share it. (Otherwise it might change without your knowledge.) Send autorelease to the old object and then send copy—not retain—to the new one, as demonstrated in Example 6-2.

Example 6-2. A setTitle: Method

```
- (void)setTitle:(NSString *)newTitle
{
    [title autorelease];
    title = [newTitle copy];
}
```

Deciding how to implement accessor methods, especially setter methods, can be tricky. There are many issues you must keep in mind, some more obvious than others. The remainder of this section discusses the most critical of these issues.

When to release

In Example 6-2, the reason title needs to be released before it is set to something else is because title is a pointer to an NSString object. So if title is set to newTitle without first autoreleasing it, then the original NSString that title pointed to will be leaked; once title is pointing to the new NSString, there is no way to release the previous value of title.

When to copy

It is often better to copy leaf value objects like NSStrings instead of just retaining them. Consider the following example:

```
NSMutableString *foo = [NSMutableString stringWithCString:"foo"];
[myWindow setTitle:foo];
[foo appendString:@"bar"];
```

If NSWindow retained (instead of copied) the string passed to it in setTitle:, the title of the window would now be foobar, instead of foo, which is probably not the intended result. Note that copy will actually just increment the reference count of an object (an implicit retain) if it can do so safely—if, for instance, the receiver is actually an immutable NSString.

Release or autorelease

Another issue is whether to release or autorelease an instance variable before changing it. If in Example 6-2 title is released instead of autoreleased, it immediately becomes invalid. So if newTitle pointed to the same object as title, the title would now point to garbage because you released what you are about to set.

Consider another possible predicament for the object invoking such a setTitle: method:

```
{
  /* ... */
  title = [myWindow title];
  [myWindow setTitle:newTitle];
  /*...*/
  // title is now garbage because it was released by setTitle:
}
```

The code following the setTitle: invocation will fail if it expects title to be a valid NSString.

A helpful rule of thumb is that Foundation objects (NSArray and NSDictionary, for example) never autorelease; they release. This is to maximize performance. However, at the Application Kit level, and in user interface classes especially, autorelease is used to maintain the general Application Kit API promise of autoreleased returns: the returned value is valid within the calling context until the autorelease pool is emptied.

When implementing your own classes, be aware of these trade-offs and dangers. Using release is likely the better choice in cases in which you work with objects that no client will ever get a handle to. Using release makes it much easier to track down retain/release bugs in your code. However, autorelease should be used for instance variables that clients are able to access.

Tips for Eliminating Deallocation Bugs

Problems in object deallocation are not unusual for beginning Cocoa programmers. You might release an object too many times or you might not release an object as many times as is needed to deallocate it. Both situations lead to nasty problems—in the first case, to runtime errors when your code references nonexistent objects; the second case leads to memory leaks.

Here are a couple of things to remember that might help you avoid deallocation bugs in Cocoa code:

- Make sure there's an `alloc`, `copy`, `mutableCopy`, or `retain` message sent to an object for each `release` or `autorelease` sent to it.

- When you add an object to a collection, it's retained; when you remove an object from a collection, it's released. Releasing a collection object (such as an NSArray) releases all objects stored in it, as well.

7

Currency Converter Tutorial

In this chapter you'll build a single window application from beginning to end, giving you an opportunity to deepen your understanding of the Cocoa programming paradigms discussed in Chapter 6, *Essential Cocoa Paradigms*. For the first time, you'll see the complete work flow typical of Cocoa application development:

1. Design the application

2. Create the project (Project Builder)

3. Create the interface (Interface Builder)

4. Define the classes (Interface Builder)

5. Implement the classes (Project Builder)

6. Build the project (Project Builder)

7. Run and test the application

The application you'll build in this chapter is called Currency Converter—a simple utility that converts a dollar amount to an amount in another currency. Currency Converter is an extremely simple application, but there's still a design behind it. This design is based upon the Model-View-Controller (MVC) paradigm, the model behind many designs for object-oriented programs. MVC separates an application into different types of objects, each with specific roles and responsibilities. This design paradigm aids in the development of a maintainable, extensible, and reusable code base, as the Currency Converter example will make clear.

Design the Currency Converter Application

An object-oriented application should be based on a design that identifies the objects of the application and clearly defines their roles and responsibilities. You normally work on a design before you write a line of code. You don't need any fancy tools for designing many applications; a pencil and a pad of paper will do.

The Model-View-Controller (MVC) Paradigm

MVC proposes three types of objects in an application—model, view, and controller—as illustrated in Figure 7-1. In MVC designs, model objects hold data and define the logic that manipulates that data, view objects represent something visible on the user interface (a window or a button, for example), and controller objects act as a mediator between model objects and view objects.

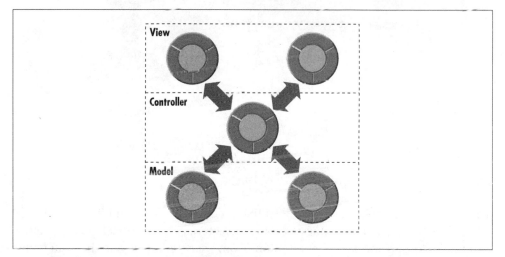

Figure 7-1. The separation of model, view, and controller objects in an MVC design

The beauty of MVC is that the controller's central, mediating role frees the model objects from having to know about the state and events of the user interface, and that frees the view objects from having to know about the programmatic interfaces of the model objects.

MVC, strictly observed, is not advisable in all circumstances. Sometimes it's best to combine roles. For instance, in a graphics-intensive application, such as an arcade game, you might have several view objects that merge the roles of view and model. In some applications, especially simple ones, you can combine the roles of controller and model; these objects join the special data structures and logic of model objects with the controller's hooks to the interface.

MVC in Currency Converter's design

Currency Converter consists of two custom objects—Converter (model) and ConverterController (controller)—as well as a user interface (view) that is implemented using a collection of ready-made Application Kit objects. The converter object is responsible for computing a currency amount and returning that value. Between the user interface and the converter object is a controller object, ConverterController. ConverterController coordinates the activity between the converter object and the UI objects. These relationships are depicted in Figure 7-2.

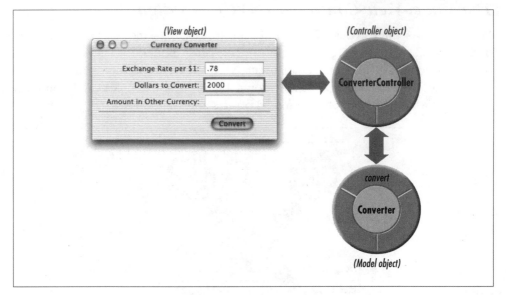

Figure 7-2. MVC in Currency Converter's design

The ConverterController class assumes the central role in the application. Like all controller objects, it communicates with the interface and model objects, and it handles tasks specific to the application. ConverterController gets the values that users enter into fields, passes these values to the converter object, gets the result back from Converter, and puts this result in a field in the interface.

The Converter class merely computes a value from two arguments passed into it by the controller and returns the result. By insulating the Converter class from implementation-specific details of the user interface, the Converter class becomes easily reusable in other applications.

This design for Currency Converter is intended to illustrate specific aspects of object-oriented programming and MVC and so may be overdesigned for something so simple. It is quite possible to have the application's controller class, ConverterController, perform the computation and do without the Converter class. However, there is no harm in concentrating on good design from the start.

Create the Currency Converter Project

Now that you have a design for Currency Converter, it's time to start building the application.

Create the Application Project

Your first step toward completing the application is to create the Project Builder project.

1. Start Project Builder.

2. Choose New Project from the File menu.

3. In the New Project panel, select the Cocoa Application project type and click the Next button.

4. Name the application **Currency Converter**.

5. If you wish, click Set to select a location to save the project in a specific location of your choice. To use the default location, go on to step 6.

6. Click Finish.

Project Indexing

It's a good idea to have Project Builder index a project once it has been created. During indexing Project Builder stores all symbols of the project (classes, methods, globals, etc.) on disk. This allows Project Builder to access project-wide information quickly.

Note that the version of Project Builder included with the first release of Mac OS X contained a bug causing project indexing to fail unless the project had first been built. If you are working with this release, simply build the project before attempting to create a project index.

To create an index, choose Index Project (Command-Option-I) from the Project menu. Once your project has been indexed, you'll be able to use Project Find to search both your project's code and the system headers for symbols. You'll also be able to access reference documentation directly from Project Find results. Creating an index for a Cocoa project the first time will take a while because Project Builder indexes all of the Cocoa headers as well as the ones in your project.

Now that your project has been indexed, you can easily access documentation for a Cocoa class or method. For example, if you look inside the main.m file in your project's Other Sources group, you'll see a call to the function NSApplicationMain.

1. Click the Find tab in Project Builder's main window. The Find pane will appear, as shown in Figure 7-3.

2. Make sure that the Find Type pop up is set to Definitions.

3. Type **NSApplicationMain** in the Find field and click the Find button.

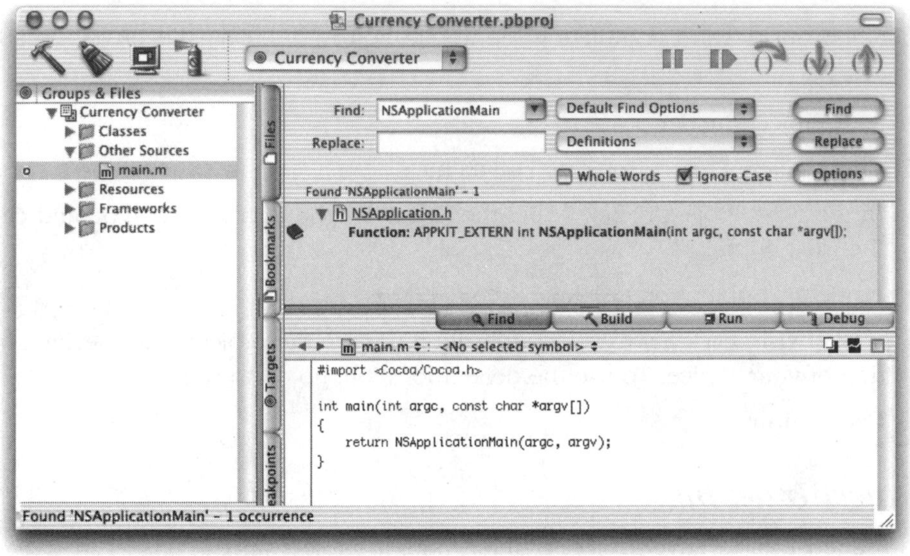

Figure 7-3. Project Builder's Find panel

As you can see, Project Builder found one definition in NSApplication.h. If you click the header filename, Project Builder will show you the definition in the document pane. If you click on the book icon just to the left of the Find result, Project Builder will launch Help Viewer and allow you to access the reference documentation for this function. Note that Help Viewer may require you to navigate to the Cocoa area of the Developer Center before searches from Project Builder function correctly.

Create the Currency Converter Interface

Currency Converter's interface is really quite simple, consisting of a few text fields and a button. However, the process of creating it will give you an opportunity to explore some of the object layout tools available in Interface Builder that make it a joy to use.

Open the Main Nib File

Begin by creating an application's user interface in Interface Builder.

1. Locate `MainMenu.nib` in the Resources group in Project Builder.

2. Double-click to open it. This will open Interface Builder and bring up the nib file.

A default menu bar and window titled Window will appear when the nib file is open.

Resize the Window

In this section you'll change the size of the application's main window to accommodate the UI objects to be added.

1. Using Figure 7-4 as a guide, make the window smaller by dragging an edge of the bottom-right corner of the window inward.

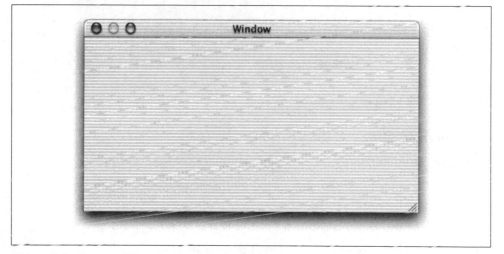

Figure 7-4. Currency Converter's main window

You can resize the window more precisely by using the Size menu of the Window Info window.

2. Choose Show Info from the Tools menu.

3. Select Size from the pop-up menu.

4. In the Content Rect area, select Width/Height from the righthand pop-up menu. In the text fields under the Width/Height menu, type **400** in the width (w) field and **200** in the height (h) field as shown in Figure 7-5.

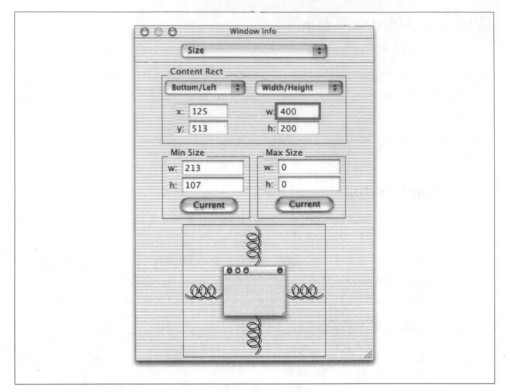

Figure 7-5. The Window Info window

Set the Window's Title and Attributes

While the Info window is open, set other attributes for the window.

1. Select Attributes from the Info window's pop-up menu and change the window's title to Currency Converter.

2. Verify that the Visible at Launch Time option is selected.

3. Deselect the Resize checkbox in the Controls area.

Place a Text Field; Resize and Initialize It

Currency Converter uses text fields to accept user input and display converted values.

1. Drag a text field object onto the Currency Converter window as shown in Figure 7-6. Notice that Interface Builder helps you place objects according to the Aqua interface guidelines by displaying pop-up guides when an object is dragged close to the proper distance from neighboring objects or the edge of the window.

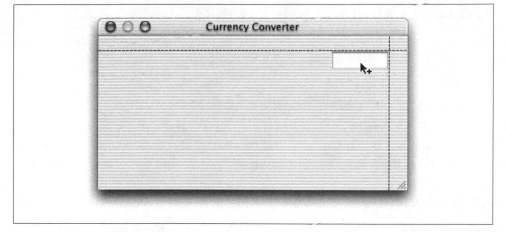

Figure 7-6. Placing a text field

2. Resize the text field by grabbing a handle and dragging in the direction you want it to grow. In this case, drag the left handle to the left to enlarge the text field, as shown in Figure 7-6.

Currency Converter needs two more text fields, both the same size as the first. You have two options: you can drag another object from the palette and make it the same size, or you can duplicate the first object.

Duplicate an Object

Using the text field you just added to the window as a template, duplicate it twice to create the remaining text field objects.

1. Select the text field, if it is not already selected.

2. Choose Duplicate (Command-D) from the Edit menu. The new text field appears slightly offset from the original field.

3. Reposition the new text field under the first text field. Notice that guides appear and assist you by snapping the second text field into place.

4. To make the third text field, type Command-D again. Notice that IB remembered the offset from the previous Duplicate command and automatically applied it to the newly created text field.

Change the Attributes of a Text Field

The bottom text field will display the results of the computation and should therefore have different attributes than the other text fields:

1. Select the third text field.

2. Bring up the Info window and choose Attributes from the pop-up menu.

3. Turn off the Editable attribute in the Options section of the Inspector so that users will not be able to alter the contents of the field. Keep the Selectable attribute so that users can copy and paste the contents to other applications.

Assign Labels to the Fields

Text fields without labels would be confusing, so add labels by using the ready-made label object from the Views palette:

1. Using Figure 7-7 as a guide, drag a Message Text object from the Views palette onto the window.

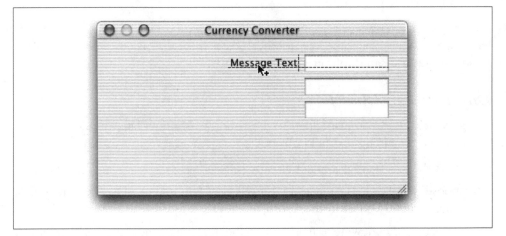

Figure 7-7. Aligning a text field with its label

2. Right-align the text; with the Message Text object selected, click on the third button from the left in the Alignment area of the Info window, as shown in Figure 7-8.

3. Duplicate the text label twice, enter the text for each, and align them, as shown in Figure 7-9.

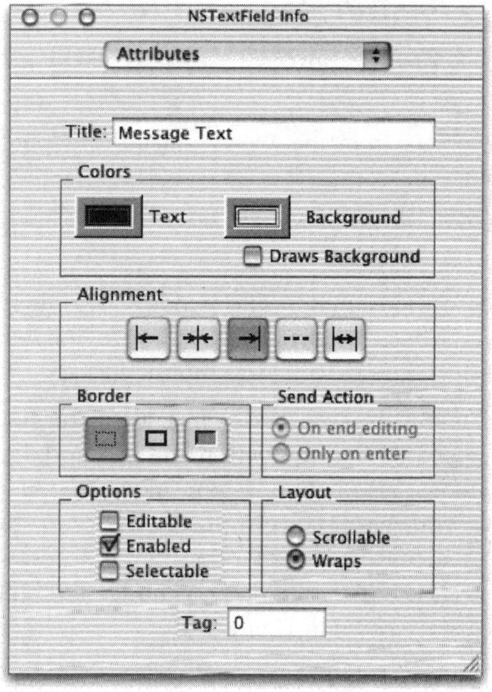

Figure 7-8. The NSTextField Info window

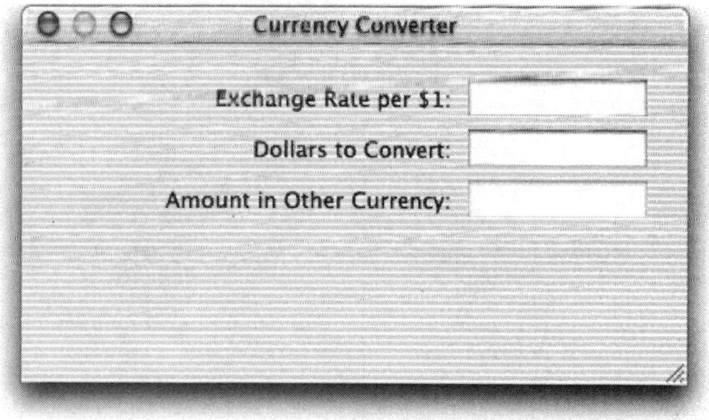

Figure 7-9. Aligning Currency Converter's text fields and labels

Add a Button to the Interface and Initialize It

The currency conversion can be invoked either by clicking a button or pressing Return:

1. Drag the button object from the Views palette and put it in the lower-right portion of the window.

2. Double-click the title of the button to select its text label and change the title to Convert.

3. Choose Attributes in the NSButton Info window, and then choose Return from the pop-up menu labeled Equiv:. This will give the button the capacity to respond to the Return key as well as to mouse clicks.

4. Align the button under the text fields. First, drag the button downward until the Aqua guide appears. With the button still selected, hold down the Option key and release the mouse button. If you move the cursor around, Interface Builder will show you the distance from the button to the object that you've indicated with the cursor. With the Option key still down and the cursor over the bottom text field, use the arrow keys to nudge the button to the exact center of the text fields as shown in Figure 7-10.

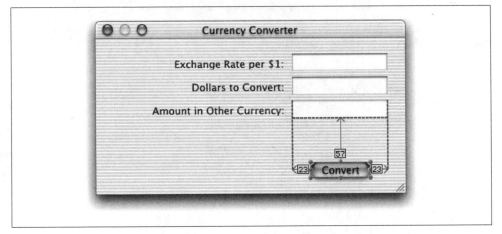

Figure 7-10. Aligning the Convert button with the text fields

Add a Horizontal Decorative Line

You've probably noticed that the final interface for Currency Converter has a decorative line between the text fields and the button. To create this line:

1. Drag a horizontal separator object from the Views palette onto the interface. It's located just beneath the Box object in the lower-righthand corner of the Views palette.

2. Using Figure 7-11 as a guide, drag the endpoints of the line until the line extends across the window.

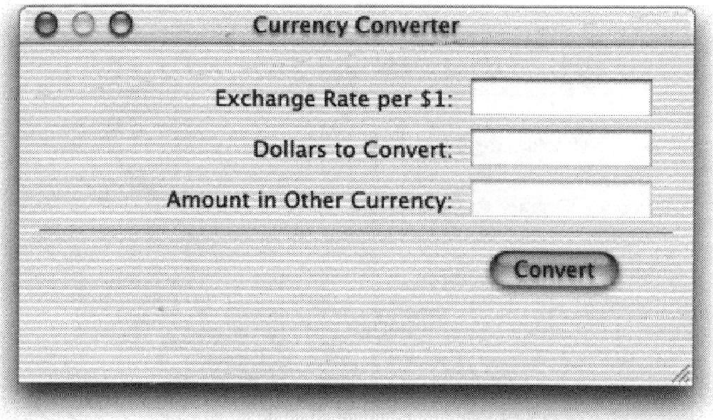

Figure 7-11. Adding a decorative line to the interface

3. Move the Convert button back up until the Aqua guide appears.

Aqua Layout and Object Alignment

In order to make an attractive user interface, you must be able to visually align interface objects in rows and columns. Eyeballing the alignments can be very difficult, and typing in x/y coordinates by hand is tedious and time consuming. Aligning Aqua interface widgets is made even more difficult because the objects have shadows and UI guideline metrics don't typically take the shadows into account. Interface Builder uses visual guides and layout rectangles to help you with object alignment.

In Cocoa, all drawing is done within the bounds of an object's frame. Because interface objects have shadows, they don't visually align correctly if you align the edges of the frames (as is done with Mac OS 9). For example, the Aqua UI guidelines say that a push button should be 20 pixels tall, but you actually need a frame of 32 pixels for both the button and its shadow. The layout rectangle is what you must align.

You can view the layout rectangles of objects in IB using Show Layout Rectangles in the Layout menu (Command-L). Also, the IB Size Inspector has a pop up to toggle between the frame and layout rectangle so you can set values by hand when appropriate.

Interface Builder gives you several ways to align objects in a window:

- Dragging objects with the mouse in conjunction with Aqua guides, as shown in Figure 7-12

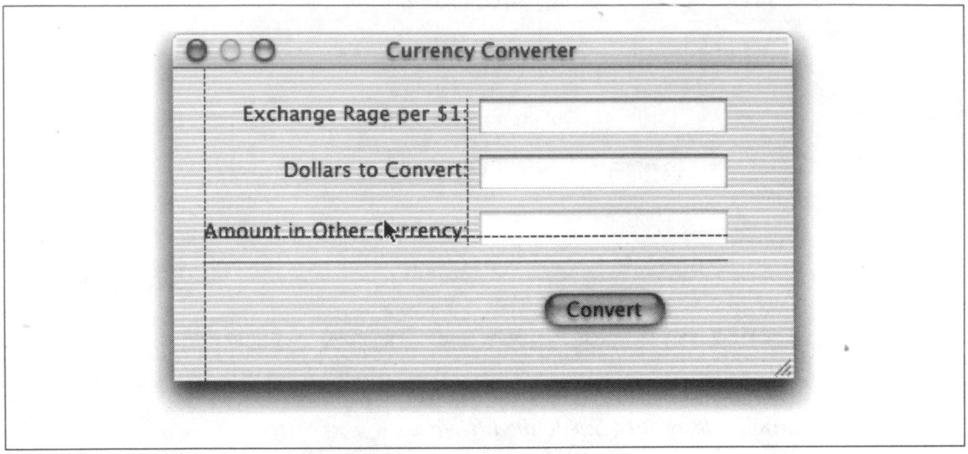

Figure 7-12. Object alignment using Aqua guides

- Pressing arrow keys (with the grid off, the selected objects move one pixel), as shown in Figure 7-13

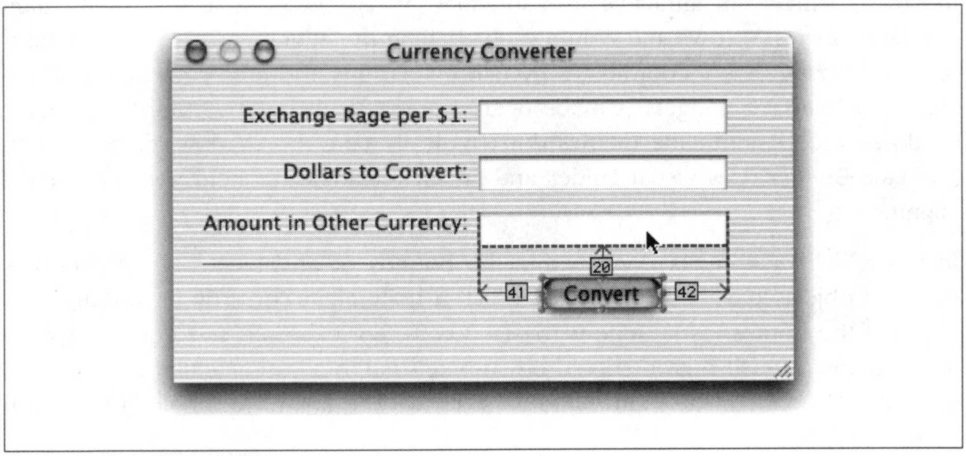

Figure 7-13. Object alignment using arrow keys

- Using a reference object to put selected objects in rows and columns, as shown in Figure 7-14
- Using the built-in alignment functions, as shown in Figure 7-15

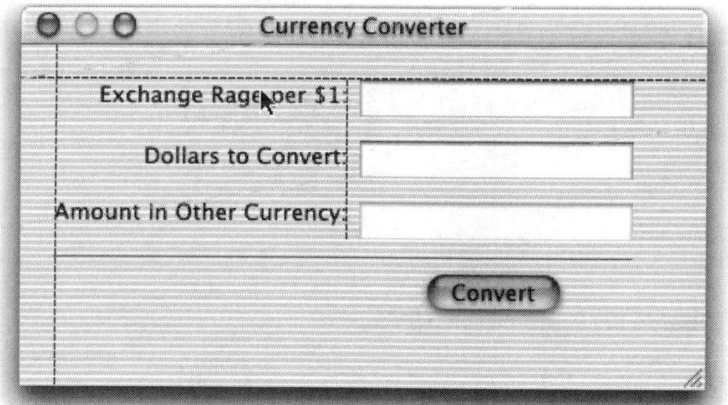

Figure 7-14. Object alignment using a reference

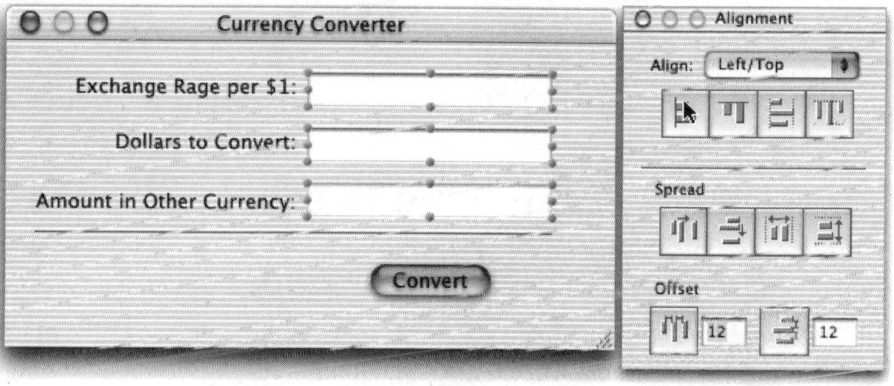

Figure 7-15. Object alignment using the Alignment palette

- Specifying origin points in the Size display of the Info window, as shown in Figure 7-16

- Using layout rectangles, as shown in Figure 7-17

Look in the Alignment and Guides submenus of the Layout menu for various alignment commands and tools. You can also use the alignment tool (choose Alignment in the Tools menu), which provides a floating window with buttons that perform various types of alignment.

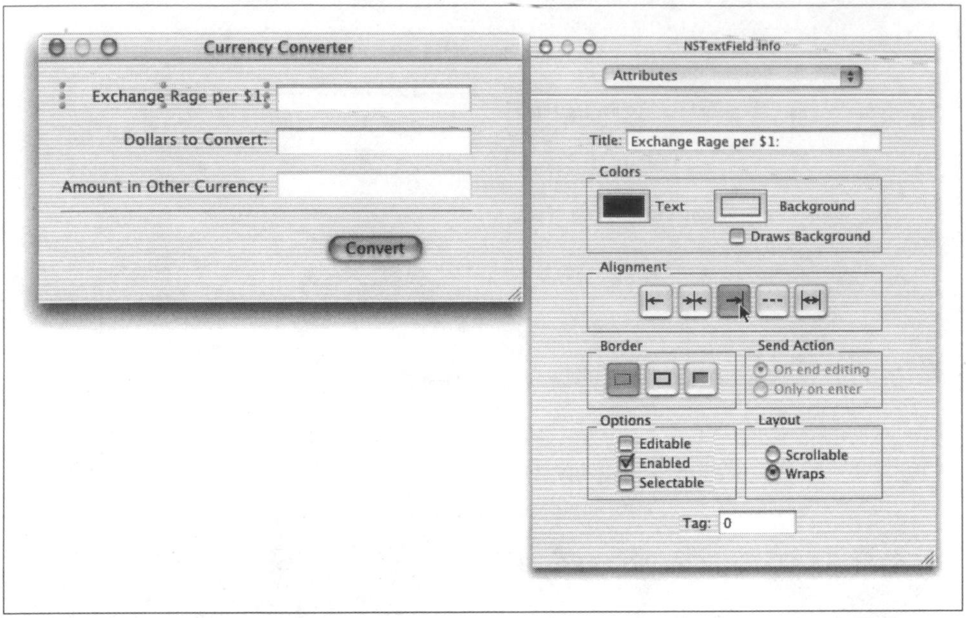

Figure 7-16. Object alignment using the Info window

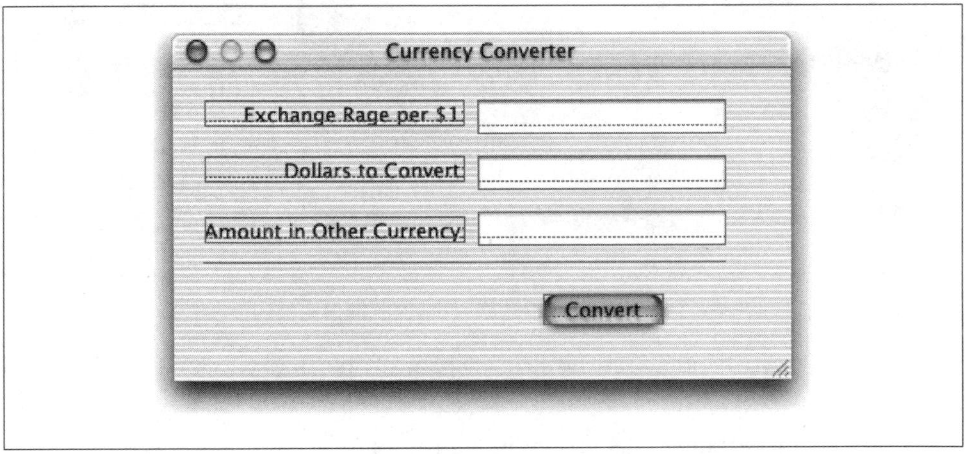

Figure 7-17. Object alignment using layout rectangles

Center the Interface Objects and Resize the Window

Currency Converter's interface is almost complete. The finishing touch is to resize the window so that all of the objects are centered and properly aligned to each edge; currently the objects are aligned only to the top and right edges.

For Currency Converter, you will continue, using the automated Aqua guides and a few Layout commands:

1. Select the third text label (Amount in Other Currency), then extend the selection (Shift-click) to include the other two.

2. Resize all the labels to their minimum width by choosing Size to Fit in the Layout menu.

3. Select Same Size from the Layout menu to make the selected text labels the same size.

4. Drag the labels toward the left edge of the window and release them when the Aqua guide appears.

5. Select all three text fields and drag them to the left, again using the guides to help you find the proper position.

6. Shorten the horizontal separator and move the button into position again under the text fields.

7. Resize the window using the guides to give you the proper distance from the text fields on the right and the Convert button on the bottom.

At this point, the application's window should look like Figure 7-18.

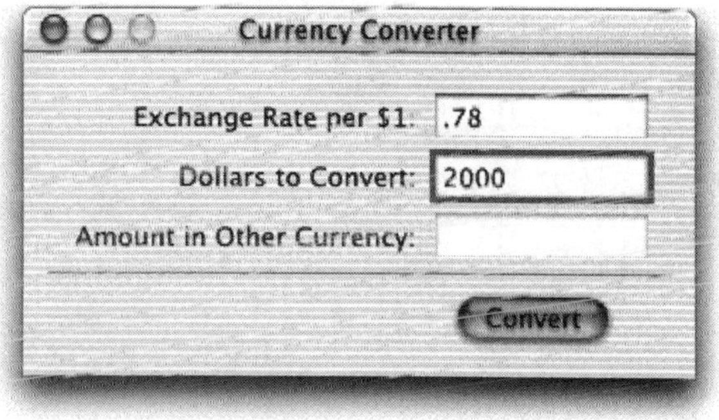

Figure 7-18. Final Currency Converter Interface

Enable Tabbing Between Text Fields

The final step in composing the Currency Converter interface has more to do with behavior than with appearance. You want the user to be able to tab from the first editable field to the second and back to the first. Many objects in Interface

Builder's palettes have an instance variable named `nextKeyView`. This variable identifies the next object to receive keyboard events when the user presses the Tab key (or the previous object if Shift-Tab is pressed). If you want interfield tabbing, you must connect fields through the `nextKeyView` variable.

In order for interfield tabbing to start from the correct text field, you need to make the text field the application window's `initialFirstResponder`—the object in the window that will be first in line to accept events from the keyboard. You will learn more about FirstResponder and the Responder chain in Chapter 8, *Event Handling*.

1. In the Instances pane of the `MainMenu.nib` window, click on the Window instance and Control-drag a connection to the first text field in Currency Converter's window. Select the `initialFirstResponder` outlet as shown in Figure 7-19 and click Connect.

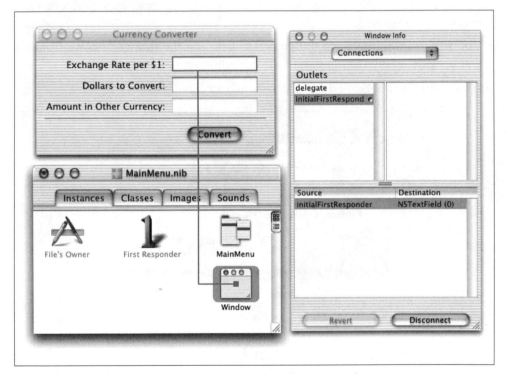

Figure 7-19. Connecting Currency Converter's initialFirstResponder

2. Select the first text field and Control-drag a connection line from it to the second text field as shown in Figure 7-20. Select nextKeyView and click Connect. The nextKeyView outlet identifies the next object to respond to events after the Tab key is pressed.

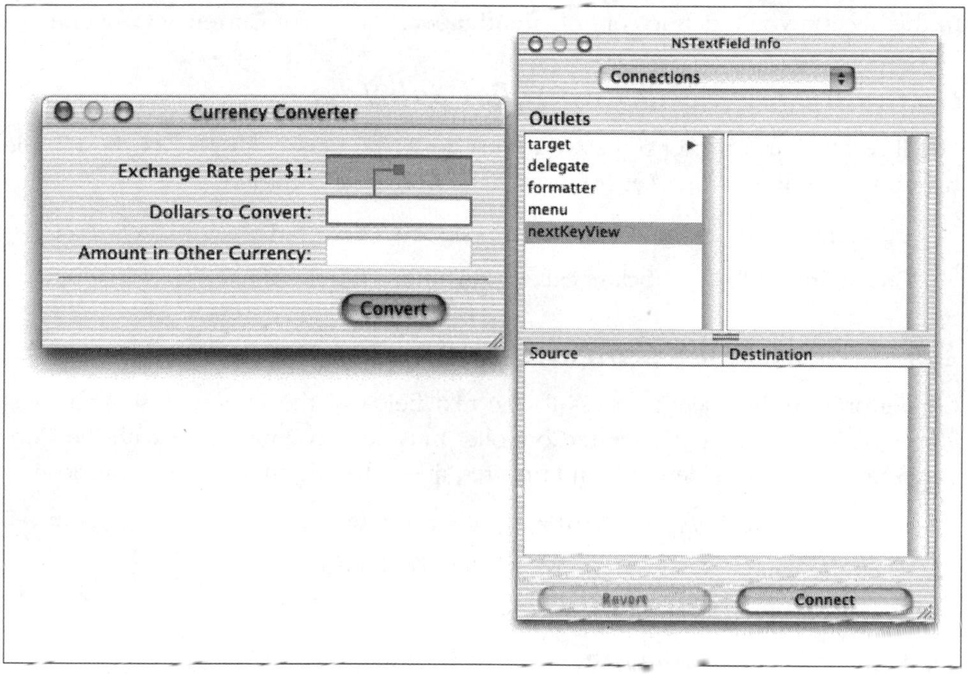

Figure 7-20. Connecting text fields for interfield tabbing

3. Repeat the step, but connect the second field to the first.

Test the Interface

The Currency Converter interface is now complete. Interface Builder lets you test an interface without having to write one line of code:

1. Choose File→Save All to save your work

2. Choose File→Test Interface.

3. Try various operations in the interface, such as tabbing and cutting and pasting between text fields.

4. When finished, choose Quit New Application from the Interface Builder Application menu to exit test mode.

Notice that the screen position of the Currency Converter window in Interface Builder is used as the initial position for the window when the application is launched. Place the window near the top-left corner of the screen so it will be in a convenient (and traditional) initial location.

Define the Classes of Currency Converter

In this section you'll define controller and model classes for Currency Converter.

Create the ConverterController Subclass

You'll recall from Chapter 6 that you must go to the Classes display of the nib file window to define a class. Let's start with the ConverterController class:

1. In Interface Builder, select the Classes display of the `MainMenu.nib` window.

2. Create an NSObject subclass called ConverterController.

Define Outlets for ConverterController

ConvertorController needs access to the text fields of the interface, so you must create outlets for them. ConverterController must also communicate with the Converter class (yet to be defined) and thus requires a fourth outlet for that purpose.

1. Select ConverterController in the Classes window.

2. Click the electrical outlet icon to the right of the class.

3. Choose Add Outlet from the Classes menu.

4. Name this outlet **rateField** and press Return.

5. Since the `rateField` outlet is still selected, all you have to do to create more outlets is press Return. Do this once to create the `dollarField` outlet, and again for the `totalField` outlet.

6. Add an outlet named `converter` to ConverterController.

Define Actions for ConverterController

ConverterController has one action method, `convert:`. When the user clicks the Convert button, a `convert:` message is sent to the target object, an instance of ConverterController. Action refers both to a message sent to an object when the user clicks a button or manipulates some other control object and to the method that is invoked.

1. Choose Add Action from the Classes menu.

2. Type the name of the method, **convert**. IB adds the : for you.

Define the Converter Class

The Converter class doesn't need to inherit any special functionality, so you'll make it a subclass of NSObject. Because instances of this model class don't communicate directly with the interface, there is no need for outlets or actions.

1. In the Classes display, make Converter a subclass of NSObject.

2. Save `MainMenu.nib`.

Connect ConverterController to the Interface

In this section you'll create an instance of ConverterController and use Interface Builder to connect the controller object's outlets to objects in the user interface.

Generate an Instance of the Class

As the final step of defining a class in Interface Builder, create an instance of your class and connect its outlets and actions:

1. Select ConverterController in the Classes window, if it is not already selected.

2. Choose Instantiate from the Classes menu. The instance will appear in the Instances view, as highlighted in Figure 7-21.

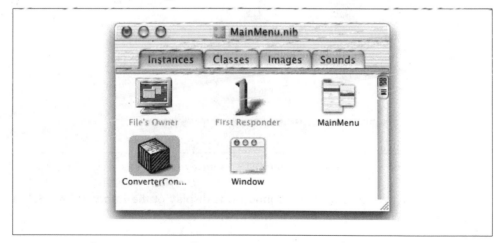

Figure 7-21. The ConverterController instance

Connect the Custom Class to the Interface

Now you can connect this ConverterController object to the user interface. By connecting it to specific objects in the interface, you initialize its outlets. Converter-Controller will use these outlets to get and set values in the interface.

1. In the Instances display of the nib file window, Control-drag a connection line from the ConverterController instance to the first text field, as shown in Figure 7-22. When the text field is outlined, release the mouse button.

Figure 7-22. Connecting the ConverterController instance to a text field

2. Interface Builder brings up the Connections display of the Info window. Select the outlet that corresponds to the first field (rateField).

3. Click the Connect button.

4. Following the same steps, connect ConverterController's dollarField and totalField outlets to the appropriate text fields.

Connect the Interface Controls to the Class's Actions

You must connect the Convert button to its action method in Interface Builder so that the button will send the message to the controller object at runtime.

1. Control-drag a connection from the Convert button to the ConverterController instance in the nib file window. When the instance is outlined, release the mouse button.

2. In the Connections display, make sure `target` in the Outlets column is selected.

3. Select `convert:` in the Actions column.

4. Click the Connect button.

5. Save the `MainMenu.nib` file.

Connect ConverterController to the Converter Class

While connecting ConverterController's outlets, you probably noticed that one outlet—converter—remains unconnected. This outlet identifies an instance of the Converter class in the Currency Converter application, but this instance doesn't exist yet.

1. Instantiate the Converter class.

2. Make an outlet connection between ConverterController and Converter. Hint: Control-drag from the ConverterController instance to the Converter instance.

3. Save `MainMenu.nib`.

Implement the Classes of Currency Converter

The final step in building the Currency Converter application is to implement the classes you defined in the previous steps.

Generate the Source Files

1. Go to the Classes display of the nib file window.

2. Select the ConverterController class.

3. Choose Create Files from the Classes menu.

4. Verify that the checkboxes in the Create column next to the .h and .m files are selected.

5. Verify that the checkbox next to Currency Converter is selected.

6. Click the Choose button.

7. Repeat for the Converter class.

8. Save the nib file.

Now we leave Interface Builder for this application. You'll complete the application using Project Builder.

Examine an Interface (Header) File in Project Builder

When Interface Builder adds the header and source files to the Currency Converter project, it tries to put them in the same group folder as other source files in the same disk folder. Since the newly created files are class implementations, move them to the Classes group if Interface Builder did not do so automatically.

1. Click Project Builder's main window to activate it.

2. Select all four files in the Groups and Files list and drag them into the Classes group, as shown in Figure 7-23.

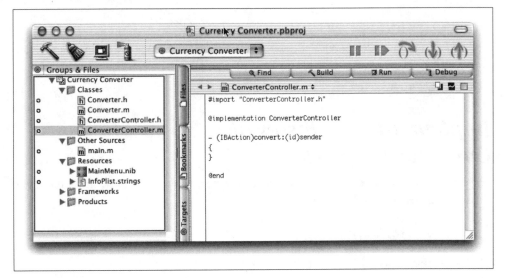

Figure 7-23. Adding the source files to the Classes group

Add a Method Declaration

You can add instance variables or method declarations to a header file generated by Interface Builder. This is commonly done, but it isn't necessary in Converter-Controller's case. But we do need to add a method to the Converter class that the ConverterController object can invoke to get the result of the computation. Let's start by declaring the method in Converter.h.

1. Select Converter.h in the project browser.

2. Insert a declaration for convertAmount:atRate::

   ```
   #import <Cocoa/Cocoa.h>
   @interface Converter:NSObject
   {
   }
   - (float)convertAmount:(float)amt atRate:(float)rate;

   @end
   ```

This declaration states that convertAmount:atRate: takes two arguments of type float and returns a float value. When parts of a method name have colons, such as convertAmount: and atRate:, they are keywords that introduce arguments.

Now you need to update both implementation files.

Implement Currency Converter's Classes

For the Converter class, implement the method you just declared in Converter.h. Method implementations go between @implementation <class name> and @end, so this is where you will add the code for Converter.

1. Select Converter.m from the Classes group in Project Builder's main window.

2. Insert the code for convertAmount:::

   ```
   #import "Converter.h"
   @implementation Converter
   - (float)convertAmount:(float)amt atRate:(float)rate
   {
       return (amt * rate);
   }
   @end
   ```

The method simply multiplies the two arguments and returns the result. Simple enough.

3. Next, update the "empty" implementation of the `convert:` method in `ConverterController.m` that Interface Builder generated for you:

```
- (IBAction)convert:(id)sender
{
    float rate, amt, total;

    amt = [dollarField floatValue];
    rate = [rateField floatValue];

    total = [converter convertAmount:amt atRate:rate];

    [totalField setFloatValue:total];
    [rateField selectText:self];
}
```

4. Make sure that `ConverterController.m` imports `Converter.h` by adding the following line at the top of the source file:

```
#import "Converter.h."
```

The `convert:` method does the following:

- Gets the floating-point values typed into the `rate` and `dollar` amount fields.

- Invokes the `convertAmount:atRate:` method and gets the returned value.

- Uses `setFloatValue:` to write the returned value in the Amount in Other Currency text field (`totalField`).

- Sends `selectText:` to the `rate` field; this selects any text in the field or, if there is no text, inserts the cursor so the user can begin another calculation.

Build and Run Currency Converter

This section explains how to build and run the application.

Build the project

You begin the build process from the Project Build panel:

1. Save source code files and any changes to the project.

2. Click the Build button on the main window.

When you click the Build button, the build process begins. When Project Builder finishes, and encounters no errors along the way, it displays Build Succeeded in the lower-left corner of the project window.

Run Currency Converter

Enter some rates and dollar amounts and click Convert. Also, select the text in a field and choose Services from the Application menu; this menu now lists the other applications that can do something with the selected text.

Of course, the more complex an application is, the more thoroughly you will need to test it. You might discover errors or shortcomings that necessitate a change in overall design, in the interface, in a custom class definition, or in the implementation of methods and functions.

Although it's a simple application, Currency Converter consolidates all of the concepts and techniques introduced in previous chapters. By now you have a much better grasp of the skills you'll need to develop Cocoa applications. To review, you have learned to:

- Design an application using the Model-View-Controller paradigm
- Compose a graphical user interface (GUI) with Interface Builder
- Test the interface
- Specify a class's outlets and actions
- Connect the class instance to the interface via its outlets and actions
- Class implementation basics
- Build an application and resolve errors

8

Event Handling

Graphical interfaces are driven by user events—mouse clicks and keystrokes. However, a running application can also receive events that don't originate from the user interface: packets arriving over a network interface, periodic timers firing, an input device being plugged into a USB port, or a CD being inserted into an attached drive. In an object-oriented world, both types of events eventually result in a message being sent to an object in your application, as depicted in Figure 8-1. This chapter focuses on events—both user- and program-generated—and how, as a programmer, you intercept, handle, and coordinate them in Cocoa.

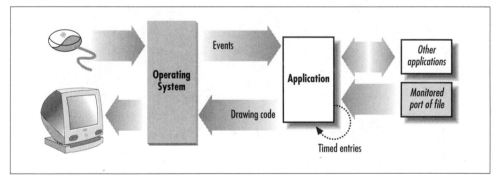

Figure 8-1. A Cocoa application receiving events

Respond to User-Generated Events

In this section you'll explore the structure of a Cocoa application from a user-event-handling perspective. You'll learn about the classes in the core program framework and delve into topics such as the view hierarchy, the event cycle, and the responder chain. Later you'll build a simple application that responds to a user's mouse click by drawing a colored dot in the application's window.

The Application Quartet

Four classes are at the core of a running application: NSResponder, NSWindow, NSView, and NSApplication (Figure 8-2). Each class plays a critical role in the two primary activities of an application: drawing the user interface and responding to events. The structure of their interaction is sometimes called the "core program framework."

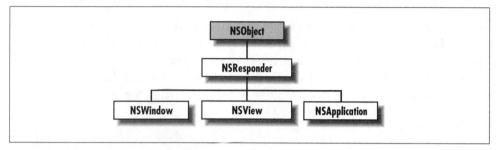

Figure 8-2. The Application Quartet class hierarchy

NSResponder

NSResponder is an abstract class, but it enables event handling in all classes that inherit from it. It defines the set of messages invoked when different mouse and keyboard events occur. It also defines the mechanics of event processing among objects in an application, especially the passing of events up the responder chain to each next responder until the event is handled. The responder chain is covered later in the section "The Event Cycle and First Responder."

NSWindow

An NSWindow object manages each physical window on the screen. It draws the window's frame area and responds to user actions that close, move, resize, and otherwise manipulate the window.

The main purpose of an NSWindow is to display an application's user interface (or part of it) in its content area: that space below the titlebar and within the window frame. A window's content is the view hierarchy it encloses, and at the root of this view hierarchy is the content view, which fills the content area. Based on the location of a user event, NSWindows assigns an NSView in its content area to act as first responder.

An NSWindow allows you to assign a custom object as its delegate and so participate in its activities.

NSView

Any object you see in a window's content area is an NSView. (Actually, since NSView is an abstract class, these objects are instances of NSView subclasses.) NSView objects are responsible for drawing and for responding to mouse and keyboard events. Each NSView owns a rectangular region associated with a particular window; it produces images within this region and responds to events occurring within the rectangle.

NSViews in a window are logically arranged in a *view hierarchy*, with the content view at the top of the hierarchy. An NSView references its window, its superview, and its subviews. It can be the first responder for events or the next responder in the event chain. An NSView's frame and bounds are rectangles that define its location on the screen, its dimension, and its coordinate system for drawing.

NSApplication

Every application must have one NSApplication object to supervise and coordinate the overall behavior of the application. This object dispatches events to the appropriate NSWindows (which, in turn, distribute them to their NSViews). The NSApplication object manages its windows and detects and handles changes in their status as well as in its own active and inactive status. The NSApplication object is represented in each application by the global variable NSApp. To coordinate your own code with NSApp, you can assign your own custom object as its delegate.

The View Hierarchy

Just inside each window's content area—the area enclosed by the titlebar and the other three sides of the frame—lies the content view. The content view is the root (or top) NSView in the window's view hierarchy, shown in Figure 8-3. Conceptually like a tree, one or more NSViews may branch from the content view, one or more other NSViews may branch from these subordinate NSViews, and so on. Except for the content view, each NSView has one (and only one) NSView above it in the hierarchy. An NSView's subordinate views are called its subviews; its superior view is known as the superview.

On the screen, enclosure determines the relationship between superview and subview: a superview encloses its subviews. This relationship has several implications for drawing on the screen:

- It permits construction of a superview simply by arrangement of subviews. (For example, an NSBrowser is an instance of a compound NSView.)

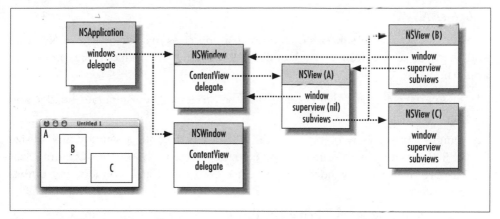

Figure 8-3. The view hierarchy

- Subviews are positioned in the coordinates of their superview, so when you move an NSView or transform its coordinate system, all subviews are moved and transformed in concert.

- Because an NSView has its own coordinate system for drawing, its drawing instructions remain constant regardless of any change in position in itself or of its superview.

The core program framework provides several ways for your application to access the participating objects so you need not define outlets or instance variables for every object in the hierarchy:

- The global variable NSApp identifies the NSApplication object. By sending the appropriate message to NSApp, you can obtain the application's NSWindow objects (windows), the key and main windows (keyWindow and mainWindow), the current event (currentEvent), the main menu (mainMenu), and the application's delegate (delegate).

- Once you've identified an NSWindow object, you can get its content view (by sending it contentView), and from that you can get all subviews of the window. By sending messages to the NSWindow object, you can also get the current event (currentEvent), the current first responder (firstResponder), and the delegate (delegate).

- You can obtain from an NSView most objects it references. You can discover its window, its superview, and its subviews.

Subclass NSView

If you make a custom subclass of NSView (or any class that inherits from NSView) and want to do custom event handling or drawing, the same basic procedure applies:

1. In Interface Builder, define a subclass of NSView. Then generate header and implementation files.

2. Drag a CustomView object from the Views palette onto a window and resize it. Then, with the CustomView object still selected, choose the Custom Class display of the Info window and select the custom class. Connect any outlets and actions.

3. Override the designated initializer, initWithFrame:, to perform any custom initialization. The argument of this method is the frame rectangle of the NSView, as set in Interface Builder.

4. Implement drawRect: to draw.

In Chapter 13, *To Do: Extended*, you'll make a subclass of NSButtonCell (which does not inherit from NSView) that uniquely responds to mouse clicks. The way custom NSViews handle events is different. If you intend your custom NSView to respond to user actions, you must do a couple of things:

- Override acceptsFirstResponder to return YES if the NSView is to handle selections. (The default NSView behavior is to return NO.)

- Override the desired NSResponder event methods (mouseDown:, mouseDragged:, keyDown:, etc.):

```
- (void)mouseDown:(NSEvent *)event {
    if ([event modifierFlags] & NSControlKeyMask){
        [self doSomething];
}
```

You can query the NSEvent argument for the location of the user action in the window, modifier keys pressed, character and key codes, and other information.

When you send display to an NSView, its drawRect: method and each of its subviews' drawRect: are invoked. This method is where an NSView renders its appearance. The argument for drawRect: is usually the bounds rectangle in which drawing is to occur. This tells the view which part of its bounds needs updating. To draw the NSView, you can do one or more of the following:

- Use the NSBezierPath, NSString, NSFont, or NSColor classes.

- Call Application Kit functions such as NSRectFill and NSFrameRect (NSGraphics.h).

- Composite an NSImage.

- Call C functions that correspond to single PDF operations.

When the state changes and you need to have the object redraw itself, invoke setNeedsDisplay: with an argument of YES.

See Appendix A, *Drawing in Cocoa*, for more information on drawing and compositing with NSView.

The Event Cycle and First Responder

The NSApplication object is, in a sense, the master controller for your application. At the core of its responsibilities is the *event loop*. One by one it picks an event from those queued by the underlying Cocoa platform and decides which object is responsible for handling the event. Then it sends a message, passing an NSEvent object describing the particulars. The event message passes from NSApplication to the appropriate window to a view (commonly a control) within the window and eventually to your target object.

This is how a button knows that it has been clicked. Your custom object responds to the button click through target/action, through delegation (which you'll learn more about in the section "Delegation"), or (in the case of custom views or controls) directly. When your application objects are finished responding to the message, control unwinds and returns to NSApplication, where it loops again, ready to process the next queued event.

This cycle—the *event cycle*—usually starts at launch time when the application (which includes all the frameworks it's linked to) sends a stream of Quartz code to the window server to have it draw the application interface. Then the application begins its main event loop and begins accepting input from the user. When users click or drag the mouse or type on the keyboard, the window server detects these actions and processes them, passing them to the application as events.

The event queue and event dispatching

When an application starts up, the NSApplication object (NSApp) starts the main event loop and begins receiving events from the window server. As NSEvents arrive, they're put in the event queue in the order they're received. On each cycle of the loop, NSApp gets the topmost event, analyzes it, and sends an event message to the appropriate object as shown in Figure 8-4. (Event messages are defined by NSResponder and correspond to particular events.) When NSApp finishes processing the event, it gets the next event and repeats the process again and again until the application terminates.

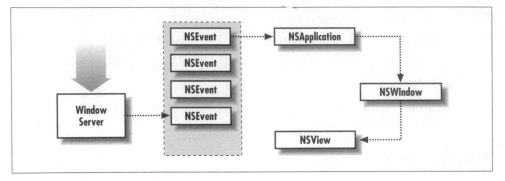

Figure 8-4. The event queue

Event routing depends on the type of the event. NSApp sends most event messages to the NSWindow in which the user action occurred. A mouse event is for-
warded by NSWindow to one of the objects in its view hierarchy: the NSView
within which the mouse was clicked. Key events are routed to the first responder.
If the NSView can respond to the event—that is, it accepts first responder status
and defines an NSResponder method corresponding to the event message—it handles the event. If the NSView cannot handle an event, it forwards the message to
the next responder in the responder chain (see the section "First responder and
the responder chain" for details). It travels up the responder chain until an object
handles it.

NSWindow handles some events, such as window-moved, window-resized, and
window-exposed events, itself and doesn't forward them to an NSView. (Since
these events are handled by NSWindow itself, they are not defined in NSResponder.) NSApp also processes a few kinds of events itself, such as application-acti-
vate and application-deactivate events.

Event types and tracing

The window server treats each user action as an event. It associates the event with
a window and reports the event to the application that created the window. Events
are objects—instances of NSEvent composed from information derived from the
user action.

All event methods defined in NSResponder (such as `mouseDown:` and `keyDown:`)
take an NSEvent as their argument. You can query an NSEvent to discover its window, the location of the event within the window, and the time the event
occurred (relative to system startup). You can also find out which (if any) modifier
keys (such as Command, Shift, Option, and Control) were pressed, the codes that
identify characters and keys, and various other kinds of information.

An NSEvent also contains the type of event it represents. There are many event types (e.g., NSEventType); they fall into four categories:

- **Keyboard events.** These events are generated when a key is pressed down, a pressed key is released, or a modifier key changes. Of these, key-down events are the most useful. When you handle a key-down event, you often determine the character or characters associated with the event by sending the NSEvent a characters message.

- **Mouse events.** These events are generated by changes in the state of the mouse button (that is, down and up) and during mouse dragging. Events are also generated when the mouse simply moves, without any button depressed.

- **Tracking-rectangle events.** These events are generated by the window server, if the application has asked it to set a tracking rectangle in a window. The window server creates mouse-entered and mouse-exited events when the cursor enters the rectangle or leaves it.

- **Periodic events.** These events are generated by timers. A periodic event notifies an application that a certain time interval elapsed. An application can request that periodic events be placed in its event queue at a certain frequency. They are usually used during a tracking loop. (These events aren't passed to an NSWindow.)

You can view events as they are sent to an application using the event-tracing feature of Cocoa. You enable event tracing for an application by setting the NSTraceEvents flag. There are several ways to do this for a given application, but they all involve using the Mac OS X command-line interface. This interface is available from the Terminal application located in /Applications/Utilities. Find and launch this application now.

To see all of the events being sent to the Project Builder application from the window server, first make sure the application is not already running, and then enter the following command into a Terminal window:

```
/Developer/Applications/Project\ Builder.app/Contents/MacOS/Project\ Builder
-NSTraceEvents YES
```

This command launches the Project Builder application and sets the NSTraceEvents flag to the value YES. Note the backslashes before the spaces separating the words "Project" and "Builder." The backslashes are necessary to let the command-line interpreter know that the following space is part of the pathname (as opposed to a space that separates different parameters of a command).

As you move the mouse over the Project Builder's user interface and interact with it by clicking buttons, you will see each event being printed out in the Terminal window. This method of enabling event tracing is "one shot," meaning that trace information will be enabled only for this Project Builder session. The next time you launch the application, it will behave normally.

Another method for enabling event tracing is to set the `NSTraceEvents` flag in the application's preferences. When you do this, event tracing will remain enabled until you turn it off by modifying the application's preferences. This method is also slightly different from the previous one because the event trace output is sent to the Mac OS X console instead of a Terminal window. The console is available from the Console application located in `/Applications/Utilities`. The console is where applications (and the operating system) can print status and debugging information. Locate and launch the Console application now.

To modify Project Builder's preferences from the command line, use the `defaults` command. This command allows you to read and write application preferences that are not available from the application's graphical user interface. Type the following into a Terminal window to enable event tracing for Project Builder:

```
defaults write com.apple.ProjectBuilder NSTraceEvents YES
```

Quit Project Builder if it is still running, and then launch it again from the Finder. You should see event trace information being printed to the Console window as you interact with Project Builder. To turn off event tracing, enter the following in the Terminal window:

```
defaults delete com.apple.ProjectBuilder NSTraceEvents
```

Though it can take time to sort through all of the event information provided by Cocoa's event-tracing facility, it can be an invaluable debugging tool.

First responder and the responder chain

Each NSWindow in an application keeps track of the object in its view hierarchy that has first responder status. This is the NSView that currently receives keyboard events for the window. By default, an NSWindow is its own first responder, but any NSView within the window can become first responder when the user clicks it with the mouse.

You can also set the first responder programmatically with the NSWindow `makeFirstResponder:` method. Moreover, the first-responder object can be a target of an action message sent by an NSControl, such as a button or a matrix. Programmatically, you do this by sending `setTarget:` to the NSControl (or its cell) with an argument of `nil`. You can do the same thing in Interface Builder by making a target/action connection between the NSControl and the First Responder icon in the Instances display of the nib file window.

Recall that all NSViews of the application, as well as all NSWindows and the application object itself, inherit from NSResponder, which defines the default message-handling behavior: events are passed up the responder chain. Many Application Kit objects, of course, override this behavior, so events are passed up the chain until they reach an object that does respond.

The series of next responders in the responder chain is determined by the interrelationships between the application's NSView, NSWindow, and NSApplication objects. For an NSView, the next responder is usually its superview; the content view's next responder is the NSWindow. From there, the event is passed to the NSApplication object.

For action messages sent to the first responder, the trail back through possible respondents is even more detailed. The messages are first passed up the responder chain to the NSWindow and then to NSWindow's delegate. Then, if the previous sequence occurred in the key window, the same path is followed for the main window. Then the NSApplication object tries to respond, and failing that, it goes to NSApplicaton's delegate.

Key window and first responder. In a multiwindowed desktop environment, there are many open windows on the screen. A user selects a window with the mouse to make it active. When this happens, the window becomes key and the window's first responder becomes the target of any events generated by the user.

If a different window is selected, it becomes key and its first responder becomes current. If no object has been selected, or if the window has no controls, the window is its own first responder. You can configure `initialFirstResponder` so that, when a window appears, the first logical control capable of using keystrokes is brought into focus as the first responder. The default object selected by the window when `initialFirstResponder` is `nil` is typically quite reasonable.

Create the Dot View Application

In this section you'll build an application using a custom NSView subclass that responds to a mouse click by drawing a colored dot. Working through this example will give you an opportunity to see how custom event handling works, and as a bonus, you'll learn how to render simple shapes using Cocoa's main drawing class: NSBezierPath.

1. Create a new Cocoa application project called Dot View.

2. Open the main nib file.

3. Title the main window Dot View.

4. Create a subclass of NSView called DotView.

5. Create the files for DotView and add them to the project.

6. Drag a custom view from the More Views palette to the window, and then add a horizontal slider and a color well, as shown in Figure 8-5.

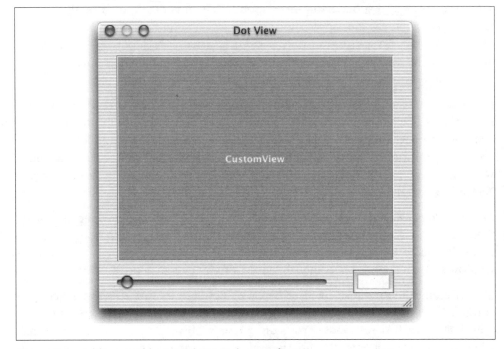

Figure 8-5. Adding a table view object to the interface

7. Select CustomView, bring up the Info window, and change the view's class to DotView.

8. Open DotView.h and add the declarations shown in Example 8-1. The three instance variables represent the attributes of the dot that the class will draw: its location in the view, its color, and its size, respectively. The method declarations are described by the brief comments in the code listing.

9. Drag DotView.h from Project Builder into Interface Builder's MainMenu.nib window. This will give Interface Builder the opportunity to parse the file and discover the actions and outlets you added to the DotView class.

10. In Interface Builder, Control-click the horizontal slider and drag a connection to the DotView. Make the target/action connection to the setRadius: method in the Connections pane of the Info window.

11. Drag a connection from the color well to the DotView, and make the target/action connection to the setColor: method.

12. Make the outlet connections from the DotView to the slider and the color well.

13. Save the nib file.

Example 8-1. DotView.h

```
#import <Cocoa/Cocoa.h>

@interface DotView : NSView {
    NSPoint center;
    NSColor *color;
    float radius;

    // Outlets for the color well and the slider
    IBOutlet NSColorWell *colorWell;
    IBOutlet NSSlider *sizeSlider;
}

// Standard view create/free methods
- (id)initWithFrame:(NSRect)frame;
- (void)dealloc;

// Drawing
- (void)drawRect:(NSRect)rect;
- (BOOL)isOpaque;

// Event handling
- (void)mouseUp:(NSEvent *)event;

// Custom methods for actions this view implements
- (IBAction)setRadius:(id)sender;
- (IBAction)setColor:(id)sender;

@end
```

Now that you have constructed the interface and defined connections between the DotView and the dot drawing controls, it's time to implement the DotView class:

1. Open `DotView.m` and add an implementation for `initWithFrame:` shown in the following code. This method initalizes DotView's instance variables:

```
- (id)initWithFrame:(NSRect)frame
{
    self = [super initWithFrame:frame];
    center.x = 50.0;
    center.y = 50.0;
    radius = 10.0;
    color = [[NSColor redColor] retain];
    return self;
}
```

2. Implement `dealloc` as shown. There's nothing unusual here:

```
- (void)dealloc {
    [color release];
    [super dealloc];
}
```

3. Implement the `awakeFromNib` method so you can initialize the color well and slider to the same values that were defined in the `initWithFrame:` method shown in step 1. To enable setup operations like this, the `awakeFromNib` message is sent to all objects in the nib when unarchiving concludes. It is not possible to do this until the nib file is unarchived because the act of unarchiving is what creates the color well and establishes the connection to the `colorWell` outlet. Before the nib file is unarchived, the outlet is uninitialized, so messages sent through the outlet will do nothing. This way, when the app first launches, the user interface controls will reflect the initial values that will be used to draw dots:

```
- (void)awakeFromNib {
    [colorWell setColor: color];
    [sizeSlider setFloatValue:radius];
}
```

4. The `drawRect:` method draws the dot in the view. First it clears the view by filling it with white. Next it computes a bounding rectangle for the dot. Then it sets the current color to the value stored in the view's instance variable, and finally it uses NSBezierPath to actually draw the rectangle in the view:

```
- (void)drawRect:(NSRect)rect {
    NSRect dotRect;

    [[NSColor whiteColor] set];
    NSRectFill([self bounds]);

    dotRect.origin.x = center.x - radius;
    dotRect.origin.y = center.y - radius;
    dotRect.size.width  = 2 * radius;
    dotRect.size.height = 2 * radius;
```

```
    [color set];
    [[NSBezierPath bezierPathWithOvalInRect:dotRect] fill];
}
```

5. Add an implementation for isOpaque. Views that redraw their whole bounds without needing any of the views behind it should override isOpaque to return YES. This is a performance optimization hint for the display subsystem:

```
- (BOOL)isOpaque {
    return YES;
}
```

6. Overriding NSResponder (the superclass of NSView) methods in the NSView subclass is the recommended way to handle events for the view. One such method is mouseUp:, which is invoked when the user releases the mouse button. Add an implementation for mouseUp:, as shown. All of the NSResponder methods receive the event as an argument. The event contains the mouse location in window coordinates; you can use convertPoint:fromView: (with nil as the view argument) to convert this point to local view coordinates. Note that once we get the new center, we call setNeedsDisplay:YES to mark that the view needs to be redisplayed (which is done automatically by the Application Kit).

```
- (void)mouseUp:(NSEvent *)event
{
    NSPoint eventLocation = [event locationInWindow];
    center = [self convertPoint:eventLocation fromView:nil];
    [self setNeedsDisplay:YES];
}
```

7. Add an implementation for setRadius:, an action method invoked by the slider on the user interface. This method lets you change the radius of the dot. It assumes the sender is a control capable of returning a floating-point number, so we ask for its value, set the DotView's instance variable, and mark the view as needing to be redisplayed. A possible optimization is to check to see if the old and new value is the same and if so, not do anything.

```
- (void)setRadius:(id)sender {
    radius = [sender floatValue];
    [self setNeedsDisplay:YES];
}
```

8. Add an implementation for setColor:, the action method invoked by the color well that lets you change the color of the dot. This method assumes the sender is a control capable of returning a color (NSColorWell can do this). setColor: gets the value from the sender, releases the previous color, and

marks the view as needing to be redisplayed. As with the `setRadius:` method, a possible optimization is to check to see if the old and new value is the same and if so, not do anything.

```
- (void)setColor:(id)sender {
    [color autorelease];
    color = [[sender color] retain];
    [self setNeedsDisplay:YES];
}
```

9. Build and run the application and create some dots as shown in Figure 8-6.

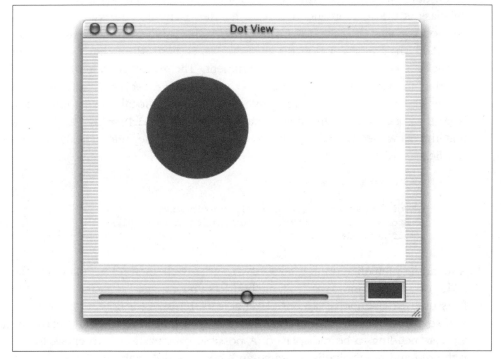

Figure 8-6. Drawing dots with the Dot View application

Dot View is a simple application, but is a great example of what makes Cocoa programming so much fun. In just a few easy steps you have created a view that can draw a circle in response to a mouse click. The size and color of the circle are dynamically configurable using the slider and color well. And you were able to build and test the project in a matter of minutes using off-the-shelf parts.

Respond to Program-Generated Events

In an object-oriented application, many situations exist in which an object must know what's going on with other objects in the system. In this section, you'll learn about two techniques for this kind of object-to-object communication in Cocoa: delegation and notification. These design patterns are so widely used in Cocoa programming that a thorough understanding of the concepts involved is absolutely critical to prepare you for developing complex applications. In fact, you'll use delegation and notification extensively to complete the advanced tutorials in Chapter 10, *Travel Advisor Tutorial*, Chapter 12, *To Do: Basics*, and Chapter 13.

Delegation

You can think of delegation as a means by which an object's behavior can be modified without needing to create a custom subclass. A delegate is a helper object that receives messages from another object when specific events occur. An object sends requests to its delegate, allowing the delegate to influence its behavior and aid in decision making.

For an object to delegate responsibility, it must declare a *delegate* outlet along with a set of delegate messages that will be sent to the delegate when "interesting" things happen. To become a delegate, an object must implement one or more of the delegate methods. There are several types of delegation messages, depending on the expected role of the delegate:

- Some messages are purely informational, occurring after an event has happened. They allow a delegate to coordinate its actions with the delegating object.

- Some messages are sent before an action will occur, allowing the delegate to veto or permit the action.

- Other delegation messages assign a specific task to a delegate, such as filling a browser with cells.

Figure 8-7 shows an object sending the message `oddBall:shouldActSilly:` to its delegate. The delegate message represents a request from the delegating object; the delegate object then has the opportunity to approve or deny the request to "act silly" by returning `true` or `false` from the delegate method implementation.

You can set a custom object to be the delegate of a framework object by making a connection in Interface Builder, or you can decide to set it programmatically using the `setDelegate:` method. Your custom classes can also define their own delegate variables and delegation protocols for client objects. Delegates (as well as outlets) are not retained because, typically, objects don't "own" their delegates.

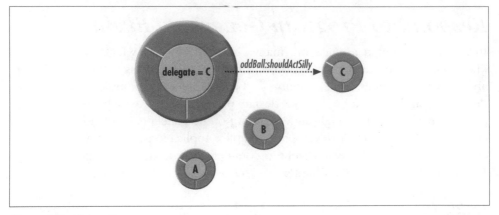

Figure 8-7. Delegation

A simple delegate example

Delegation is commonly used in Cocoa to modify the behavior of windows. For each type of event in the life of a window that is suitable for input by a delegate—resizing, hiding, moving, and closing, among others—NSWindow declares a delegate method. Not every delegate wants to provide input for all possible events in the life of a window, so Cocoa allows a delegate to implement only the delegate methods it is interested in. There is a mechanism for the delegating object to discover which delegate methods its delegate implements, therefore unimplemented delegate messages will simply not be sent.

For example, the `windowShouldClose:` method is NSWindow's delegate method for window closing. After the user clicks a window's close button, but before the window closes, the window object sends a `windowShouldClose:` message to its delegate. Typically, a delegate implements the code necessary for the user to save changes to the window's contents in its `windowShouldClose:` method. The value returned to the window object from the delegate method determines if the window actually closes or remains onscreen.

In the following example you will implement a delegate class for NSWindow that can respond to the `windowShouldClose:` method by displaying a standard Window Closing dialog.

1. Create a new Project Builder project called Delegate and open the main nib file.

2. Create a new subclass of NSObject called MyDelegate.

3. Instantiate MyDelegate.

4. In the Instances pane of the MainMenu.nib window, Control-drag a connection from Window to MyDelegate, as shown in Figure 8-8.

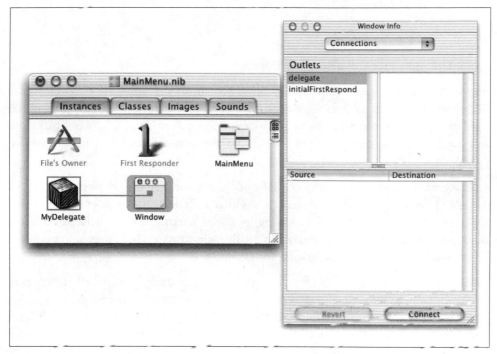

Figure 8-8. Control dragging from Window to MyDelegate

5. Make sure the delegate outlet is selected in the Connections pane of the Window Info window and click Connect.

6. Save the nib file.

7. Create the files for the MyDelegate class and add them to the project.

You have established the delegate relationship between Window and MyDelegate in the nib file. Now implement the delegate method for MyDelegate:

1. Open MyDelegate.h and add the following method declaration.

    ```
    - (BOOL)windowShouldClose:(NSWindow *)sender;
    ```

2. Open MyDelegate.m and add the following method implementation:

    ```
    - (BOOL)windowShouldClose:(NSWindow *)sender
    {
        int answer;

        answer = NSRunAlertPanel(@"Close", @"Are you certain?",
                    @"Close", @"Cancel", nil);
    ```

```
switch (answer) {
    case NSAlertDefaultReturn:
        return YES;
    default:
        return NO;
}
}
```

3. Build and run the example application.

As you can see, when you click the close button on the application's window, a dialog box appears asking permission to close the window. In a fully functional application where the window actually contained edited data, you would use the `windowShouldClose` delegate method to save the contents of the window before closing it.

Use sheets.   Another example of delegation appears in the implementation of Aqua's sheets—a new type of dialog box that is attached to a document. Sheets slide out from the window title (Figure 8-9), making their relationship to a document clear. Sheets are modal only for the window to which they are attached, so you can proceed to other tasks before dismissing them.

Adding support for sheets is more complicated than using a standard dialog box because the function that displays an alert sheet—`NSBeginAlertSheet`—is asynchronous. In other words, `NSBeginAlertSheet` does not wait for the user to dismiss the sheet before returning control to the caller. Instead, it returns immediately after presenting the sheet. To discover the result of the user's interaction with the sheet, you must pass `NSBeginAlertSheet` a reference to a delegate object, along with a method selector to invoke as a callback when the sheet is dismissed. When the callback is invoked, you are passed the result code indicating which button the user clicked. Unlike the previous window delegate example, sheets use a temporary or "modal" delegate. The delegate relationship lasts only until the sheet is dismissed.

The parameter list for `NSBeginAlertSheet` is a bit daunting at first glance, but it's really not difficult to use. Here is a brief parameter summary:

*   `title`. The title of the sheet; displayed near the top of the sheet in a bold font.
*   `defaultButton`. The label for the sheet's default button; typically OK.
*   `alternateButton`. The label for the sheet's alternate button; typically Cancel.
*   `otherButton`. The label for a third button. If you pass `nil`, only two buttons will appear on the sheet.
*   `docWindow`. A reference to the NSWindow to which the sheet will be attached.

Figure 8-9. Aqua Sheets

- modalDelegate. A reference to the object that will respond when the user dismisses the sheet.

- didEndSelector. A selector for a method implemented by the modalDelegate. The method will be invoked when the modal session is ended, but before the sheet is dismissed.

- didDismissSelector. A selector for a method implemented by the modalDelegate. The method will be called after the sheet is dismissed. It is useful for any extra cleanup that might be necessary. Pass NULL if you don't need this functionality.

- contextInfo. Additional data that you can define to be passed to the modal delegate as a parameter of the didEnd and didDismiss methods.

- msg. An optional message string that appears near the bottom of the sheet. The string can include printf-style percent escape sequences.

- optional params. These printf-style parameters can be used to format the msg string.

Now that you've learned what the parameters are for, go ahead and implement an alert sheet. All you have to do is add the call to NSBeginAlertSheet and implement the delegate method that will handle the result of the user's interaction with the sheet. Here are the steps:

1. In Project Builder, open MyDelegate.h , and add the following method declaration. This is the method that will be invoked when the modal session has ended (the user has clicked a button).

```
- (void)didEndShouldCloseSheet:(NSWindow *)sheet
        returnCode:(int)returnCode
        contextInfo:(void *)contextInfo;
```

2. Open MyDelegate.m.

3. Modify the windowShouldClose method as shown.

Notice that sender (a reference to the delegating window) is being passed for the contextInfo as well as the docWindow parameter. The value of contextInfo will be passed back to the modal delegate as a parameter of the didEnd method, and so it can be used to determine which window to close.

```
- (BOOL)windowShouldClose:(NSWindow *)sender
{
    NSBeginAlertSheet(@"Close",               // sheet title
        @"OK",                                 // default button label
        @"Cancel",                             // alternate button label
        nil,                                   // other button label
        sender,                                // document window
        self,                                  // modal delegate
        @selector(didEndShouldCloseSheet:returnCode:contextInfo:),
                                               // didEnd selector
        NULL,                                  // didDismiss selector
        sender,                                // context Info
        @"Should this window close?",          // message
        nil);                                  // params for msg string

    // Don't decide to close window until results of sheet
    // interaction are known.
    return NO;
}
```

4. Add the implementation for didEndShouldCloseSheet:

```
- (void)didEndShouldCloseSheet:(NSWindow *)sheet
        returnCode:(int)returnCode
        contextInfo:(void *)contextInfo
```

```
    {
        if (returnCode == NSAlertDefaultReturn)
            [(NSWindow *)contextInfo close];
    }
```

5. Build and run the application.

Find delegate methods programmatically. If you're curious about the other delegate methods for a class, you can look in the class's header file. There is also a way to find out what methods are being called at runtime. As you've already learned, it's possible for a delegating object to query its delegate to discover which delegate methods it implements. The delegating object performs this query by sending a `respondsToSelector:` message to its delegate. By overriding this method in the MyDelegate class, you can examine every query the object receives.

The code to do this is simple. Add the following method implementation to `MyDelegate.m`:

```
- (BOOL)respondsToSelector:(SEL)aSelector
{
    NSLog(@"respondsToSelector: %@",NSStringFromSelector(aSelector));
    return [super respondsToSelector:aSelector];
}
```

This method simply prints the method name that the sender is asking about. Compile and run the application and examine the output in the Run pane of Project Builder's main window.

Notification

Another very common way to communicate events between objects in Cocoa is *notification*. A notification is a message that is broadcast to all objects in an application that are interested in the event the notification represents. As does the informational delegation message, the notification informs these observers that this event took place (Figure 8-10).

Notifications can also pass along relevant data about the event. Notification differs from delegation in that notification does not allow an observer to interfere with the event. Also, an object can have many observers, but only one delegate.

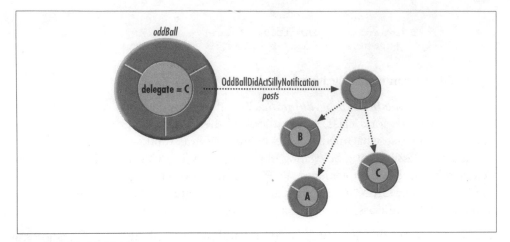

Figure 8-10. Notification

Here's the way the notification process works:

- Objects interested in an event that happens elsewhere in the application—say the addition of a record to a database—register themselves with a notification center (an instance of NSNotificationCenter) as observers of that event. During the registration process, the observer specifies that one of its methods should be invoked by the notification center when the event occurs.

- The object that adds the record to the database (or some such event) posts a notification (an instance of NSNotification) to a notification center. The notification object contains a tag identifying the notification, the ID of the object posting the notification, and, optionally, a dictionary of supplemental data.

- The notification center then sends a message to each registered observer, invoking the method previously specified by each and passing in the notification.

Notifications allow an object to synchronize its behavior and state with multiple objects in an application, without having to know the identity of those objects. With notification queues, it is also possible to post notifications asynchronously and coalesce groups of similar notifications.

Register to receive a notification

A class that posts notifications defines the names of those notifications in its header file as static NSString objects. For example, NSTableView (which you'll explore in detail in Chapter 9, *Data Functionality)* displays data as rows and columns. It defines four notifications in NSTableView.h that allow other objects to monitor changes to the table view:

```
APPKIT_EXTERN NSString *NSTableViewSelectionDidChangeNotification;
APPKIT_EXTERN NSString *NSTableViewColumnDidMoveNotification;
APPKIT_EXTERN NSString *NSTableViewColumnDidResizeNotification;
APPKIT_EXTERN NSString *NSTableViewSelectionIsChangingNotification;
```

An object that wants to receive one of these notifications must import NSTableView.h and use the notification name when registering with the notification center. For example:

```
[[NSNotificationCenter defaultCenter] addObserver:self
        selector:@selector(tableViewSelectionChanged:)
        name:NSTableViewSelectionDidChangeNotification
        object:someTableView];
```

The selector parameter is the name of a method implemented by the observing object that will be invoked by the notification center when it receives the specified notification from someTableView.

Note that a delegate of an object that posts notifications is automatically registered as an observer of those notifications. Cocoa registers the delegate using the selectors declared as an informal protocol accompanying the notification names. For example, NSTableView declares the following informal protocol:

```
@interface NSObject(NSTableViewNotifications)
- (void)tableViewSelectionDidChange:(NSNotification *)notification;
- (void)tableViewColumnDidMove:(NSNotification *)notification;
- (void)tableViewColumnDidResize:(NSNotification *)notification;
- (void)tableViewSelectionIsChanging:(NSNotification *)notification;
@end
```

When an object is made the delegate of a table view, it will automatically be registered to receive all of these notifications using the selectors from the informal protocol. If that delegate object wants to respond to one of the notifications, it need implement only the associated method declared in the informal protocol.

A simple notification example

In this section you'll create an application that demonstrates a simple notification using a text field. All text fields post the notification NSControlTextDidChangeNotification when their text is modified. This application has a simple controller class that registers itself as an observer of the text field object so it will be notified when NSControlTextDidChangeNotification messages are posted from the text field.

Create a new project. Begin by creating a Project Builder project for the Notification application and open its main nib file.

1. Create a new Cocoa application project called Notification.

2. Open the main nib file.

Add a text field and controller class. Add a text field object to the application's main window. As you'll soon see, adding, modifying, or deleting text in the text field will prompt the application's controller to post notifications.

1. Drag a text field object onto the window.

2. Subclass NSObject and call the new class MyController.

3. Add an outlet to MyController called `textField`.

4. Instantiate MyController.

5. Drag a connection from MyController to the text field object.

6. Connect the `textField` outlet.

7. Create the files for MyController and add them to the project.

Make MyController an observer. The notification center is like a bulletin board. Objects register themselves as being interested in a given notification from a specific object or, alternatively, from any object. Typically there is only one notification center in an application. It is an instance of NSNotificationCenter and can be accessed using the `defaultCenter` class method.

Objects generally register themselves as observers in their initialization method. Objects archived in nib files must wait until they have been unarchived and sent the `awakeFromNib` message. Override MyController's `awakeFromNib` method to make the class an observer of the text field's `NSControlTextDidChangeNotification`. Add the following method implementation:

```
- (id) awakeFromNib
{
    [[NSNotificationCenter defaultCenter] addObserver:self
            selector:@selector(textDidChange:)
            name:NSControlTextDidChangeNotification
            object:textField];
}
```

MyController sends `addObserver:selector:name:object:` to the default notification center, requesting that a `textDidChange:` message be sent back to MyController whenever the `textField` object posts `NSControlTextDidChangeNotification`. If you wanted to be notified of every `NSControlTextDidChangeNotification` posted to the notification center, you would pass `nil` for the `object:` parameter.

Now add the following implementation of the textDidChange: method to MyController:

```
- (void)textDidChange:(NSNotification *)notification
{
    NSLog(@"Notification received - %@\n", [notification name]);
}
```

The textDidChange: method simply prints the name of the notification.

Notification centers do not retain observer objects, so you should be careful to remove any observers before they are deallocated. This is to prevent the notification center from sending a message to an object that no longer exists. Because MyController registers itself as an observer in its init method, the object should remove itself from the notification center in its dealloc method. Add the following implementation for dealloc to MyController.m.

```
- (void)dealloc
{
    [[NSNotificationCenter defaultCenter] removeObserver:self];

    [super dealloc];
}
```

If an object registers another object with the notification center and then doesn't release it after removing it from the notification center, the application will leak memory. The rule to follow is: if object A registers object B with a notification center, object A is responsible for removing object B from the notification center as well as releasing object B.

Build and run the application. When you add or modify text in the text field object, you should see the notification log appear in Project Builder's Run pane.

9

Data Functionality

This chapter uses a simple tutorial application called Expenses to introduce two of Cocoa's data handling features that are used in many types of applications. You need to be familiar with these features to complete the advanced tutorials in Chapter 11, *Cocoa's Multiple-Document Architecture*; Chapter 12, *To Do: Basics*; and Chapter 13, *To Do: Extended*.

The first section of the chapter covers table views—user interface objects that display data as rows and columns. Implementing a table view will deepen your understanding of the interaction between controls, cells, and their enclosing objects. Your work with table views will also provide an introduction to the concept of data sources—helper objects that provide the data to a table view for display.

In the final section of this chapter, you'll use Cocoa's archive/unarchive mechanism to "flatten" a group of data objects (also known in object-oriented parlance as *serialization*) so they can be saved to persistent storage and later retrieved for use.

Table Views and Data Sources

Table views are objects that display data as rows and columns. In a table view, a row typically maps to one object in your data model, while a column maps to an attribute of the object for that row. Some columns may hold derived or calculated values. Often, only a subset of an object's attributes appear in the table view. See Figure 9-1

An NSTableView is actually several objects, bound together in a scroll view. Inside the scroll view is an instance of NSTableView, in which data is displayed and edited. At the top of the table view is an NSTableHeaderView object. Beneath the

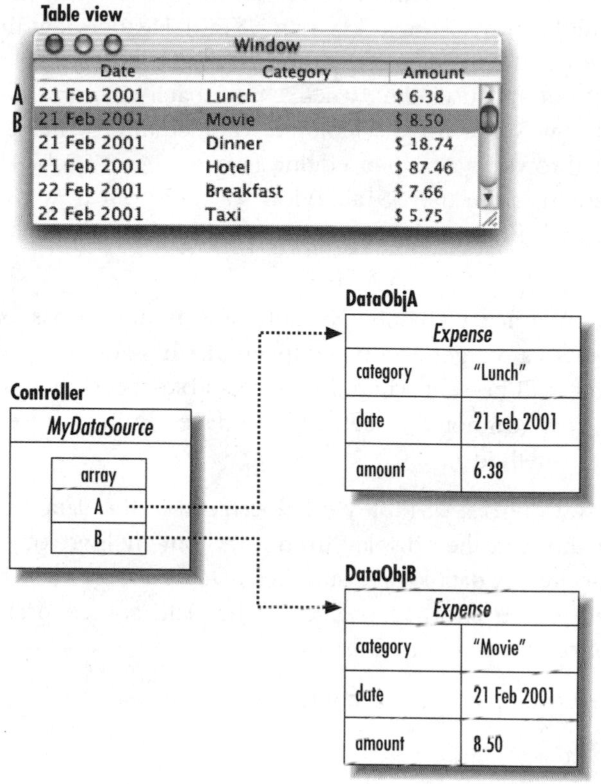

Figure 9-1. Mapping a data model to a table view's rows and columns

header view are one or more columns (instances of NSTableColumn). A column in a table view has several configurable attributes:

- **Header cell**. This cell is the column title.

- **Identifier**. This is an object value, most often a string, that is used to map a column to an attribute in the data model object. The identifier might be the attribute name or a number that acts as a tag.

- **Data cell**. This is a single object value within a table view. It is possible to configure a column to use a custom cell if your application requires it. NSTextFieldCell is the default `dataCell` type.

- **Formatter**. Like a text field, a table view column can use a formatter. The formatter applies to all cells in the column.

An NSTableView owns one or more NSTableColumns that define the columns the table shows. A table view also may own an NSTableHeaderView that is tiled above it in its scroll view. A table view uses the NSTableColumns inside it to figure out how to lay itself out and uses the `dataCell` from each column to draw and/or edit each individual row value for that column. (For editing, it makes a copy of the `dataCell` that it throws away when editing is over.) An NSTableHeaderView uses the NSTableColumns from the NSTableView to figure out how to lay itself out. It uses the `headerCell` from each column to actually draw the column heading for that column.

Like most user interface elements, NSTableView is a subclass of NSControl. As such, it supports a target/action connection. In addition, you can set a `doubleAction` that will be sent when the user double-clicks anything other than an editable cell. This cannot be set in Interface Builder; use NSTableView's `setDoubleAction:` method.

Unlike simpler NSControls, NSTableView doesn't store the data it displays. Instead, table views get the data they display from a custom "helper" object that you provide—its data source. A data source supplies data to a table view by implementing the NSTableDataSource informal protocol. The data source protocol for a table view consists of only two required methods:

```
-(int)numberOfRowsInTableView:(NSTableView *)tableView;
```

and:

```
-(id)tableView:(NSTableView *)tableView
    objectValueForTableColumn:(NSTableColumn *)tableColumn row:(int)row;
```

The first method provides a way for the table view to ask its data source how many rows of data are in the data model. The second method is used by the table view to retrieve an object value from the data model using row and column numbers as coordinates. If the user is allowed to enter or modify data in the table, you must implement a third method for saving changes back to the data source.

In MVC terms, a data source is a controller object that communicates with a model object (typically an array) and the view object (typically a table view or outline view). Figure 9-2 shows these relationships.

Several other Application Kit classes (such as NSOutlineView and NSComboBox) declare analogous informal protocols so that other objects can act as a data source for them.

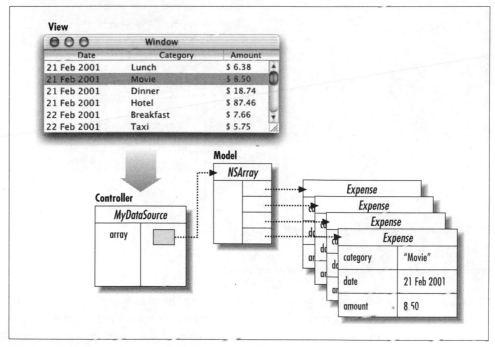

Figure 9-2. Data source as an MVC controller object

A Very Simple Table

In this section you'll implement a very simple application with a data source that supplies data to a table view for display. Later in the chapter you'll extend the application so that it functions as a utility for tracking daily expenses.

Create the project

Begin by creating a new Project Builder project for the application.

1. Create a new Cocoa application project called Expenses.

2. Open the main nib file.

Add the table view

The only UI object the Expenses application requires is a table view. Add it to the window now.

1. Drag the table view object from the Tabulation Views palette as shown in Figure 9-3.

2. Resize the table view to fill the window.

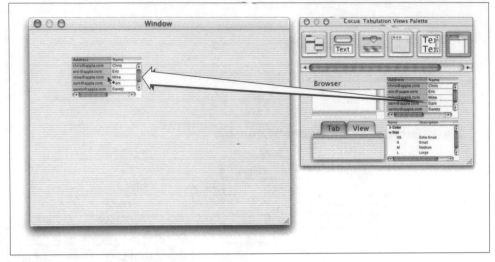

Figure 9-3. Adding a table view object to the interface

If you test the interface now, you'll see that resizing the window doesn't affect the table view. If you want to make the table view resize along with the window, you must modify the Autosizing settings in the Size pane of the table view's enclosing NSScrollView:

1. Click the table view once to bring up the NSTableView Info window.

2. Select the Size pane and click the lines so they match those shown in Figure 9-4.

The Autosizing box represents the view enclosing the currently selected object—in this case, the window enclosing the table view. The beveled square represents the selected object, while the springs and lines indicate freedom of movement. The settings shown earlier dictate that the distance between the edges of the table view and the enclosing window are fixed (the straight lines extending from the beveled square to the Autosizing box), but the size of the table view is flexible (the springs inside the beveled square). Clicking a line changes it to a spring and vice versa. Experiment with different settings and test the interface each time to see what happens.

To completely configure the table view, you must set attributes of the NSTable-View object as well as the NSTableColumn object:

1. Select the NSTableView.

2. Set the attributes in the Attributes pane of the NSTableView Info window as shown in Figure 9-5.

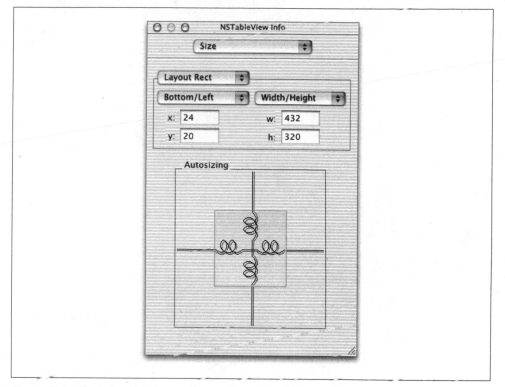

Figure 9-4. Changing the size attributes of an NSTableView

Configure the table columns

In this section you'll make the table columns equal width and give the columns titles.

1. Make the columns' width equal. Select the leftmost column (you may have to double-click), hold the cursor over the right edge of the column, and wait for the cursor to change to a pair of horizontally opposed arrows. Drag the column edge so the column view is divided into two equal parts. When you are done, Command-click on the selected column to deselect it.

2. Double-click the column header. Type **Column 1** and press Return.

3. Repeat for the second column and name it **Column 2**.

4. One at a time, select the column headings and bring up the Table Column Info window. Select the Attributes pane and center the headings.

When you're finished, the window should look something like Figure 9-6.

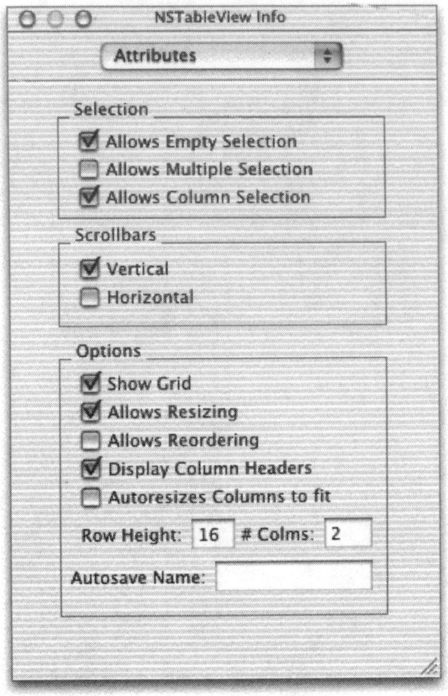

Figure 9-5. NSTableView attributes

Declare the data source class

A data source can be any object in your application that supplies the NSTableView with data. Later in the chapter, you'll build a complex data model for a table view, but for the first incarnation of this example, you'll create a dedicated simple data source object that will supply test data to the table view.

1. Create a subclass of NSObject and name it **MyDataSource**.

2. Instantiate the MyDataSource class.

3. Draw a connection from the table view object to the data source object in the Instances window. Make sure you have selected the table view and not its surrounding scroll view before you draw the connection. The table view will turn a darker shade of gray when selected.

4. Select the `dataSource` outlet in the Connections pane of the Info window and click Connect.

5. Create the files for MyDataSource, and add them to the Project Builder project.

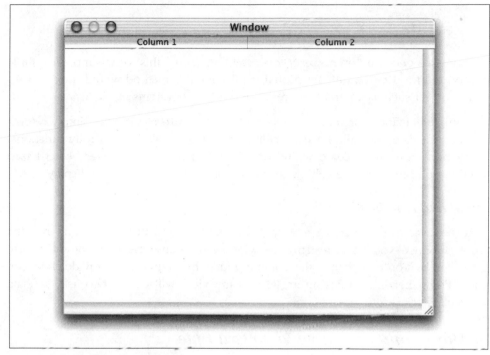

Figure 9-6. A table view with two columns

Implement the data source methods

The MyDataSource class needs only two methods to be able to feed data to the table for display—one to tell the table view how many rows of data to display and the other to return values for the cells in the table. To be compatible with the table view, the elements of data (usually records of some sort) must be identifiable through zero-based indexing.

1. Open MyDataSource.h in Project Builder and add the following declarations:

```
- (int)numberOfRowsInTableView:(NSTableView *)tableView;
- (id)tableView:(NSTableView *)tableView
       objectValueForTableColumn:(NSTableColumn *)tableColumn
       row:(int)row;
```

2. Open MyDataSource.m and add the following method implementations:

```
- (int)numberOfRowsInTableView:(NSTableView *)tableView
{
    return 10;
}


- (id)tableView:(NSTableView *)tableView
       objectValueForTableColumn:(NSTableColumn *)tableColumn
       row:(int)row
```

```
    {
        return [NSCalendarDate date];
    }
```

The implementation for `numberOfRowsInTableView:` in this very simple example always returns 10. In a fully functional application this method would query a container object such as an array and return the number of items in the array.

The implementation for `tableView:objectValueForTableColumn:row:` simply returns the current date and time for each cell in the table. Similarly, in a fully functional implementation, this method would retrieve data from the container object based on the requested row and column and return it to the table view for display.

Build and run the project

That's all there is to making a very simple table. Build the project and run the application. As you'll see, resizing the window will cause the table view to resize accordingly. You can change the column widths by dragging the divider between the column headings. Clicking an item in the view will cause it to ask the data source for an update.

A More Complete Table View Example

Though you have built a working table view, its implementation is unrealistically minimal. The data source class doesn't have a true data model, and there is no way for the user to modify data in the table. In this section you'll modify the Expenses application to address these shortcomings. The new version of the table view example will function as a very simple expenses application.

Create an expense class

The first thing you need to add to the table view application is a data model class. Since you are creating an expense-tracking application, you need a class that will represent an expense. Create a class that stores three pieces of data: the date of the expense, the category, and the amount.

1. In Project Builder, open the Expenses example project (if it's not already open).

2. Choose New File from the File menu.

3. An Assistant dialog box will appear. Choose Objective-C Class from the list.

4. Name the new file **Expense.m** and click Finish. Project Builder will create the header and implementation files, insert default templates, and add them to the project.

5. Open `Expense.h` and add the following instance variable declarations. Remember to insert these declarations between the curly braces.

```
NSCalendarDate *date;
NSString *category;
NSDecimalNumber *amount;
```

6. Add the following accessor method declarations. Remember to insert these declarations between the closing curly brace and the `@end` directive.

```
- (NSCalendarDate *)date;
- (void)setDate:(NSCalendarDate *)value;
- (NSString *)category;
- (void)setCategory:(NSString *)value;
- (NSDecimalNumber *)amount;
- (void)setAmount:(NSDecimalNumber *)value;
```

7. In `Expense.m`, add the next line between the `#import` and `@implementation` directives:

```
static NSString *defaultCategory = @"Food";
```

8. In the implementation section, add an `init` method:

```
- (id)init {
    self = [super init];
    [self setDate: [NSCalendarDate date]];
    [self setCategory: defaultCategory];
    [self setAmount: [NSDecimalNumber zero]];
    return self;
}
```

9. Add a corresponding `dealloc` method:

```
- (void)dealloc {
    [date release];
    [category release];
    [amount release];
    [super dealloc];
}
```

10. Finally, add the accessor method implementations:

```
- (NSCalendarDate *)date {
    return date;
}

- (void)setDate:(NSCalendarDate *)value {
    [date autorelease];
    date = [value copy];
}

- (NSString *)category {
    return category;
}
```

```
- (void)setCategory:(NSString *)value {
    [category autorelease];
    category = [value copy];
}

- (NSDecimalNumber *)amount {
    return amount;
}

- (void)setAmount:(NSDecimalNumber *)value {
    [amount autorelease];
    amount = [value copy];
}
```

Now you have a fully functional Expense class. When the modifications to the Expenses application are completed, the data source object will contain an array of Expense objects. Each row in the table view will have a corresponding Expense object in the array. Each column in the table view for a given row will correspond to an instance variable in that row's Expense object.

Add a new column to the table view

Create a third column for the table view. The three columns will display the date, category, and amount of each expense.

1. Open the main nib file.

2. Select the NSTableView object, and in the Attributes pane of the Info window, change the number of columns to three.

3. Resize the three columns so that they are of equal width. The newly created third column will appear out of sight to the right of the second. You'll have to select the second column and move its right edge to the left to reveal the third column.

Configure the table columns

Rename the table columns and add formatters to make the application's UI more attractive.

1. Rename the three columns **Date**, **Category**, and **Amount**, respectively.

2. Use the Info window to center the third column's label.

3. Select the Date column and drag a date formatter onto the Date column heading box. You'll see the outline of the heading box highlight when the cursor enters it. In the Formatter pane of the Date column's Info window, choose a

date format that appeals to you. Also, select the Allow Natural Language box. This is a nice feature of the formatter that lets you use strings like "today," "yesterday," and "tomorrow" for entering dates.

4. Repeat step 3 for the Amount column, using a number formatter instead of a date formatter.

Add table column identifiers

A column identifier is an object value, most often a string, that is used to map a column to an attribute in the data model object. When the table view sends a message to the data source asking for data, the column identifier is included so the data source can determine which column needs data—and therefore which attribute in the data model to retrieve.

In Interface Builder, select each column of the table view and use the Attributes pane of the Info window (Figure 9-7) to set a column identifier.

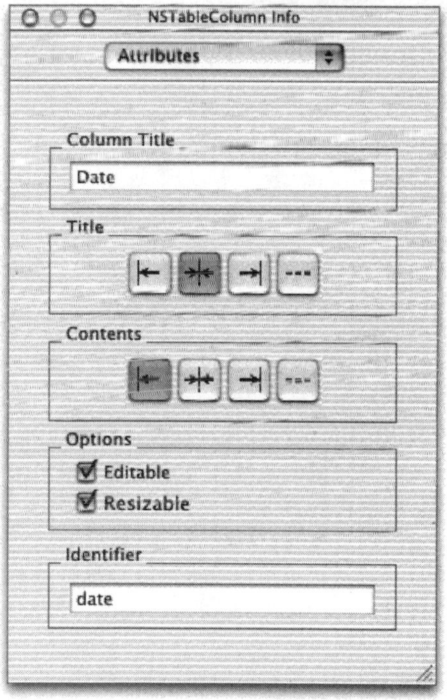

Figure 9-7. Adding a column identifier to a table view column

Use "date" for the Date column, "category" for the Category column, and "amount" for the Amount column. You could use any string value as an identifier, but as you'll soon see, there is a reason for using these particular strings.

Update the data source class

Now that your work with the user interface is complete, you must make some modifications to the data source class so it can use the Expense class you created earlier. The new implementation of the data source from earlier in the chapter will maintain an array of Expense objects as its data model.

1. In Project Builder, open `MyDataSource.h`.

2. Add an instance variable for the array of Expense objects:

   ```
   NSMutableArray *expenses;
   ```

3. Add method declarations for the accessor methods:

   ```
   - (NSMutableArray *)expenses;
   - (void)setExpenses:(NSMutableArray *)newExpenses;
   ```

4. Open `MyDataSource.m` and import `Expense.h`:

   ```
   #import "Expense.h"
   ```

5. Add implementations for the accessor methods:

   ```
   - (NSArray *)expenses {
       return expenses;
   }

   - (void)setExpenses:(NSMutableArray *)newExpenses {
       [expenses autorelease];
       expenses = [newExpenses retain];
   }
   ```

6. Add implementations for the `init` and `dealloc` methods:

   ```
   - (id)init {
       self = [super init];
       [self setExpenses: [NSMutableArray array]];
       return self;
   }

   - (void)dealloc {
       [expenses release];
       [super dealloc];
   }
   ```

7. Change the implementation of numberOfRowsInTableView: so it returns the number of items in the array of Expense objects:

```
- (int)numberOfRowsInTableView:(NSTableView *)tableView
{
    return [expenses count];
}
```

8. Change the implementation for tableView:objectValueForTableColumn:row: so it retrieves a value from the array of Expense objects.

This method uses a column identifier to retrieve data from an Expense object. It accomplishes this in an especially clever way that bears some explanation. First, the column identifier is retrieved from the table column object that was sent as a message parameter. Next, an Expense object is retrieved from the array of expenses using a row number that was also sent as a message parameter.

Now for the tricky bit: since the table column identifier string you assigned in Interface Builder is the same as the name of an instance variable in the Expense object, you can use *key-value coding* to retrieve the proper attribute value from the Expense object in one step. Key-value coding is a kind of shorthand used for accessing instance variables. If an object has an instance variable, then you can use the variable name as a parameter of the message valueForKey: and get the value of that variable from the object in one simple step:

```
- (id)tableView:(NSTableView *)tableView
    objectValueForTableColumn: (NSTableColumn *)tableColumn
    row: (int)row
{
    NSString *identifier = [tableColumn identifier];
    Expense *expense = [expenses objectAtIndex: row];

    return [expense valueForKey: identifier];
}
```

Key-value coding substantially simplifies the implementation of the data source method. Without this convenience, you would have to test the string value of the column identifier against a list in an elaborate if ... then statement to decide which of the Expense object's accessor methods to call. Instead of one line, you would have to do the following:

```
id value = nil;

if ([identifier isEqual: @"date"])
    value = [expense date];
else if ([identifier isEqual: @"category"])
    value = [expense category];
```

```
        else
            value = [expense amount];

    return value;
```

Seed the Expense array with test data

You could build and run the application now, but since you haven't yet implemented a way to add data to the empty array of expenses, you wouldn't see anything. In this section you will use the awakeFromNib method to fill an Expense array
with data and set the data source object to use the test data.

1. Add a method to MyDataSource.m that creates an array of Expense objects filled
   with test data and declare it in MyDataSource.h. Each object is created using
   the current date, the default expense category, and a dollar amount equal to
   the loop counter:

   ```
   - (NSMutableArray *)generateTestData
   {

       NSMutableArray *array = [NSMutableArray array];
       int index;

       for (index = 0; index < 15; index++) {
           Expense *exp = [[Expense alloc] init];
           [exp setAmount:
                   (NSDecimalNumber *)[NSDecimalNumber numberWithInt:index]];
           [array addObject: exp];
           [exp release];
       }

       return array;
   }
   ```

2. Implement awakeFromNib for MyDataSource.m:

   ```
   - (void)awakeFromNib
   {
       [self setExpenses: [self generateTestData]];
   }
   ```

Build and test the application

Build the application and try it. You should see something similar to Figure 9-8.

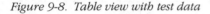

Date	Category	Amount
27 Mar 2001	Food	$ 0.00
27 Mar 2001	Food	$ 1.00
27 Mar 2001	Food	$ 2.00
27 Mar 2001	Food	$ 3.00
27 Mar 2001	Food	$ 4.00
27 Mar 2001	Food	$ 5.00
27 Mar 2001	Food	$ 6.00
27 Mar 2001	Food	$ 7.00
27 Mar 2001	Food	$ 8.00
27 Mar 2001	Food	$ 9.00
27 Mar 2001	Food	$ 10.00
27 Mar 2001	Food	$ 11.00
27 Mar 2001	Food	$ 12.00
27 Mar 2001	Food	$ 13.00
27 Mar 2001	Food	$ 14.00

Figure 9-8. Table view with test data

Modify values in the table view

For users to be able to change a value in the table and have the new value be copied back to the associated attribute in the data source's array of Expense objects, you need implement only one more method: `tableView:setObject-Value:forTableColumn:row:`. Here's an implementation that uses key-value coding:

```
- (void)tableView:(NSTableView *)tableView
   setObjectValue:(id)object
   forTableColumn:(NSTableColumn *)tableColumn
   row:(int)row
{
    NSString *identifier = [tableColumn identifier];
    Expense *expense = [expenses objectAtIndex: row];

    [expense takeValue: object forKey: identifier];
}
```

Enter data in the table view

Build and run the application again. Double-click a cell in the table to enter a new value. You should see the new value in the table when you press Return. Try entering the string "tomorrow" in one of the date cells.

Further Exploration

Some commonly used NSTableView methods that you might want to try out include:

- `reloadData`. This method forces the table view to reload from the data source.

- `noteNumberOfRowsChanged`. This informs the table view that the size of the data source has changed.

- `selectedRow`. This method returns the index of the currently selected row.

- `editColumn:row:withEvent:select:`. This method is used with NSTextField's `selectText` method; it allows you to put an individual cell into edit mode programmatically.

NSTableView defines some delegate methods including `textShouldBeginEditing`, `textShouldEndEditing`, `tableView:willDisplayCell:forTableColumn:row:`, and `tableView:shouldEditTableColumn:row:`. You can make your data source be the table view's delegate and implement these methods to more closely follow the user's interaction with the table view and modify its behavior.

NSTableView also posts some notifications like `NSTableViewSelectionDidChangeNotification` and `NSTableViewColumnDidMoveNotification`, which you can also use to help your data source track changes in the table view.

A good way to explore NSTableView and how it interacts with a data source is to modify the example application so you can add and delete expenses.

Also, examine and run the example application OutlineView in `/Developer/Examples/AppKit`. NSOutlineView is slightly more complicated than NSTableView, but with what you've learned here you should have no problem understanding how it works.

Flatten the Object Network: Coding and Archiving

Virtually all applications need a way to make some of their objects persistent. For example, the Expenses application that you created in the previous section doesn't save the state of the data model, so you'll lose all of your expenses information as soon as you quit. Cocoa applications typically use coding and archiving to store document contents and other critical application data to disk for later retrieval. Some applications may also use coding and archiving to send objects over a network to another application. (For instance, in case you want to send a set of expenses to a friend.)

In this section you will modify the simple expense-tracking application from the previous section to use coding and archiving so it can save and reload the array of expenses.

NSCoder and NSArchiver

Coding, as implemented by NSCoder, takes a connected group of objects such as those in an application (an *object graph*) and serializes that data, capturing the state, structure, relationships, and class memberships of the objects. A subclass of NSCoder, NSArchiver extends this behavior by storing the serialized data in a file.

When archiving an object graph's root object, archive not only that object, but all other objects the root object references, all objects those second-level objects reference, etc. To be archived, though, objects must conform to the NSCoding protocol (consisting of the encodeWithCoder: and initWithCoder: methods).

Add Coding and Archiving to the Expenses Application

1. Open the main nib file in Interface Builder.

2. In the Instances pane of the MainMenu.nib window, Control-drag a connection from the Window instance to the MyDataSource instance. In the Connections pane of the Info window, make MyDataSource the delegate of Window.

3. In Project Builder, open the TableView example project.

4. Open Expense.h and modify the class declaration as follows. Adding <NSCoding> declares that the Expense class conforms to the coding protocol.

   ```
   @interface Expense : NSObject <NSCoding>
   {
   ```

5. Open Expense.m and add the NSCoding methods. The most frequently used NSCoder method, encodeObject:, encodes (serializes) a single object. For nonobject types, you can use encodeValueOfObjCType:at:. The order of decoding should be the same as the order of encoding; since date is encoded first, it should be decoded first. NSCoder defines decode methods that correspond to the encode methods, which you should use. As in any init method, end by returning self—an initialized instance:

   ```
   - (id)initWithCoder:(NSCoder *)coder {
       [self setDate: [coder decodeObject]];
       [self setCategory: [coder decodeObject]];
       [self setAmount: [coder decodeObject]];
       return self;
   }
   ```

```
- (void)encodeWithCoder:(NSCoder *)coder {
    [coder encodeObject: [self date]];
    [coder encodeObject: [self category]];
    [coder encodeObject: [self amount]];
}
```

6. Add the following implementation of the `windowShouldClose:` delegate method
   to MyDataSource. This method first displays a standard alert asking users if
   they want to save the contents of the window. If they click Save, a Save dialog
   box (NSSavePanel) is displayed so the users can name the file and choose a
   directory in which to save it. The `setRequiredFileType:` method tells the Save
   panel to append `.expenses` to the filename so that the file has a recognizable
   type. If the user clicks Save, NSArchiver encodes the entire array of Expense
   objects and saves them to disk. If the user cancels, the window is closed and
   nothing is saved:

```
- (BOOL)windowShouldClose:(NSWindow *)sender
{
    NSSavePanel *sp;
    int answer;

    answer = NSRunAlertPanel(@"Save Expenses",
        @"Do you want to save?",
        @"Save",
        @"Don't Save",
        nil);

    if (answer == NSAlertDefaultReturn) {
        sp = [NSSavePanel savePanel];
        [sp setRequiredFileType:@"expenses"];
        answer = [sp runModal];
        if (answer == NSOKButton ) {
            [NSArchiver archiveRootObject:[self expenses]
                    toFile:[sp filename]];
        }
    }

    return YES;
}
```

7. Finally, modify the implementation of `awakeFromNib` so it prompts the users for
   a file to load. This method now presents a standard open dialog box, so the
   users can choose an archived data file to load. The types array means that the
   users can't choose any file, only valid expenses files (or at least files with a
   `.expenses` file extension). If they choose a file, NSUnarchiver is invoked to
   restore the array of expense objects from the archive. If the users cancel, the
   test data is generated as before:

```
- (void)awakeFromNib
{
    NSOpenPanel *op;
```

```
        int answer;

        op = [NSOpenPanel openPanel];
        answer = [op runModalForTypes: [NSArray arrayWithObject:@"expenses"]];

        if (answer == NSOKButton) {
            [self setExpenses: [NSUnarchiver unarchiveObjectWithFile:
                    [op filename]]];
        } else {
            [self setExpenses:[self generateTestData]];
        }
}
```

10

Travel Advisor Tutorial

In this chapter you'll expand your repertoire of Cocoa programming techniques to:

- Use forms and table views (beyond the simple introduction in Chapter 9, *Data Functionality*)

- Group objects in Interface Builder

- Add images to applications

- Format and validate fields

- Make connections for simple printing

- Use collection objects and string objects

- Reuse custom objects from other applications

The vehicle for exploring these topics is an application called Travel Advisor. Travel Advisor is a forms-based application used for entering, viewing, and deleting records on countries to which the user travels. This example application will give you another chance to work with design using Model-View-Controller (MVC) and also provides a chance to explore more deeply many of the Cocoa programming techniques to which you've been introduced in previous chapters.

Travel Advisor Design

Travel Advisor is much like Currency Converter in its basic design, but the application is considerably more complex. Figure 10-1 shows Travel Advisor's user interface. To use Travel Advisor, you enter a country name along with travel-related information associated with that country. When you click Add, the name of the country appears in the table of country records. After you've entered data on several countries, you can select a particular country from the table and the information on that country appears in the forms. You can save all of your travel information to disk before you quit the application, so no data is lost between sessions. The application also allows you to do temperature and currency conversions.

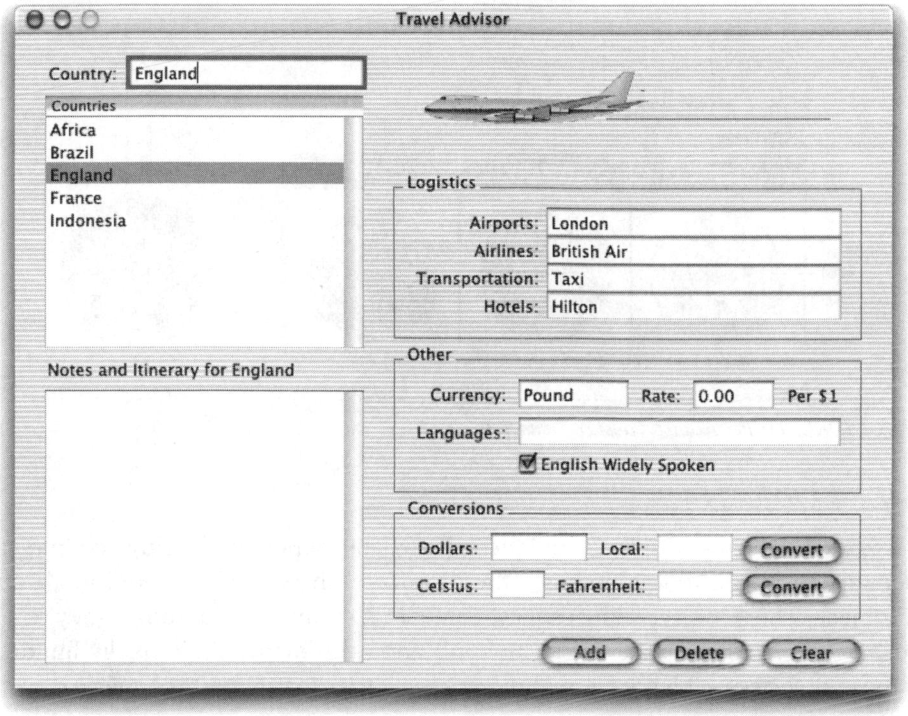

Figure 10-1. Travel Advisor's user interface

Travel Advisor is based on the Model-View-Controller paradigm. A Controller object (TAController) manages a user interface comprised of Application Kit objects, and the controller sends messages to the Model objects to get the results of various data manipulations. The high-level design is depicted in Figure 10-2.

Because one of the computations required for Travel Advisor is the conversion of various currencies, the Converter object from the Currency Converter project can be reused without modification.

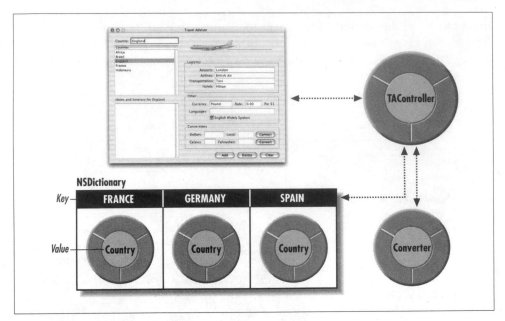

Figure 10-2. Travel Advisor design overview

Model Objects

Travel Advisor must display a unique set of data, depending on the country the user selects. To make this possible, the data for each country is stored in a Country object. These objects encapsulate data on a country (in a sense, they're like records in a relational database). The application can manage potentially hundreds of these objects, tracking each without recourse to a "hardwired" connection.

Another Model object in the application is the instance of the Converter class. This instance does not hold any data, but does provide some specialized behavior.

View Objects

Travel Advisor's view objects are all off-the-palette Application Kit objects: text fields, checkboxes, buttons, and so on.

Controller Objects

The Controller object for the application is TAController. Like all Controller objects, TAController is responsible for mediating the flow of data between the user interface (the View part of the paradigm) and the Model objects that encapsulate that data—the Country objects. Based on user choices in the interface, TAController can find and display the requested Country object; it can also save changes made by users to the appropriate Country object.

What makes this possible is an NSDictionary object (called a dictionary from here on). A dictionary, as you learned in Chapter 6, *Essential Cocoa Paradigms,* is a container that stores objects and permits their retrieval through key-value associations. The key is a unique identifier that can be used to "look up" the associated object. To get the object, you send a message to the dictionary using the key as an argument (objectForKey:). For example:

```
NSColor *aColor = [aDictionary objectForKey: @"BackgroundColor"];
```

In this example, aDictionary holds one or more NSColor objects, each associated with a string key. When the dictionary object receives the objectForKey: message, it looks for an object associated with the argument BackgroundColor.

In Travel Advisor (as shown later in this chapter) a Country object holds the name of a country as an instance variable; this country name also functions as the dictionary key. When you store a Country object in the dictionary, you also store the country name (in the form of an NSString) as the object's key. Later you retrieve the object by sending the dictionary the message objectForKey: with the country name as argument.

How TAController manages data

The TAController class plays a central role in the Travel Advisor application, as shown in Figure 10-3. As the application's Controller object, it transfers data from the Model objects (Country instances) to the fields of the interface and, when users enter or modify data, back to the correct Country object. The TAController must also coordinate the data displayed in the table view with the current object, and it must do the right thing when users select an item in the table view or click the Add or Delete button. All custom code specific to the user interface resides in TAController. The mechanics of this activity requires an array.

Storing data source information

TAController also manages the data source for the table view that is used to display a list of available countries. TAController stores the keys to the dictionary containing all of the known Country objects in an array object (NSArray), sorted alphabetically. When the table view requests data for display, the TAController "feeds" it the sorted list of objects in the array.

Creation of Country objects

Another important point of design is the manner in which the Country objects are created. Instead of Interface Builder creating them, the TAController object creates Country objects in response to users clicking the Add button.

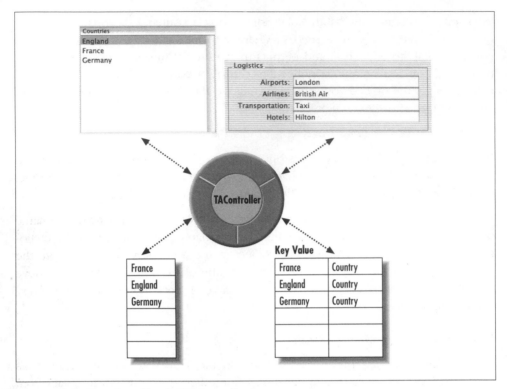

Figure 10-3. Data handling by TAController

Delegation and notification

An essential aspect of design not evident from the Figure 10-3 are the roles delegation and notification play. You'll see how these design patterns are used as you construct the application.

Create the Travel Advisor Interface

In creating the interface of Travel Advisor, you'll be exercising the capabilities of Interface Builder much more than you did with Currency Converter. Here is an overview of the steps you'll take in this section to complete the Travel Advisor interface:

1. Create the application project.

2. Open the application's nib file.

3. Customize the application's window.

4. Add text fields, labels, and buttons to the window.

5. Add a form object to the window.

6. Group the user interface objects.

7. Add a text view.

8. Add and configure a table view.

9. Add an image to the interface.

10. Add a menu and menu items.

11. Add formatters.

12. Make connections for interfield tabbing and printing.

13. Test the interface.

Get Started

You should be familiar with many of the objects on the Travel Advisor interface because you've encountered them them in Chapter 7, *Currency Converter Tutorial.* Figure 10-4 points out the objects that are new to you in this tutorial.

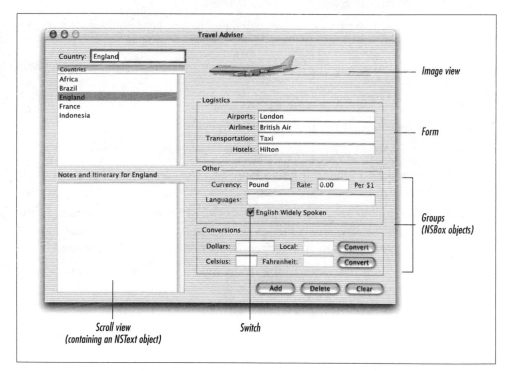

Figure 10-4. New interface elements

Create the Application Project

Start by creating a new project for the application.

1. Start Project Builder.

2. Choose New Project from the File menu.

3. In the New Project panel, select the Cocoa Application project type and click the Next button.

4. Name the application **Travel Advisor**.

5. If you wish, click Set to select a location to save the project in a specific location of your choice. To use the default location, go on to step 6.

6. Click Finish.

Customize the Application Window

Rename and resize the application's main window.

1. Open the Resources group in the project browser.

2. Double-click `MainMenu.nib`. (This will launch Interface Builder if it is not already running.)

3. Bring up Interface Builder's Info window (Command-Shift-I) if it's not already open.

4. Change the window title to **Travel Advisor**.

5. In the Controls area, turn off the Resize attribute.

6. Click the Window Info's pop-up menu and select Size.

7. In the Content Rect area of the Info window, verify that the left pop-up menu says Top/Left.

8. Set the x field to 30 and the y field to 80. This sets the starting location of the Travel Advisor window when the application first launches. Note that moving the Travel Advisor window in Interface Builder will change these values.

9. Also in the Content Rect area of the Info window, verify that the right pop-up menu says Width/Height.

10. Set the width to 700 and the height to 520.

Add the Text Fields, Labels, and Buttons to the Window

Complete the first phase of the application's user interface.

1. Position, resize, and initialize the objects, as shown in Figure 10-5. Hint: liberal use of the Duplicate function (Command-D) will make this step go much more quickly.

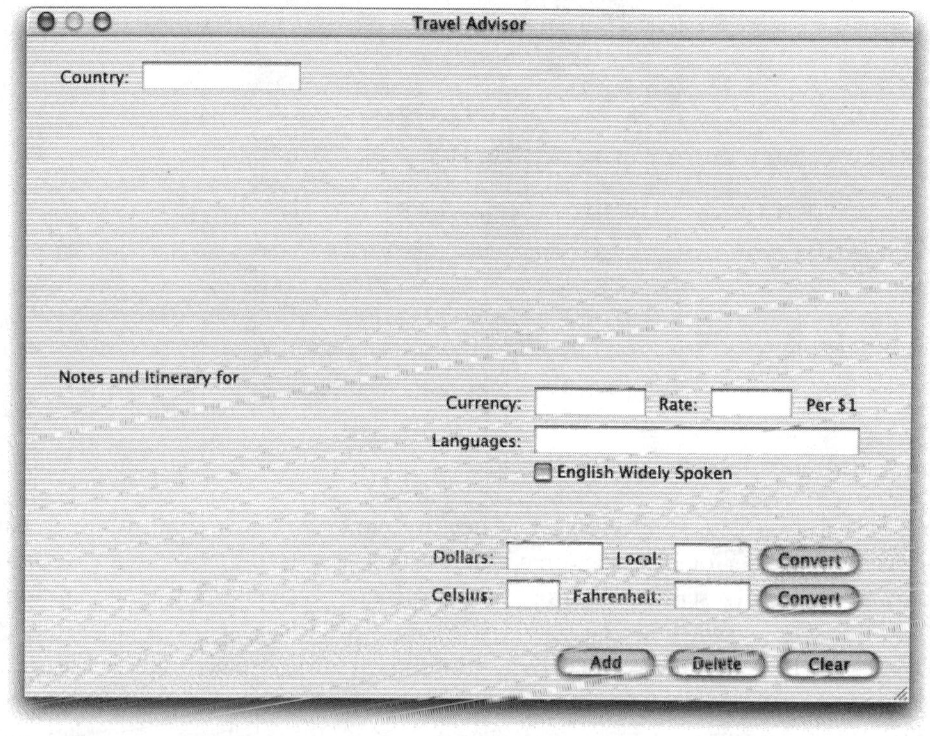

Figure 10-5. Initial layout of Travel Advisor's interface

2. Use the Info window (Command-Shift-I) to change the attributes of the text fields labeled Local and Fahrenheit so they are not editable, as shown in Figure 10-6. These fields are used to display the results of computations, so there is no need for the user to be able to edit them.

More about buttons

If in Interface Builder you select the English Widely Spoken switch and bring up the Attributes Info window, you can see that the switch is simply a type of button. (See Figure 10-7.)

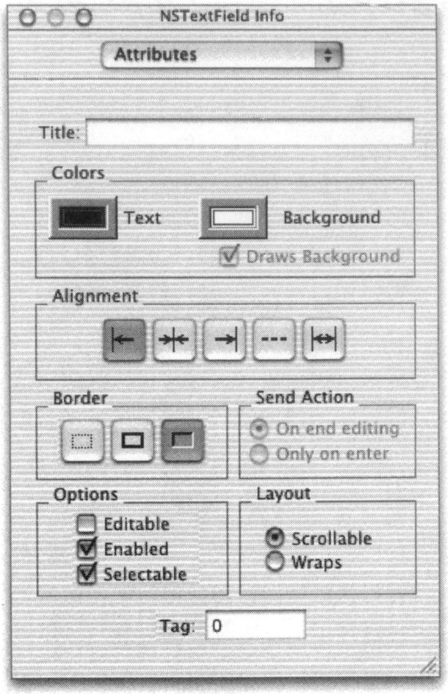

Figure 10-6. Text field Attributes Info window

Buttons are two-state control objects. They are either off or on, and this state can be set by the user or set programmatically using setState:. For certain types of buttons (especially standard buttons like Currency Converter's Convert button), when the state is switched, the button sends an action message to a target object. Toggle-type buttons, such as switches and radio buttons, visually reflect their state. Applications can learn of this state with the state message. You can make your own buttons, associating icons and titles with a button's off and on states and positioning titles and icons relative to one another.

Add a Form Object to the Interface

Add the form object that will hold logistical information about a country.

1. Drag the form object from Interface Builder's Views palette as shown in Figure 10-8.

2. Increase the size of the form's fields by dragging the resize handle sideways. Make the fields the same width as the Languages field in the Other section of the Travel Advisor's UI.

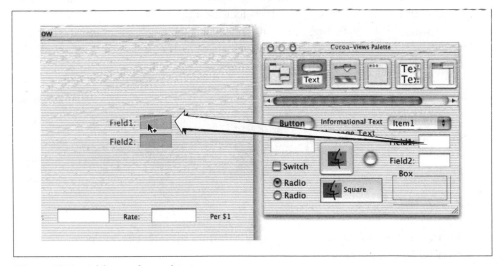

Figure 10-7. Checkbox Attributes Info window

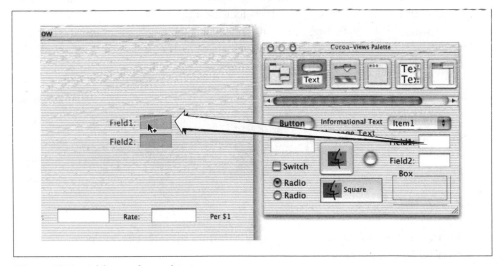

Figure 10-8. Adding a form object

3. Create two more form fields by Option-dragging the bottom-middle resize handle downward.

4. Remove the spacing between the text fields by Command-dragging the bottom-middle resize handle upward.

5. Rename the field labels as shown. (Tip: Use the Tab key to move between fields in the form.)

6. Right-align the labels so that the form looks like Figure 10-9.

Figure 10-9. Finalized form object

Group the Objects on the Interface

To make titled sections of the fields, forms, and buttons on the Travel Advisor interface, group selected objects. By grouping them, you put them in a box.

1. Select the two Convert buttons along with the Dollars, Local, Celsius, and Fahrenheit labels and text fields. To select the objects as a group, drag a selection rectangle around them or Shift-click each object. (To make a selection rectangle, start dragging from an empty spot on the window.) When all the objects are selected, they should look like Figure 10-10.

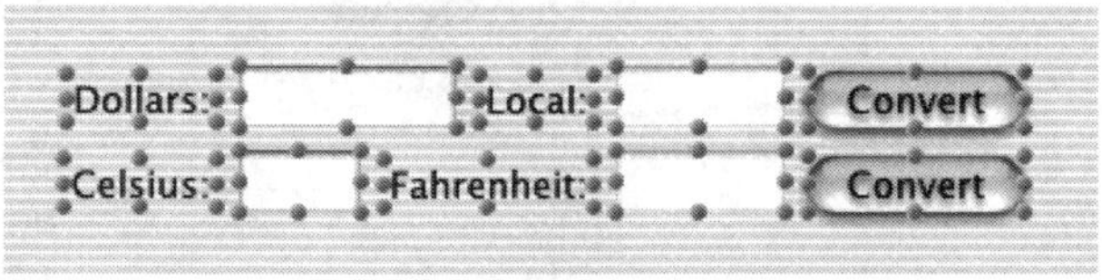

Figure 10-10. Selecting objects for grouping

2. Choose Layout → Group In → Box (Command-G). The objects are now enclosed by a titled box.

3. Double-click Title to select it.

4. Rename Title as **Conversions**.

5. Repeat for the next two groups, Logistics and Other, as shown in Figure 10-11.

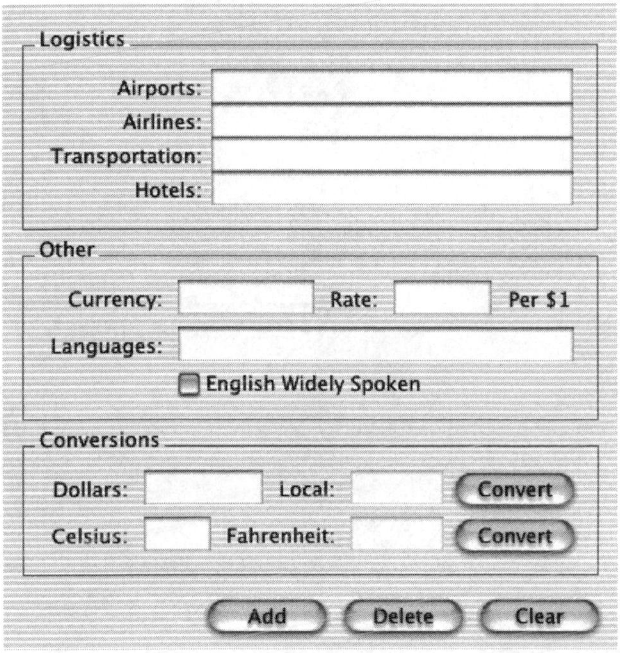

Figure 10-11. Grouped objects

Boxes are a useful way to organize and name sections of an interface. In Interface Builder you can move, copy, paste, and perform other operations with the box as a unit. For Travel Advisor, you don't need to change the default box attributes, but you can choose a different box style if you wish.

The box, an instance of NSBox, is the superview of all of its grouped objects. (A view, simply put, is any object visible in a window.) As was discussed in Chapter 8, *Event Handling*, a superview encloses its subviews and is the next in line to respond to user actions if its subviews cannot handle them.

Add the Text View

The text view on the DataViews palette consists of a text object (an instance of NSTextView) enclosed within a scroll view (an instance of NSScrollView). This object allows users to enter, edit, format, and scroll through arbitrary-length text with minimal programmatic involvement on your part.

1. Drag the text view from the DataViews palette and drop it on the lower-left corner of the window, as shown in Figure 10-12.

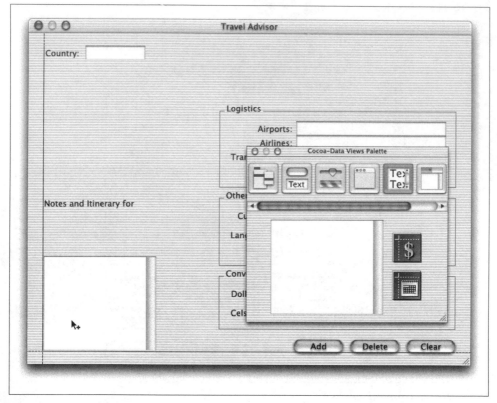

Figure 10-12. Adding a text view object

2. Resize the text view so it occupies the entire lower-left portion of the Travel Advisor window.

3. Resize the Notes and Itinerary For label so that its right edge is aligned with the text view. This will leave some extra space to programmatically insert the name of the country currently being viewed.

You don't need to change any of the default attributes of the text view (but you might want to look at the attributes that you can set, if you're curious).

Add and Configure the Table View

As you discovered in Chapter 9, a table view is an object used to display and edit tabular data. Often that data consists of a set of related records, with rows for individual records and columns for the common fields (attributes) of those records. Table views are ideal for applications that have a database component.

In this section you will configure a table view to display the list of available countries:

1. Drag the table view object from the Tabulation Views palette, (see Figure 10-13).

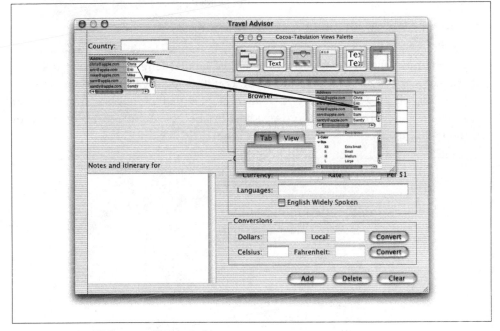

Figure 10-13. Adding a table view object

2. Resize the table view to fill the area between the Country field and Notes label.

3. Set the title of the first column to Countries. Double-click the column header to insert the cursor. Type **Countries**, then click anywhere outside the column or press Return.

4. Make the table contain only one column. First, delete the unneeded column by selecting it (click on the column header) and pressing Delete. Next, hold the cursor over the right edge of the Countries column, wait for the cursor to change to a pair of horizontally opposed arrows, and then click and drag the column edge so that it's flush with the right edge of the view. If you go too far to the right, a horizontal scrollbar will appear at the bottom of the view. If this

happens, just slide the column edge back to the left and try again. When you are done, click outside the table view to deselect the column.

5. Resize the Country text field so that its right edge is aligned with the table.

To configure the table view, you must set attributes of two component objects: the NSTableView object and the NSTableColumn object:

1. Select the table view.

2. Set the NSTableView attributes, as shown in Figure 10-14. Since this is a single-column view and country names are of limited length, you need only the vertical scroller in case there are more countries than can be shown at once. Whether to show the grid is a matter of personal preference, but turn off Resizing and Reordering. The user shouldn't be able to affect the contents of the table directly.

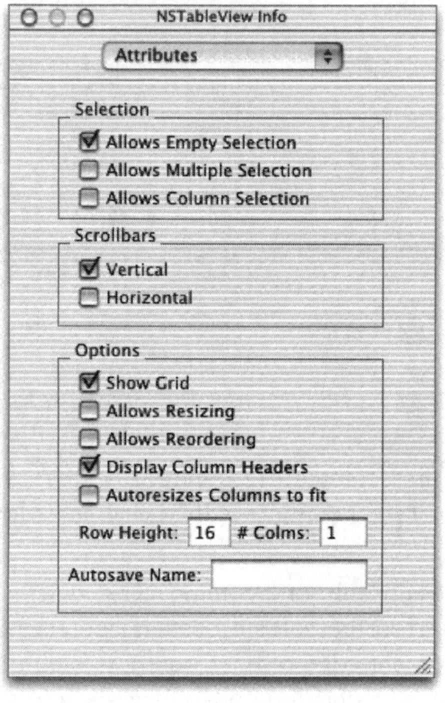

Figure 10-14. Table view Attributes Info window

3. Double-click the table's interior and select the Countries column label.

4. Set the NSTableColumn attributes, as shown in Figure 10-15.

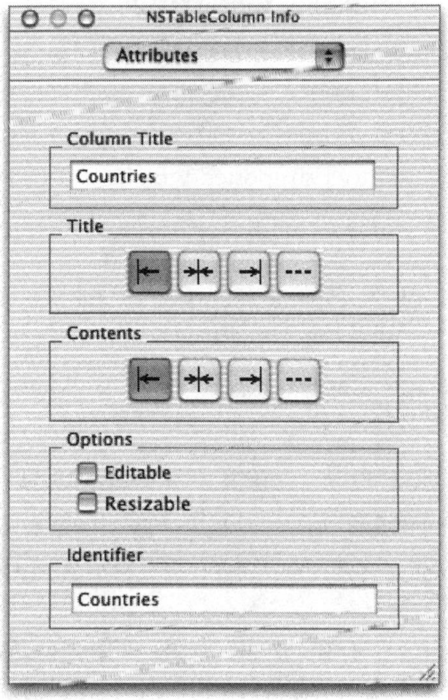

Figure 10-15. Table column Attributes Info window

5. In the Identifier field, type the name with which you want to identify the column programmatically. For Travel Advisor, make this name the same as the column title.

Add an Image to the Interface

When used tastefully, images can add a very nice visual touch to an interface. Sometimes buttons are the preferred objects for holding images—for instance, when you want a different image for the various button states. But when buttons are disabled, any image they display is dimmed. For decorative images, use image views (NSImageView) instead of buttons.

Tag Image File Format (TIFF) is the preferred image file format for use with Cocoa. You can use any of the formats supported by the NSImage class, including:

• Portable Document Format (PDF)

• Apple's PICT format

- Bitmap data in Windows Bitmap format (BMP)

- Untagged (raw) bitmap data

- Other image data supported by an NSImageRep subclass registered with the NSImage class

- Data that can be filtered to a supported type by a user-installed filter service

Consult the reference documentation for NSImage and NSImageRep for additional information. Note that Cocoa also accepts any of the image formats supported by QuickTime, but the use of QuickTime incurs extra memory and performance overhead and is not recommended for static images in the application's user interface.

To make managing image files easier, Interface Builder can reference and use images included in your Project Builder project:

1. In Project Builder, choose New Group from the Project menu.

2. Name the group **Images** and put it in the Resources group.

3. Choose Add File from the Project menu and add `Airplane.tiff` included with the example files.

4. In Interface Builder, drag an image view onto the window from the More Views palette, as shown in Figure 10-16.

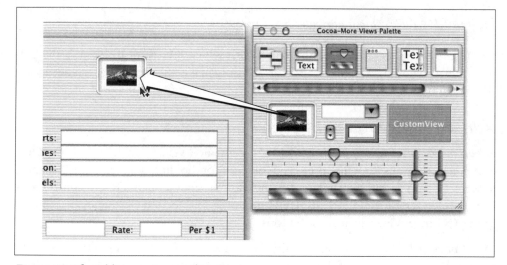

Figure 10-16. Adding an image view object

5. Click on the Images tab in the `MainMenu.nib` window.

6. Drag the proxy for the image onto the image view.

It's also possible to add images directly from Interface Builder. When you drop an image over a button or image view, Interface Builder adds the image file to the project (if the project is currently open in Project Builder) and includes a reference to it in the nib file.

Now configure the image's properties:

1. In Interface Builder, bring up the Attributes Info window for the image view and set the attributes as shown in Figure 10-17.

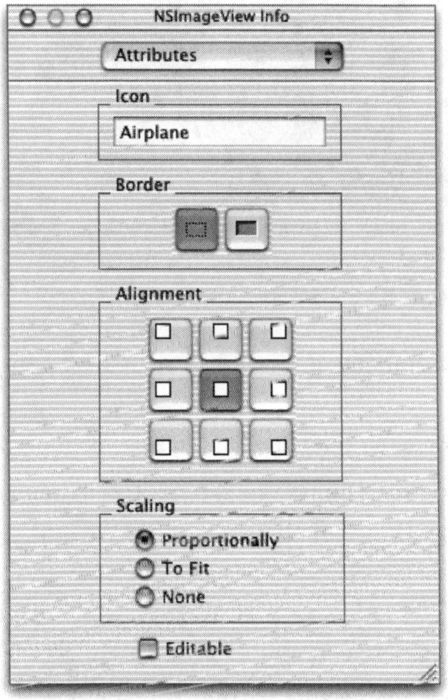

Figure 10-17. Image view Attributes Info window

2. Make the image view (and the enclosed image) small enough to fit between the titlebar and the Logistics group.

3. Add a "velocity" line behind the airplane. (Tip: Use a horizontal separator.)

Add a Menu and Menu Items

Travel Advisor's menu contains default submenus and commands. You need a submenu and menu commands that are not included in the default set and that are not found on the Menus palette. Use the Submenu and the Item cells to create customized menus and menu items, respectively.

1. In Interface Builder, select the Menus palette. The palette window will look like Figure 10-18.

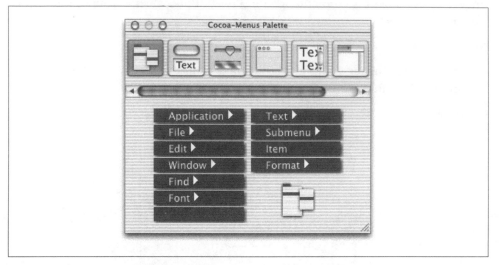

Figure 10-18. Menus palette

2. Drag the generic Submenu item and drop it between the Edit and Window submenus.

3. Double-click Submenu to select the menu title; change the name to **Records**.

4. Click the new Records menu to expose the Item command.

5. Click the Item and duplicate it three times (making four altogether) using Command-D.

6. Change the command names to **Add**, **Delete**, **Next**, and **Previous**. (Tip: Use the Tab key to move between entries in the menu.)

7. Add Command-key equivalents to the right of the Next and Previous commands: Command-Option-N and Command-Option-P. To make the key assignment, double-click the area to the right of the menu command (a small square will appear), and then type the key equivalent you wish to assign. The Records menu should look like Figure 10-19.

8. In the File menu, change Print . . . to Print Notes . . . .

Add Formatters

As you learned in Chapter 6, formatters are objects that translate the values of certain objects to specific onscreen representations. In this section you'll add formatters to some of the text fields on the user interface to more appropriately display currency values.

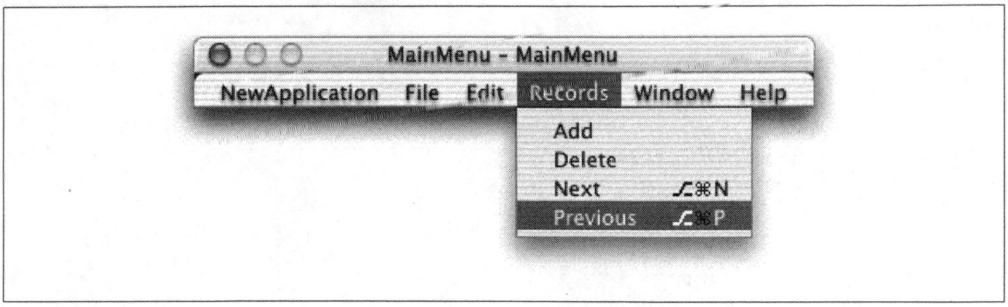

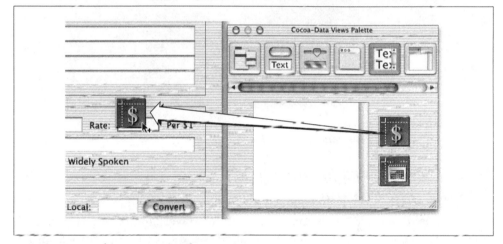

Figure 10-19. Records menu items

1. Select the DataViews palette in the Palette window.

2. Drag a number-formatter object and drop it over the Rate field, as shown in Figure 10-20.

Figure 10-20. Adding a number formatter

3. Click on the Rate field to select it and bring up the Info window (Command-Shift-I), if it is not already visible.

4. In the Formatter display of the Info window shown in Figure 10-21, specify a rate format by selecting the table view row with the 9999.99 format.

5. Repeat for the Dollars and Local fields, but apply a suitable format.

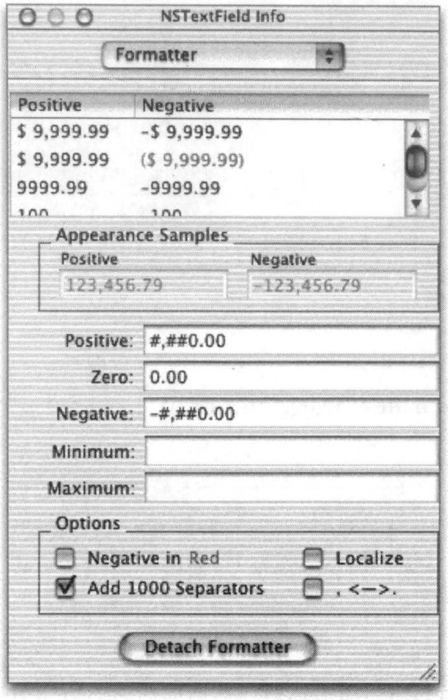

Figure 10-21. Text field Formatter Info window

Make Connections for Interfield Tabbing and Printing

You can now connect many of the objects on the Travel Advisor interface through outlets and actions defined by the Application Kit. As you'll remember from the previous tutorials, objects are connected in Interface Builder by Control-clicking on a source object and dragging a connecting line to the destination object.

Windows in Cocoa have an `initialFirstResponder` outlet for the object in the window that should be the initial focus of events. Text fields have a `nextKeyView` outlet that you connect so that users can tab from field to field. Forms also have a `nextKeyView` outlet for tabbing. (The fields within a form are already interconnected, so you don't need to connect them.)

1. Make a connection from the window icon in the nib file window to the Country field.

2. Select `initialFirstResponder` in the Connections display of the Info window and click Connect.

3. In top-to-bottom sequence, connect the fields and the form through their nextKeyView outlets. Start by connecting the Country field to the Logistics form.

4. When you reach the Languages field, connect it with the Country field, making a loop.

5. Connect the editable text fields in the Conversions section in a similar loop.

The Application Kit also has preset actions to which you can connect your application. The NSTextView object in the scroll view can print its contents as can all objects that inherit from NSView. To take advantage of this capability, "hook up" the menu command with the NSTextView action method for printing:

1. Click on the Print Notes menu command to select it. The Connection area of the NSMenuItem Info window shows a preexisting connection to FirstResponder.print. Disconnect the connection to FirstResponder.

2. Connect the Print Notes menu command to the text object in the scroll view.

3. Select the print: action method in the Connections display of the Info window.

4. Click the Connect button.

Test the Interface

You're finished with the Travel Advisor interface. Save your work (Command-S) and test it by choosing Test Interface (Command-R) from Interface Builder's File menu. Try the following:

- Press the Tab key repeatedly. Notice how the cursor jumps between the fields of the form and how it loops from the Languages field to the Country field. Press Shift-Tab to make the cursor go in the reverse direction.

- Enter some text in the text view, then click the Print Notes menu item. The Print dialog box is displayed. Print the text object's contents.

- Also in the text view, press the Return key repeatedly until a scrollbox appears in the scrollbar.

Define the Classes of Travel Advisor

Travel Advisor has three classes: Country, Converter, and TAController. Only TAController has outlets and actions. And, rather than defining the Converter class, you are simply going to add it to the project from the Currency Converter project and reuse it.

Specify the Country and TAController Classes

Subclass NSObject to create the Country and TAController classes.

1. In Interface Builder, bring up the Classes display of the nib file window.

2. Select NSObject as the superclass.

3. Choose Subclass from the Classes menu.

4. Type **Country** in place of `MyObject`.

5. Repeat for TAController.

Specify TAController's Outlets and Actions

Now that the interface has been laid out, you can define the outlets that let TAController communicate with the UI objects. While here, you can also add the outlet for the Converter object that will be reused from the Currency Converter project.

1. Select TAController and choose Add Outlet from the Classes menu.

2. Add the following outlets:

   celsiusField
   commentsField
   commentsLabel
   converter
   countryField
   countryTableView
   currencyDollarsField
   currencyLocalField
   currencyNameField
   currencyRateField
   englishSpokenSwitch
   fahrenheitField
   languagesField
   logisticsForm

In addition to outlets, you must specify actions so that the UI objects can message TAController.

1. Select TAController and choose Add Action from the Classes menu:

2. Define the following action methods:

   addRecord:
   blankFields:
   convertCurrency:
   convertTemp:
   deleteRecord:
   handleTVClick:

nextRecord:
prevRecord:
switchClicked:

Reuse the Converter Class

In Cocoa there are many ways to reuse objects. For example, subclassing an existing class to obtain slightly different behavior is one way to reuse the functionality of the superclass. Another way is to integrate an existing class—like the Converter class—into your project.

1. In Project Builder, select the Classes group in the project browser.

2. Choose Add Files from the Project menu and navigate to the Currency Converter project directory. Select both `Converter.m` and `Converter.h`. Click Open.

3. When asked if you want to add the file to the Travel Advisor target, make sure the Copy checkbox is checked and the Travel Advisor target selected before you click Add.

4. Open Travel Advisor's `MainMenu.nib` file.

5. Drag the `Converter.h` file from Project Builder to the `MainMenu.nib` window in Interface Builder. Interface Builder parses the header file, looking for the superclass and all declared outlets and actions. The Classes panel of the nib file will now list Converter as a subclass of NSObject.

When you're finished with this procedure, the Converter class is copied both to the Travel Advisor project and to the Travel Advisor main nib file.

Generate TAController and Converter Instances

You don't need to instantiate the Country class in the nib file because it is not involved in any outlet or action connections. However, you must create an instance of TAController for making connections to other objects. TAController interacts behind the scenes with users as they manipulate the application's interface and mediates the data coming from and going to Country objects. It therefore needs access to interface objects and should be made the target of action messages. It also needs to connect to a Converter object, so instantiate Converter, too.

Make Connections to the TAController Instance

The TAController outlets need to be connected to the interface objects and the Converter object so that they can communicate with these objects at runtime. Remember to make the connections (Control-click and drag) in the direction that messages will flow. For example, TAController will send messages to the Celsius text field to draw text into it. So to connect these objects you would Control-click on the TAController instance and drag the connection to the Celsius text field.

1. Connect TAController to the outlets listed in the following table. After making the first few connections in the list, it may seem as if Interface Builder is reading your mind because the proper outlet will already be selected in the Connections Info window each time you make a new connection. This is simply an artifact of the fact that the list in the table happens to be in alphabetical order. This makes things go more quickly for the purposes of the tutorial. If you connect the TAController instance to the interface objects in a different order, you'll have to search through the list in the Info window each time to select the proper outlet for the connection you're making.

Outlet	Make Connection to
celsiusField	Text field labeled Celsius
commentsField	Text object within scroll view
commentsLabel	Label that reads Notes and Itinerary for
converter	Instance of Converter class (cube in Instances display)
countryField	Text field labeled Country
countryTableView	The area underneath the Countries column
currencyDollarsField	Text field labeled Dollars
currencyLocalField	Text field labeled Local
currencyNameField	Text field labeled Currency
currencyRateField	Text field labeled Rate
englishSpokenSwitch	Switch (button) labeled English Widely Spoken
fahrenheitField	Text field labeled Fahrenheit
languagesField	Text field labeled Languages
logisticsForm	Form in group (box) labeled Logistics; the form is selected when a gray line borders all four fields.

2. Connect the TAController instance to control objects in the interface via its actions as listed in the following table. Remember, for actions, you drag connections from the interface object to the TAController instance.

Action	Make Connection from
addRecord:	Add button (and also the Add item in the Records menu)
blankFields:	Clear button
convertCurrency:	Convert button to the right of the Local field
convertTemp:	Convert button to the right of the Fahrenheit field
deleteRecord:	Delete button (and also the Delete item in the Records) menu
handleTVClick:	The table view (you must double-click the area beneath the Countries column to select it)
nextRecord:	The Next Record item in the Records menu
prevRecord:	The Previous Record item in the Records menu
switchClicked:	The English Widely Spoken switch

View Connections in Outline Mode

The nib file window of Interface Builder gives you two modes in which to view the objects in a nib file and to make connections between those objects. So far you've been working in the icon mode of the Instances display, which pictorially represents objects such as windows and custom objects.

Outline mode, as the phrase suggests, represents objects in a hierarchical list: an outline. The advantages of outline mode are that it represents all objects as well as graphically indicating the connections between them.

You can enter outline mode from the Instances view of the `MainMenu.nib` window. Simply click the outline view icon directly above the view's vertical scrollbar.

As you can see in Figure 10-22, this outline view is showing the connection between the Add button on the main Travel Advisor window and the TAController instance. A connection is identified by a black line linking the two objects, as well as an icon (a crosshair for an action, an electrical outlet for outlet) and text label. In outline view, a right-pointing triangle shows connections from an object, while a left-pointing triangle shows connections to an object. You can connect objects through their outlets and actions in outline mode by Control-clicking a connection line, much as you would in icon mode.

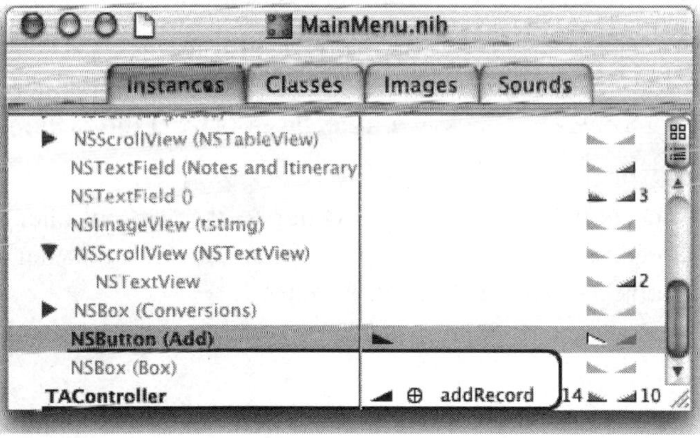

Figure 10-22. Nib file outline view

About File's Owner

Every nib file has one owner, represented by the File's Owner icon in a nib file window. The owner is an object, external to the nib file, that relays messages between the objects unarchived from the nib file and the other objects in your application.

You specify a file's owner programmatically, in the second argument of NSBundle's `loadNibNamed:owner:`. The File's Owner icon in Interface Builder is a "proxy" object for that owner. Although you can assign owners to this object in Interface Builder, this doesn't necessarily guarantee anything about the file's real owner.

In the main nib file, File's Owner always represents NSApp, the global NSApplication constant. The main nib file is created automatically when you create an application project; it is loaded when an application is launched.

Nib files other than the main nib file—auxiliary nib files—contain objects and resources that an application may load only when it needs them (for example, an Info panel). You must specify the owner of auxiliary nib files.

You can determine or change the class of the current nib file's owner in Interface Builder by selecting the File's Owner icon in the nib file window and then displaying the Custom Class Info window. You'll get to practice this technique when you learn how to create multidocument applications in Chapter 11, *Cocoa's Multiple-Document Architecture*.

Connect the Delegate Outlet

You're now going to make TAController the delegate of the NSApp object using the File's Owner proxy. As the delegate of NSApp (the NSApplication object), TAController will receive messages from it as certain events happen.

Among many other messages, NSApp sends a message to its delegate notifying it that the application is about to terminate. Later, you will implement TAController so that, when it receives this message, it archives (saves) the dictionary containing the Country objects.

1. Drag a connection line from File's Owner to the TAController object. Notice that the direction of the connection is from the File's Owner (which is the application object) to the TAController object.

2. In the Connections display of the Info window, select `delegate` and click Connect.

Generate Source Code Files

When you generate the header and implementation files for the classes of Travel Advisor, you are finished with the Interface Builder portion of development.

1. Save `MainMenu.nib`.

2. Select the TAController class in the Classes display of the nib file window.

3. Choose Create Files from the Classes menu.

4. Choose the Travel Advisor project directory.

5. Repeat for the Country class.

You don't need to do this for the Converter classes because you already imported the files from the Currency Converter project.

After you've generated the files, switch to Project Builder and make sure that the newly added files are in the Classes group, as shown in Figure 10-23. This won't affect the way Project Builder treats the files, but it helps keep the project consistently organized.

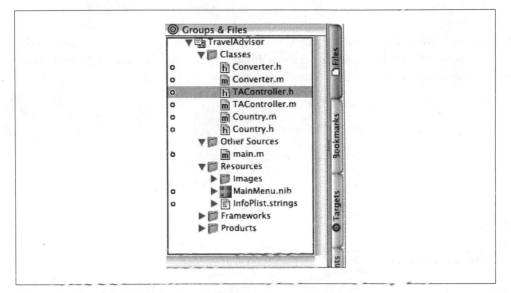

Figure 10-23. Project Builder Groups & Files

Implement the Classes of Travel Advisor

Now that the user interface for Travel Advisor has been created and the connections between objects specified in Interface Builder, you can proceed with the implementation of the application's classes.

Reuse Currency Converter

Using Interface Builder, you have already set up an action so that clicking the Convert button will invoke TAController's convertCurrency: method. Now all you have to do to is write the code to get numeric values from the user, invoke the Converter object using those values, and send the result back to the user interface for display:

1. Open `TAController.m` by clicking it in Project Builder's Groups & Files view.

2. At the top of the file, add the following line. This gives TAController access to the Converter class's methods:

   ```
   #import "Converter.h"
   ```

3. Now modify the empty declaration of the `convertCurrency:` method, as shown. This is not the most compact form you can use to express a solution in Objective-C, but it clearly delineates the steps involved in solving this problem. First, the values that the user entered are retrieved from the user interface. Next, the `converter` object's `convertAmount:atRate:` method is invoked to perform the conversion operation. Finally, the value of `currencyLocalField` is set to reflect the result returned by the Converter object:

   ```
   - (IBAction)convertCurrency:(id)sender
   {
       float rate, dollars, result;

       dollars = [currencyDollarsField floatValue];
       rate = [currencyRateField floatValue];
       result = [converter convertAmount:dollars atRate:rate];

       [currencyLocalField setFloatValue:result];
   }
   ```

Build and Test the Application

Before moving on, go ahead and build Travel Advisor to make sure that currency conversion actually works as expected:

1. Click the Build button in Project Builder, or type Command-B.

2. Click the Run button to launch Travel Advisor.

3. Enter reasonable values in the Rate and Dollars fields. Notice that the value in the Dollars field is automatically formatted with the dollar symbol.

4. Click the Convert button next to the Local field.

Did you get a correct value back? If so, congratulations—you're already a hotshot Cocoa programmer! If nothing happened, open `MainMenu.nib` in Interface Builder and verify that you correctly connected the Convert button action to the TAController instance. If you got an incorrect value back, verify that you correctly connected TAController's outlets to the corresponding text fields. If you find you made a mistake, save the nib file, rebuild the application, and try again.

Implement Temperature Conversion

Implement TAController's `convertTemp:` method: You've already specified and connected the necessary outlets (Celsius, Fahrenheit) and action (`convertTemp:`), so all that remains is the method implementation. The formula you'll need is:

```
F = (9/5)C + 32
```

There's no need to implement a new Converter class for such a simple task. Simply put the code inline in TAController's `convertTemp:` method:

```
- (IBAction)convertTemp:(id)sender
{
    [fahrenheitField setFloatValue:
            (((9.0/5.0) * [celsiusField floatValue]) + 32.0)];
}
```

If you have problems getting temperature conversion to work, remember to check the outlet and action connections in Interface Builder.

Implement the Country Class

The Country class is Travel Advisor's Model object, storing the information on a given country and providing methods to access as well as archive the data.

Declare instance variables

Although it has no outlets, the Country class defines a number of instance variables that correspond to the fields on Travel Advisor's user interface.

1. In Project Builder, select `Country.h`.

2. Add the declarations from Example 10-1. These instance variables hold the attribute information that describes a country. In addition to declaring instance variables, this declares that the Country class adopts the NSCoding protocol.

Example 10-1. Country Instance Variables

```
@interface Country : NSObject <NSCoding>
{
    NSString *name;
    NSString *airports;
    NSString *airlines;
    NSString *transportation;
    NSString *hotels;
    NSString *languages;
    BOOL     englishSpoken;
    NSString *currencyName;
    float    currencyRate;
    NSString *comments;
}
```

Methods for the Country class

Now you must declare the methods that the Country class supports. These methods fall into the following three categories:

- Object initialization and deallocation
- Object archiving and unarchiving
- Accessor methods

Declare the Methods.   Add the method declarations for the class between the brace that closes the instance variable section and the @end statement. After the instance variables, add the declarations from the following code:

```
/* Initialization and De-allocation
*/
- (id)init;
- (void)dealloc;

/* Archiving and Unarchiving */
- (void)encodeWithCoder:(NSCoder *)coder;
- (id)initWithCoder:(NSCoder *)coder;

/* Accessor Methods */
- (NSString *)name;
- (void)setName:(NSString *)str;

- (NSString *)airports;
- (void)setAirports:(NSString *)str;

- (NSString *)airlines;
- (void)setAirlines:(NSString *)str;

- (NSString *)transportation;
- (void)setTransportation:(NSString *)str;

- (NSString *)hotels;
- (void)setHotels:(NSString *)str;

- (NSString *)languages;
- (void)setLanguages:(NSString *)str;

- (BOOL)englishSpoken;
- (void)setEnglishSpoken:(BOOL)flag;

- (NSString *)currencyName;
- (void)setCurrencyName:(NSString *)str;

- (float)currencyRate;
- (void)setCurrencyRate:(float)val;

- (NSString *)comments;
- (void)setComments:(NSString *)str;
```

Implement the Country object's init method

The init method first invokes super's (the superclass's) init method so that inherited instance variables will be initialized. You should always do this first in an init method. The init method also initializes the NSString instance variables to an empty string. @"" is a compiler-supported construction that creates an immutable constant NSString object from the text enclosed by the quotes. Being constants, these objects cannot be deallocated, so they do not obey the regular reference-counting technique. They do accept retain and release messages sent to them, although they are ignored, allowing these strings to be treated like regularly allocated NSStrings.

1. Open Country.m.

2. Fill in the implementation of the init method from Example 10-2.

Example 10-2. Implementation of Country's init Method

```
- (id)init
{
    [super init];

    [self setName:@""];
    [self setAirports:@""];
    [self setAirlines:@""];
    [self setTransportation:@""];
    [self setHotels:@""];
    [self setLanguages:@""];
    [self setCurrencyName:@""];
    [self setComments:@""];

    return self;
}
```

You don't need to initialize nonobject instance variables to null values (nil, zero, NULL, and so on) because the runtime system does it for you. But you should initialize instance variables that take other starting values. Also, don't substitute nil when empty objects are expected, and vice versa. The Objective-C keyword nil represents a null "object" with an ID (value) of zero. An empty object (such as @"") is a true object; it just has no "real" content. By returning self you're returning a true instance of your object; up until this point, the instance is considered undefined.

Implement the dealloc method

In this method you release objects that you've created, copied, or retained (that don't have an impending autorelease). For the Country class, release all objects held as instance variables. If you had other retained objects, you would release them, and if you had dynamically allocated data, you would free it. When this method completes, the Country object is deallocated. The `dealloc` method should send `dealloc` to `super` as the last thing it does, so that the Country object isn't released by its superclass before it's had the chance to release all objects it owns.

Add the implementation of the `dealloc` method from Example 10-3.

Example 10-3. Implementation of Country's dealloc Method

```
- (void)dealloc
{
    [name release];
    [airports release];
    [airlines release];
    [transportation release];
    [hotels release];
    [languages release];
    [currencyName release];
    [comments release];

    [super dealloc];
}
```

Implement the accessor methods

For "get" accessor methods (at least when the instance variables, like Travel Advisor's, hold immutable objects), simply return the instance variable. For accessor methods that set object values, first send `autorelease` to the current instance variable, then copy (or retain) the passed-in value to the variable. You'll recall that the `autorelease` message causes the previously assigned object to be released at the end of the current event loop, keeping current references to the object valid until then.

If the instance variable has a nonobject value (such as an integer or float value), you don't need to autorelease and copy; just assign the new value.

In many situations you can send retain instead of copy to keep an object around. But for value-type objects, such as NSStrings and our Country objects, copy is better.

1. Select `Country.m` in the project browser.

2. Write the code that obtains and sets the values of the class's instance variables using the standard format shown:

```
- (NSString *)name
{
    return name;
}

- (void)setName:(NSString *)str
{
```

```
            [name autorelease];
            name = [str copy];
    }
```

Statically Type TAController's Outlets

Interface Builder provides outlet declarations in the `TAController.h` file that are typed as `id`. Though it takes a little extra time, it's good programming practice to statically type objects unless dynamic typing is necessary.

1. Open `TAController.h` and forward-declare the Converter class. Add the `@class` statement near the top of the file, just before the `@interface` statement.

   ```
   @class Converter;
   ```

   The `@class` directive simply lets the compiler know about the Converter class without having to include all of the declarations in the class's header file. TAController's implementation file needs access to the full class definition, so the class header file, which was added previously in this chapter, is imported there.

2. Modify the instance variable declarations as shown in Example 10-4.

Example 10-4. TAController Instance Variables

```
@interface TAController : NSObject
{
    IBOutlet Converter *converter;
    IBOutlet NSTextField *countryField;
    IBOutlet NSTableView *countryTableView;

    IBOutlet NSTextField *commentsLabel;
    IBOutlet NSTextView *commentsField;

    IBOutlet NSTextField *celsiusField;
    IBOutlet NSTextField *fahrenheitField;

    IBOutlet NSTextField *currencyNameField;
    IBOutlet NSTextField *currencyDollarsField;
    IBOutlet NSTextField *currencyLocalField;
    IBOutlet NSTextField *currencyRateField;

    IBOutlet NSTextField *languagesField;
    IBOutlet NSButton *englishSpokenSwitch;

    IBOutlet NSForm *logisticsForm;
}
```

Add New Instance Variables to TAController.h

1. Add the instance-variable declarations shown next. The variables countryDict and countryKeys identify the dictionary and the array used to keep track of Country objects. The Boolean recordNeedsSaving flag indicates whether the user has modified the information in any field of the user interface.

```
NSMutableDictionary *countryDict;
NSMutableArray *countryKeys;
BOOL recordNeedsSaving;
```

2. Add the enum declaration shown here between the last @class directive and the @interface directive. This declaration is not essential, but the enum constants provide a clear and convenient way to identify the cells in the Logistics form. Methods such as cellAtIndex: identify the editable cells in a form through zero-based indexing. This declaration gives each cell in the Logistics form a meaningful, human-readable, designation:

```
enum LogisticsFormIndices {
    LGAirports=0,
    LGAirlines,
    LGTransportation,
    LGHotels
};
```

Implement the blankFields: Method

The blankFields: method clears whatever appears in Travel Advisor's fields by inserting empty string objects and zeros. Add the implementation from Example 10-5 to TAController.m.

Example 10-5. Implementation of the blankFields: Method

```
- (void)blankFields:(id)sender
{
    [countryField setStringValue:@""];

    [[logisticsForm cellAtIndex:LGAirports] setStringValue:@""];
    [[logisticsForm cellAtIndex:LGAirlines] setStringValue:@""];
    [[logisticsForm cellAtIndex:LGTransportation] setStringValue:@""];
    [[logisticsForm cellAtIndex:LGHotels] setStringValue:@""];

    [languagesField setStringValue:@""];
    [englishSpokenSwitch setState:NSOffState];

    [currencyNameField setStringValue:@""];
    [currencyRateField setFloatValue:0.0];
    [currencyDollarsField setFloatValue:0.0];
    [currencyLocalField setFloatValue:0.0];

    [celsiusField setFloatValue:0.0];
```

Example 10-5. Implementation of the blankFields: Method (continued)

```
    [fahrenheitField setFloatValue:0.0];

    [commentsLabel setStringValue:@"Notes and Itinerary for"];
    [commentsField setString:@""];

    [countryField selectText:self];
}
```

In `blankFields:`, the `countryField` is first set to an empty string. Next, the four cells of the Logistics form are cleared. Notice how the `cellAtIndex:` message is sent to the form object using `enum` constants to address each cell in the form.

The `setState:` message affects the appearance of two-state toggled controls, such as a switch button. With an argument of `YES`, the check mark appears; with an argument of `NO`, the check mark is removed. The `setString:` message sets the textual contents of NSText objects.

Recall that `blankFields:` is an action that is connected to the Clear button on the user interface, so you can test the method now. Build Travel Advisor, enter values for all of the fields, and click the Clear button to see if the `blankFields:` method is working properly. Debug if necessary.

Note that when you build the project, you'll get compiler warnings because you haven't yet supplied implementations for all of the methods declared in `Country.h`. These warnings can be ignored for the purposes of testing; you'll implement the missing methods later in the chapter.

TAController and Data Mediation

TAController acts as the mediator of data exchanged between a source of data and the display of that data. Data mediation involves taking data from fields in the user interface, storing it somewhere, and putting it back into the fields later. TAController has two private methods related to data mediation: `populateFields:` puts Country instance data into the fields of Travel Advisor's user interface, and `extractFields:` updates a Country object with the information in the fields.

Implement the extractFields: method

The controller's `extractFields:` method retrieves values from the application's user interface objects and stores the values in the current Country object's instance variables.

1. Add the following method declaration to TAController.h:

   ```
   - (void)extractFields:(Country *)aRec;
   ```

2. Because you've referenced a Country object, you need to forward-declare the Country class:

   ```
   @class Country;
   ```

3. Open TAController.m and import Country.h:

   ```
   #import "Country.h"
   ```

   Although the interface file now declares the existence of a Country object, the implementation file needs to know about its methods.

4. Enter the code from Example 10-6 for the extractFields: method in TAController.m.

Example 10-6. Implementation of the extractFields: Method

```
- (void)extractFields:(Country *)aRec
{
    [aRec setName:[countryField stringValue]];

    [aRec setAirports:[[logisticsForm
            cellAtIndex:LGAirports] stringValue]];
    [aRec setAirlines:[[logisticsForm
            cellAtIndex:LGAirlines] stringValue]];
    [aRec setTransportation:[[logisticsForm
            cellAtIndex:LGTransportation] stringValue]];
    [aRec setHotels:[[logisticsForm
            cellAtIndex:LGHotels] stringValue]];

    [aRec setCurrencyName:[currencyNameField stringValue]];
    [aRec setCurrencyRate:[currencyRateField floatValue]];
    [aRec setLanguages:[languagesField stringValue]];
    [aRec setEnglishSpoken:[englishSpokenSwitch state]];

    [aRec setComments:[commentsField string]];
}
```

Now that you have an implementation for extractFields:, test it. TAController's addRecord: method is connected to the Add button on the user interface. One of the things addRecord: will need to do is get the data from the UI, so add the call to extractFields: in the implementation of addRecord: and set a breakpoint at the invocation of extractFields::

```
- (IBAction)addRecord:(id)sender
{
    Country *aCountry = [[Country alloc] init];

    [self extractFields:aCountry];
}
```

Build and debug the app, step through the code, and see if the data you enter in the UI makes it into the Country object properly. Experiment with the use of the gdb command po to print information about an object in the gdb Console pane.

Implement the populateFields: method

The controller's populateFields: method is the inverse of extractFields:. It takes values from the current Country object's instance variables and displays them in the user interface.

1. Add the following method declaration to TAController.h:

   ```
   - (void)populateFields:(Country *)aRec;
   ```

2. Open the TAController.m file and enter the code from Example 10-7 for the populateFields: method.

Example 10-7. Implementation of the populateFields: Method

```
- (void)populateFields:(Country *)aRec
{
    [countryField setStringValue:[aRec name]];

    [[logisticsForm cellAtIndex:LGAirports] setStringValue:
            [aRec airports]];
    [[logisticsForm cellAtIndex:LGAirlines] setStringValue:
            [aRec airlines]];
    [[logisticsForm cellAtIndex:LGTransportation] setStringValue:
            [aRec transportation]];
    [[logisticsForm cellAtIndex:LGHotels] setStringValue:
            [aRec hotels]];

    [currencyNameField setStringValue:[aRec currencyName]];
    [currencyRateField setFloatValue:[aRec currencyRate]];
    [languagesField setStringValue:[aRec languages]];
    [englishSpokenSwitch setState:[aRec englishSpoken]];

    [commentsLabel setStringValue:[NSString stringWithFormat:
            @"Notes and Itinerary for %@", [aRec name]]];
    [commentsField setString:[aRec comments]];

    [countryField selectText:self];
}
```

The first thing populateFields: does is display the name of the current country in the Country field. The value is retrieved from the name instance variable of the Country record (aRec) passed into the populateFields: method. The object returned by the expression [aRecname] is used as the argument of the setString-Value: method, which sets the text content of the receiver (in this case, the countryField object). Next, the remainder of the user interface elements are updated. Finally, the `selectText:` message is sent to Country field so that any text is selected, or if there is no text, the cursor is inserted into the field.

Get the Table View to Work

The table view in Travel Advisor has only one column and is used to display the list of countries for which the application contains travel information. You've already explored table views and data sources in Chapter 9, so the steps in this section of the tutorial should be straightforward.

Implement the behavior of the table view's data source

Implement TAController's `awakeFromNib` method. Designate `self` as the data source:

```
- (void)awakeFromNib
{
    [countryTableView setDataSource:self];
    [countryTableView sizeLastColumnToFit];
}
```

The `[countryTableView setDataSource:self]` message identifies the TAController object as the table view's data source. The table view will commence sending NSTableDataSource messages to TAController. (You can effect the same thing by setting the NSTableView's `dataSource` outlet in Interface Builder.)

Implement two methods of the NSTableDataSource informal protocol

To fulfill its role as data source, TAController must implement two methods of the NSTableDataSource informal protocol: `numberOfRowsInTableView:` and `tableView:objectValueForTableColumn:row:`, as shown in Example 10-8.

Example 10-8. Implementation of the NSTableDataSource Protocol

```
- (int)numberOfRowsInTableView:(NSTableView *)theTableView {
    return [countryKeys count];
}

- (id)tableView:(NSTableView *)theTableView
    objectValueForTableColumn:(NSTableColumn *)theColumn
    row:(int)rowIndex
{
    if ([[theColumn identifier] isEqualToString:@"Countries"])
        return [countryKeys objectAtIndex:rowIndex];
    else
        return nil;
}
```

The first method returns the number of country names in the countryKeys array. The table view uses this information to determine how many rows to create.

The second method evaluates the column identifier to determine if it's the correct column (it should always be Countries). If it is, the method returns the country name from the countryKeys array that is associated with rowIndex. This name is then displayed at rowIndex of the column. (Remember, the array and the cells of the column are synchronized in terms of their indexes.)

The NSTableDataSource informal protocol has another method, table-View:setObjectValue:forTableColumn:row:, which you won't implement in this tutorial. This method allows the data source to extract data entered by users into table view cells; since Travel Advisor's table view is read-only, there is no need to implement it.

If you had an application with multiple table views, each table view would invoke these NSTableView delegation methods (as well as the others). By evaluating the theTableView argument, you could distinguish which table view was involved.

Implement the country-selection method

Finally, you have to have the table view respond to mouse clicks in it, which indicate a request that a new record be displayed. As you recall, you defined in Interface Builder the handleTVClick: action for this purpose. This method must do a number of things:

- Save the current Country object or create a new one.

- If there's a new record, resort the array providing data to the table view.

- Display the selected record.

- Implement the handleTVClick: Method from Example 10-9. This method responds to user selections in the table view.

Example 10-9. Implementation of the handleTVClick: Method

```
- (IBAction)handleTVClick:(id)sender
{
    Country *aRec;
    NSString *countryName;
    int index = [sender selectedRow];

    if (index == -1) return;
    countryName = [countryKeys objectAtIndex:index];

    if (recordNeedsSaving) {
        [self addRecord:self];
        index = [countryKeys indexOfObject:countryName];
        [countryTableView selectRow:index byExtendingSelection:NO];
    }
```

Example 10-9. Implementation of the handleTVClick: Method (continued)

```
    aRec = [countryDict objectForKey:countryName];
    [self populateFields:aRec];
}
```

The first thing `handleTVClick:` does is identify which row (and hence country) the user selected. If no row is selected, NSTableView's `selectedRow` method returns -1 and `handleTVClick:` exits. Otherwise, the row index is used to get the country's name.

When any Country-object data is added or altered, Travel Advisor sets the record-NeedsSaving flag to YES (you'll learn how to do this later on). If `recordNeedsSaving` is YES, the code calls the `addRecord:` method, which will update a modified record or insert a new one, as appropriate. Because inserting a new record will alter the contents of the table, the selected row may need to be updated to highlight the correct country. To do this, the current position of the country's name within `countryKeys` is obtained, using the `indexOfObject:` method. The corresponding row is then selected within the table view.

Finally, the country's name is used as the key to get the associated Country instance from the dictionary. It then calls `populateFields:` to update the window with the country's instance-variable values.

Optional exercise

Users often like to have key alternatives to mouse actions such as clicking a table view. One way of acquiring a key alternative is to add a menu command in Interface Builder, specify a key as an attribute of the command, define an action method that the command will invoke, and then implement that method.

The methods `nextRecord:` and `prevRecord:` should be invoked when users choose Next or Previous from the Records menu or type the key equivalents Command-Option-N and Command-Option-P. In `TAController.m`, implement these methods, keeping the following hints in mind:

1. Get the index of the selected row (`selectedRow`).

2. Increment or decrement this index, according to which key is pressed (or which command is clicked).

3. If the start or end of the table view is encountered, "wrap" the selection. (Hint: use the count of the `countryKeys` array.)

4. Using the index, select the new row, but don't extend the selection.

5. Simulate a mouse click on the new row by sending `handleTVClick:` to `self`.

Build the Project

Now is a good time to take a break and build Travel Advisor. See if there are any errors in your code or in the nib file.

Add and Delete Records

When users click Add Record to enter a Country record, the `addRecord:` method is invoked. You want this method to do a few things besides adding a Country object to the application's dictionary:

- Ensure that a country name has been entered.

- Make the table view reflect the new record.

- If the record already exists, update it (but only if it's been modified).

- Implement the `addRecord:` method from Example 10-10.

Example 10-10. Implementation of the addRecord: Method

```
- (IBAction)addRecord:(id)sender
{
    Country *aCountry;
    NSString *countryName = [countryField stringValue];

    //  Is there country data to be saved?
        if (recordNeedsSaving && ![countryName isEqualToString:@""])
{
        aCountry = [countryDict objectForKey:countryName];

        //  Is current object already in dictionary?
        //  ...  aCountry will be nil if new
            if (!aCountry) {
            //  Create Country obj, add to dict, add name to keys array
            aCountry = [[[Country alloc] init] autorelease];
            [countryDict setObject:aCountry forKey:countryName];
            [countryKeys addObject:countryName];

            //  Sort array and update table view
            [countryKeys sortUsingSelector:@selector(compare:)];
            [countryTableView reloadData];
            [countryTableView selectRow:
                    [countryKeys indexOfObject:countryName]
                    byExtendingSelection:NO];
        }

        //  Update the country object
        [self extractFields:aCountry];
        recordNeedsSaving = NO;

        [commentsLabel setStringValue:[NSString stringWithFormat:
                @"Notes and Itinerary for %@", countryName]];
```

Example 10-10. Implementation of the addRecord: Method (continued)

```
        [countryField selectText:self];
    }
}
```

This method adds a Country object to the NSDictionary "database." This section of code verifies that a country name has been entered and that its fields are flagged as modified. It then sees if there is a Country object with the given name in the dictionary. If there's no object for the key, `objectForKey:` returns nil. In this case, the code creates a new Country object and adds it to the dictionary and adds its name to the keys array. The array is then sorted and the table view is updated. The `reloadData` message forces the table view to update its contents. The `selectRow:byExtendingSelection:` message highlights the new record in the table view.

Immediately following the innermost `if` block, the `aCountry` variable is a reference to an object stored in `countryDict`. This Country object is updated with the information in the application's fields (`extractFields:`) and the `recordNeedsSaving` flag is reset. Finally, the label over the text view is updated to reflect the just-added country and the country name field is highlighted.

In Example 10-10, note the expression `if (!aCountry)`. For objects, this is shorthand for `if (aCountry == nil)`; in the same vein, `if (aCountry)` is equivalent to `if (aCountry != nil)`. Also note that the newly created Country object is sent an `autorelease` message when created. Because Country objects are being stored within a dictionary, which retains its values, `addRecord:` does not want ownership of the newly created Country object. By autoreleasing it, the dictionary will be the sole owner of the object at the end of the current event loop.

• Implement the `deleteRecord:` method. Although similar in structure to `addRecord:`, this method is a little simpler because you don't need to worry about whether a Country record has been modified. Once you've deleted the record, remember to update the table view and clear the fields of the application.

Field Validation

The NSControl class gives you an API for validating the contents of cells. Validation verifies that the values of cells fall within certain limits or meet certain criteria. In Travel Advisor, we want to make sure that the user does not enter a negative value in the Rate field.

The request for validation is a message, `control:isValidObject:`, that a control sends to its delegate. The control, in this case, is the Rate field.

1. In `awakeFromNib`, make TAController a delegate of the field to be validated: the Rate field:

   ```
   [currencyRateField setDelegate:self];
   ```

2. Implement the `control:isValidObject:` method to validate the value of the field:

   ```
   - (BOOL)control:(NSControl *)control isValidObject:(id)obj
   {
       if (control == currencyRateField) {
           if ([obj floatValue] <= 0.0) {
               NSRunAlertPanel(@"Travel Advisor",
                   @"Rate cannot be zero or negative.", nil, nil, nil);
               return NO;
           }
       }
       return YES;
   }
   ```

Because you might have more than one field's value to validate, this example first determines which field is sending the message. It then checks the field's value (passed in as the second object); if it is negative, it displays a message box and returns NO, blocking the entry of the value. Otherwise, it returns YES and the field accepts the value.

The previous example calls `NSRunAlertPanel` simply to inform the user why the value cannot be accepted. Although Travel Advisor doesn't evaluate it, the function returns a constant indicating which button the user clicks in the message box. The logic of your code could therefore branch according to user input. In addition, the function allows you to insert variable information (using `printf`-style conversion specifiers) into the body of the message.

Application Management

At this point you've finished the major coding tasks for Travel Advisor. All that remains to be implemented are a half dozen or so methods. Some of these methods perform tasks that every application should do. Others provide bits of functionality that Travel Advisor requires. In this section you'll:

* Archive and unarchive the TAController object.

* Implement TAController's `init` and `dealloc` methods.

* Save data when the application terminates.

* Mark the current record when users make a change.

* Obtain and display converted currency values.

The data that users enter into Travel Advisor should be saved in the file system or archived. The best time to initiate archiving in Travel Advisor is when the application is about to terminate. Earlier you made TAController the delegate of the application object (NSApp). Now respond to the delegate message application-Terminate:, which is sent just before the application terminates.

Implement the delegate method applicationShouldTerminate:, as shown in Example 10-11.

Example 10-11. Implementation of the applicationShouldTerminate: Method

```
- (NSApplicationTerminateReply)applicationShouldTerminate:(id)sender
{
    NSString *storePath = [NSHomeDirectory()
            stringByAppendingPathComponent:@"Documents/TravelData.travela"];

    // save current record if it is new or changed
    [self addRecord:self];
    if (countryDict)
        [NSArchiver archiveRootObject:countryDict toFile:storePath];

    return NSTerminateNow;
}
```

This function constructs a pathname for the archive file, TravelData. This file is stored in the Documents folder of the user's home directory.

If the countryDict dictionary exists, TAController archives it with the NSArchiver class method archiveRootObject:toFile:. Since the dictionary is designated as the root object for archiving, all objects that the dictionary references (that is, the Country objects it contains) will be archived too.

Implement TAController's methods for initializing and deallocating itself

Implement the init and dealloc methods from Example 10-12.

Example 10-12. Implementation of the init and dealloc Methods

```
- (id)init
{
    NSString *storePath = [NSHomeDirectory()
            stringByAppendingPathComponent:@"Documents/TravelData.travela"];
    [super init];

    countryDict = [NSUnarchiver unarchiveObjectWithFile:storePath];

    if (!countryDict) {
        countryDict = [[NSMutableDictionary alloc] init];
        countryKeys = [[NSMutableArray alloc] initWithCapacity:10];
    } else {
```

Example 10-12. Implementation of the init and dealloc Methods (continued)

```
        countryDict = [[NSMutableDictionary alloc]
                initWithDictionary:countryDict];
        countryKeys = [[NSMutableArray alloc]
                initWithArray:[[countryDict allKeys]
                sortedArrayUsingSelector:
                @selector(caseInsensitiveCompare:)]];
    }

    recordNeedsSaving = NO;
    return self;
}

- (void)dealloc
{
    [countryDict release];
    [countryKeys release];
    [super dealloc];
}
```

The init method locates the archive file TravelData in the user's Documents directory and returns the path to it.

The unarchiveObjectWithFile: message unarchives (that is, restores) the object whose attributes are encoded in the specified file. The object that is unarchived and returned is the NSDictionary of Country objects (countryDict).

If no NSDictionary is unarchived, the countryDict instance variable remains nil. If this is the case, TAController creates an empty countryDict dictionary and an empty countryKeys array. Otherwise, it retains the instance variable and builds the country keys array.

The [countryDict allKeys] message returns an array of keys (country names) from countryDict, the unarchived dictionary that contains Country objects as values. The sortedArrayUsingSelector: message sorts the items in this "raw" array using the caseInsensitiveCompare: method defined by the class of the objects in the array, in this case NSString (this is an example of polymorphism and dynamic binding). The sorted names go into a temporary (autoreleased) NSArray—since that is the type of the returned value—and this temporary array is used to create a mutable array, which is then assigned to countryKeys. A mutable array is necessary because users may add or delete countries.

The dealloc method releases the objects created by the init method. It then calls its superclass's implementation of dealloc to continue the process until the object itself is freed.

Implement notification to track modified records

When users modify data in fields of Travel Advisor, you want to mark the current record as modified so later you'll know to save it. The Application Kit broadcasts a notification whenever text in the application is altered. To receive this notification, add TAController to the list of the notification's observers.

1. In the `awakeFromNib` method, make TAController an observer of all objects posting `NSControlTextDidChangeNotification`:

```
[[NSNotificationCenter defaultCenter] addObserver:self
        selector:@selector(textDidChange:)
        name:NSControlTextDidChangeNotification object:nil];
```

2. You also need to observe the notes field; it isn't a control text object:

```
[[NSNotificationCenter defaultCenter] addObserver:self
        selector:@selector(textDidChange:)
        name:NSTextDidChangeNotification object:commentsField];
```

3. Implement `textDidChange:` to set the `recordNeedsSaving` flag. Two of the editable fields of Travel Advisor hold temporary values used in conversions and so are not saved. The `if` statement checks if these fields are the ones originating the notification and, if they are, returns without setting the flag. (The object message obtains the object associated with the notification.)

```
- (void)textDidChange:(NSNotification *)notification
{
    if (([notification object] == currencyDollarsField) ||
        ([notification object] == celsiusField)) return;

    recordNeedsSaving = YES;
}
```

4. Implement the `switchClicked:` action method to learn of changes to the English Widely Spoken switch:

```
- (IBAction)switchClicked:(id)sender
{
    recordNeedsSaving = YES;
}
```

Implement Archiving and Unarchiving

In this section you'll implement the methods for archiving and unarchiving the Country class. Once this step is complete, the application will be able to save the entire dictionary of countries to disk, so you won't lose your travel information when the application terminates.

1. Implement the `encodeWithCoder:` method in `Country.m` as shown:

```
- (void)encodeWithCoder:(NSCoder *)coder
{
    [coder encodeObject:[self name]]];
    [coder encodeObject:[self airports]]];
    [coder encodeObject:[self airlines]]];
    [coder encodeObject:[self transportation]]];
    [coder encodeObject:[self hotels]]];
    [coder encodeObject:[self languages]]];
    [coder encodeValueOfObjCType:"s" at:&englishSpoken];
    [coder encodeObject:[self currencyName]]];
    [coder encodeValueOfObjCType:"f" at:&currencyRate];
    [coder encodeObject:[self comments]]];
}
```

2. Implement the `initWithCoder:` method as shown:

```
- (id)initWithCoder:(NSCoder *)coder
{
    [self setName:[coder decodeObject]];
    [self setAirports:[coder decodeObject]];
    [self setAirlines:[coder decodeObject]];
    [self setTransportation:[coder decodeObject]];
    [self setHotels:[coder decodeObject]];
    [self setLanguages:[coder decodeObject]];
    [coder decodeValueOfObjCType:"s" at:&englishSpoken];
    [self setCurrencyName:[coder decodeObject]];
    [coder decodeValueOfObjCType:"f" at:&currencyRate];
    [self setComments:[coder decodeObject]];

    return self;
}
```

Build and Run the Application

When Travel Advisor is finished building, start it up by double-clicking the icon in the Finder. Then put the application through the following tests:

- Enter a few records. Make up geographical information if you have to—you're not trusting your future travels to this application. Not yet, anyway.

- Click the items in the table view and notice how the selected records are displayed. Press Command-Option-N and Command-Option-P and observe what happens.

- Enter values in the conversion fields to see how they're automatically formatted. Try to enter a negative value in the Rate field.

- Quit the application and then start it up again. Notice how the application displays the same records that you entered.

III

Multiple-Window Applications

11

Cocoa's Multiple-Document Architecture

Document-based applications are one of the more common types of applications developed today. They provide a framework for generating identically contained, but uniquely composed, sets of data that can be stored in files. Word processors and spreadsheet applications are two well-known examples of document-based applications. Before investigating how document-based applications are structured, let's consider exactly what such an application does. It:

- Creates new documents

- Opens existing documents that are stored in files

- Saves documents under user-designated names and locations

- Reverts to saved documents

- Closes documents (usually after prompting the user to save changes)

- Prints documents and allows the page layout to be modified

- Represents data of different types internally

- Monitors and sets the document's edited status and validates menu items

- Manages document windows, including setting the window titles

- Handles application and window delegation methods (such as when the application terminates)

Cocoa's remarkable multiple-document architecture consists of a set of three classes—NSDocument, NSDocumentController, and NSWindowController—which provide the features in the preceding list almost entirely "for free." Using the multiple-document architecture drastically simplifies the work developers must do to implement a multidocument application. Once you understand how the architecture works, you can have a multidocument application up and running, literally in minutes.

This chapter begins with an overview of Cocoa's multiple-document architecture and explains the interactions between NSDocument, NSDocumentController, and NSWindowController. The final part of the chapter guides you through the implementation of a simple multidocument RTF text-editing application.

Architectural Overview

From a user's perspective, a *document* is a unique body of information usually contained in its own window. Users can create an unlimited number of documents and save each to a file.

From a programming perspective, a document comprises the objects and resources unarchived from an auxiliary nib file and the controller object that loads and manages these things. This document controller is the owner of the auxiliary nib file containing the document interface and related resources. To manage a document, the document controller makes itself the delegate of its window and its "content" objects. It tracks edited status, handles window-close events, and responds to other conditions.

When users choose the New (or equivalent) command, a method is invoked in the application's controller object. In this method, the application controller creates a document-controller object that loads the document nib file in the course of initializing itself. A document thus remains independent of the application's "core" objects, storing state data in the document controller. If the application needs information about a document's state, it can query the document controller.

When users choose the Save command, the application displays a Save panel and enables users to save the document in the file system. When users choose the Open command, the application displays an Open panel, allowing users to select a document file and open it.

Three Application Kit classes provide an architecture for document-based applications. These classes are NSDocumentController, NSDocument, and NSWindowController. Objects of these classes divide and orchestrate the work of creating, saving, opening, and managing the documents of an application. They are tiered in a one-to-many relationship, as depicted in Figure 11-1.

Multidocument applications have one NSDocumentController, which creates and manages potentially many NSDocument objects (one for each New or Open operation). In turn, an NSDocument object creates and manages one or more NSWindowController objects, one for each of the windows displayed for a document.

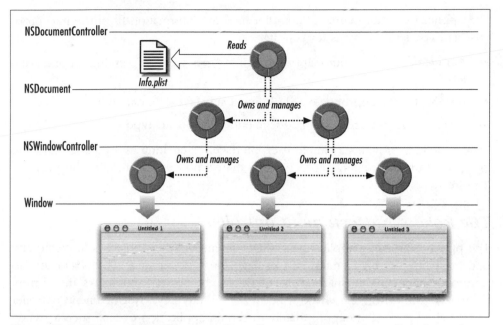

Figure 11-1. NSDocument, NSDocumentController, und NSWindowController relationships

Some objects also have responsibilities analogous to NSApplication and NSWindow delegates. NSDocument, NSDocumentController, and NSWindowController can be, but are not by default, the delegate of the application or windows.

In addition to these three Application Kit classes, the multiple-document architecture uses information in the application's info property list to determine what types of data the application can work with. The information is stored in the property list as an array of document types. Each document type entry in the array includes the following information (packaged as a dictionary):

- The name of the document type

- An array of filename extensions such as rtf and txt that correspond to a document's data type

- An array of Mac OS–style type identifiers such as TEXT and PICT, which also correspond to a document's data type

- A string that determines the role of the application when interacting with the data. An application can be an Editor or a Viewer for a given data type

- The name of the NSDocument subclass in your application that handles the data type

The application's NSDocumentController uses the information from the info property list to do several things for you. It:

- Automatically filters out inappropriate file types when presenting an open dialog box

- Instantiates the appropriate NSDocument subclass for a data type

- Prevents the user from saving documents of a specific type

Project Builder provides a simple user interface for creating and editing entries in an application's document type array, so there's no need to modify the property list directly.

The Role of NSDocumentController

The primary job of an application's NSDocumentController object is to create and open documents and to track and manage these documents. The NSDocument-Controller maintains an internal list of document objects and tracks the current document (the document whose window is currently key). NSDocumentController is hardwired to respond appropriately to certain application events, such as when the application starts up, when it terminates, when the system powers off, and when documents are opened or printed from the Finder. For example, when a user chooses New from the File menu, an NSDocumentController:

1. Allocates an instance of the NSDocument subclass specified in the first entry in the application's document type array

2. Initializes the instance by invoking your NSDocument subclass's `init` method

When the user chooses Open from the File menu, an NSDocumentController:

1. Displays the Open panel, filtering the file list using the data type(s) from the application's info property list (`Info.plist`), and gets the user's selection

2. Uses type information from the file and data to allocate an instance of the appropriate NSDocument subclass

3. Initializes the object by invoking its `initWithContentsOfFile:ofType:`, which causes the contents of the file to be loaded into the document instance

If you wish, you can make a custom document controller and implement the delegate methods invoked as a result of the same events. However, the default NSDocumentController object is an adequate application controller for most situations, and you should not need to subclass it. If you require additional behavior, such as displaying About panels and handling application preferences, it is recommended that a custom controller object rather than a subclass of NSDocumentController perform these duties.

The Role of NSDocument

The primary job of an NSDocument object is to represent, manipulate, store, and load the persistent data associated with a document. Based on the document types it claims to understand (as specified in the DocumentTypes array in the info property list), a document object must be prepared to:

- Provide other objects in the application the data displayed in its window(s). The document object must be able to provide the data in any of the supported formats.

- Load data into internal data structures and display it in windows. The document object must be able to accept the data in any of the supported formats.

- Store document data in a file at a specified location in the file system.

- Read document data stored in a file.

With the assistance of its window controllers, an NSDocument manages the display and capture of the data in its windows. By some special hardwiring of the Application Kit, the NSDocument associated with the key window is made the recipient of first responder action messages when users save, print, revert, and close documents. It also knows how to run and manage the Save panel and the Page Layout panel.

A fully implemented NSDocument knows how to track its edited status, print document data, and perform undo and redo operations. As you'll discover as you work through the tutorials in Chapter 12, *To Do: Basics* and Chapter 13, *To Do: Extended*, these behaviors aren't provided completely by default, but NSDocument does go a long way to assist you in implementing each.

For edited-status tracking, NSDocument provides an API for updating a document change counter. For undo/redo operations, NSDocument creates an NSUndoManager when one is requested, responds appropriately to Undo and Redo menu commands, and updates the change counter when undo and redo operations are performed.

NSDocument facilitates the display of the Page Layout panel and the subsequent modification of the NSPrintInfo object used in printing.

The Role of NSWindowController

NSWindowController manages one window associated with a document, which is usually stored in a nib file. If a document had multiple windows, each window would have its own window controller. For example, a document might have a main data-entry window and a window listing records for selection; each window would have its own NSWindowController. When requested by its owning

NSDocument, an NSWindowController loads the nib file containing a window and displays it. It also assumes responsibility for properly closing windows (after ensuring that they are saved).

Subclasses of NSWindowController are optional. Applications can often use the default instance. Subclasses can augment NSWindowControllers to perform different nib-loading and setup tasks or to customize the titles of windows.

Some applications may want to subclass NSWindowController to move the user-interface-specific logic out of the NSDocument class so it can concentrate on model-specific functionality. The Sketch application in `/Developer/Examples/AppKit` uses this technique.

Implement a Document-Based Application

It is possible to put together a document-based application without having to write very much code. If your requirements are minimal, the Application Kit provides you with a default NSWindowController instance and a default NSDocumentController instance. You just have to create a multidocument project, compose the human interface, implement a subclass of NSDocument, and add any other custom classes or behavior required by your application.

The following procedures step you through the creation of a very simple rich text (RTF) editor. In a few minutes, and with only a few lines of code, you'll have an application that—without Cocoa's help—would have taken days or weeks to construct and debug.

The Document-Based Application Package

Project Builder provides a Document-Based Application project template to expedite the development of these kinds of applications. This project type provides the following things:

- **The application's main nib file.** This nib file contains a standard Cocoa application menu bar. The menu items in the File and Edit menus are already connected to appropriate first responder action methods.

- **A nib file for the application's document.** This nib file contains a single window to which other UI items can be added. A subclass of NSDocument named MyDocument has been made File's Owner of the nib file. It (and therefore the MyDocument subclass) has an outlet to its window.

- **A skeletal NSDocument subclass implementation.** The project includes `MyDocument.h` and `MyDocument.m`, which are derived from the definition of the NSDocument subclass in the document nib file. The latter file includes commented "stub" definitions for the important methods.

- **A document type entry in the info property list.** In the Application Settings pane of the Targets display is a simple user interface for modifying the `Info.plist` file. The file contains placeholder values for global application keys as well as the document type array.

The remainder of this chapter describes what you must do to create a document-based application starting from this template.

Create the Project

1. Launch Project Builder and choose New Project from the File menu.

2. Create a Cocoa Document-Based Application project called Simple RTF Edit.

3. Open the Resources group; double-click `MyDocument.nib` to open this file in Interface Builder.

The nib file is quite simple. There's only a single window with a default text string. If you select the File's Owner instance and bring up the Inspector, you'll notice in the Attributes pane that File's Owner is set to correspond to an instance of MyDocument. Also, in the Connections pane, you'll see an outlet with a connection to the window. If you like, open the `MainMenu.nib` file as well. As mentioned previously, many of the application's menu items were already connected to appropriate first responder action methods. These methods are implemented by the application's NSDocumentController and are listed in Table 11-1.

Table 11-1. Target/Action Configuration for Default Multidocument Application

File Menu Command	First Responder Action
New	newDocument:
Open	openDocument:
Save	saveDocument:
Save As	saveDocumentAs:
Save To	saveDocumentTo:
Save All	saveAllDocuments:
Close	closeDocument:
Revert	revertDocumentToSaved:
Print	printDocument:
Page Layout	runPageLayout:

Now open `MyDocument.m` and examine the skeletal implementation of this NSDocument subclass. There are four methods:

- `- (NSString *)windowNibName`. This method returns the name of the nib file for the class. The application's NSDocumentController uses this method to locate and load the nib file for the document object.

- `- (void)windowControllerDidLoadNib:(NSWindowController *)aController`. This method provides an opportunity for any initialization once the document object's nib file has been loaded.

- `- (NSData *)dataRepresentationOfType:(NSString *)aType`. For the NSDocumentController to save a document's data to disk, you must provide an implementation for this method that returns an NSData object containing the document's data in the specified format (data type).

- `- (BOOL)loadDataRepresentation:(NSData *)data ofType:(NSString *)aType`. Similarly, you must provide an implementation of this method, which loads (and typically displays) document data when it is passed to you by the document controller.

Go ahead and build the project and experiment with it. As you'll see, the entire infrastructure is already there. Now all you have to do is fill in a few blanks to create a text editor.

Compose the Interface

In this section you'll define the look and feel of the application's document. All you have to do is modify the default nib file created by Project Builder's template to add a text view that will allow the user to view and edit RTF text.

1. Open `MyDocument.nib` if it isn't already open.

2. Make the document window smaller and remove the default text object that says Your Document Contents Here.

3. Drag an NSTextView to the window from the DataViews pane of the palette.

4. Move and resize the scroll view so that it occupies the entire window. Turn off the scroll view's border using the Attributes pane of the Info window.

5. With the scroll view selected, bring up the Size pane in the Inspector. Change the resize options so the scroll view will follow changes in the window size.

6. In Project Builder, open MyDocument.h and add a declaration for the text view's outlet:

```
IBOutlet NSTextView *textView;
```

7. Drag MyDocument.h from Project Builder Groups & Files listing onto Interface Builder's MyDocument.nib window. This gives Interface Builder the opportunity to parse the outlet so you can use it for connections.

8. In the Instances pane, drag a connection from the File's Owner instance (remember this is a proxy for a MyDocument instance) to the text view and connect the textView outlet. Warning: do not generate an instance of MyDocument to make this connection. You want to connect the File's Owner, which at runtime will be a true instance of MyDocument.

9. Save the nib file.

Now the user interface for this simple text editor is complete.

Modify the Info Property List

The Simple RTF Edit application handles only one kind of data, RTF. It's very simple to modify the application's info property list to add support for this document type:

1. In Project Builder, select the Targets pane in the main window.

2. Select the default target, Simple RTF Edit.

3. Select Application Settings for the target.

4. Scroll down to the Document Types editor shown in Figure 11-2.

5. Modify the default document type entry, as shown in the illustration. Simply click on the entry to select it, enter the values into the Type Information area, and click Change.

The Application Settings pane of the target window allows you to create and modify a variety of application-wide properties. Critical values like the name of the executable and the name of the main Cocoa class are provided by default. Many of the other properties are important for a full-fledged application, but can remain unset for this simple example. You will learn more about these properties when you construct the final tutorial application in the next chapter. For now, don't worry about them.

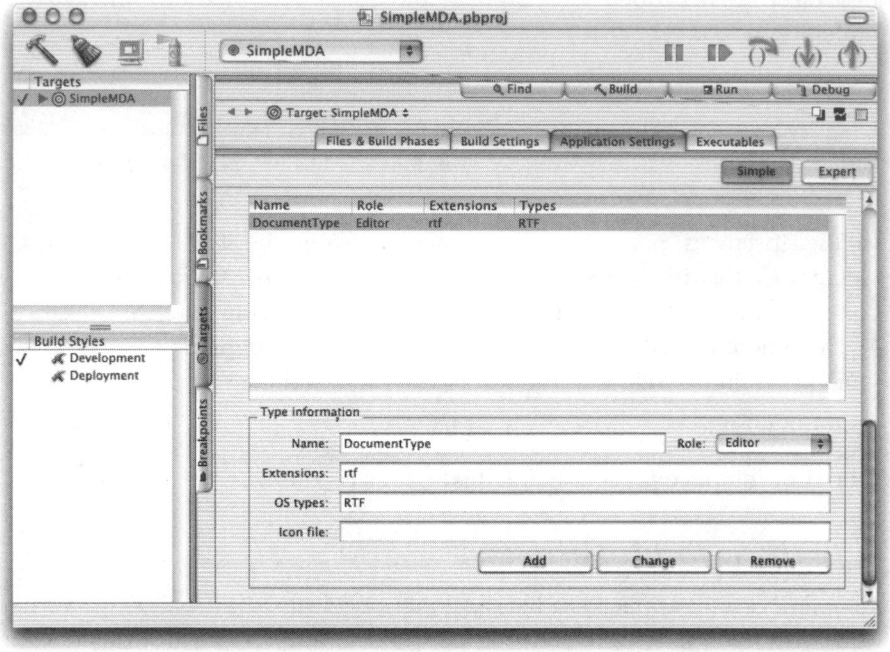

Figure 11-2. Project Builder's Document Types editor

Subclass NSDocument

Every application that takes advantage of the Application Kit's architecture for document-based applications must create at least one subclass of NSDocument. The architecture requires that you override some NSDocument methods and recommends overriding several others in certain situations. The most common cases will be covered in the rest of this section.

Data-based primitives

The `dataRepresentationOfType:` method has to be implemented to create and return document data (packaged as an NSData object) of a supported type, usually in preparation for writing that data to a file. The `loadDataRepresentation:ofType:` method must be implemented to convert an NSData object containing document data of a certain type into the document's internal data structures and display that data in a document window; the NSData object usually results from the document reading a document file. Subclasses must override these methods.

Location-based primitives

By default, the `writeToFile:ofType:` method writes data to a file after obtaining the data from `fileWrapperRepresentationOfType:`, which gets it from `dataRepresentationOfType:`. The `readFromFile:ofType:` method reads data from a file, creates an NSFileWrapper object from it, and gives this object to `loadFileWrapperRepresentation:ofType:`; if this object represents a simple file, it is passed to the `loadDataRepresentation:ofType:` method for processing. You must override `loadFileWrapperRepresentation:ofType:` to handle an object that represents a directory.

Subclasses can override any of these methods instead of the data-based primitives if the way NSDocument reads and writes document data is not sufficient; their override implementations, however, must also assume the loading duties of the data-based primitives.

Window controller creation

NSDocument subclasses must also create their window controllers. They can do this indirectly or directly. If a document has only one nib file (with one window in it), the subclass can simply override `windowNibName` to return the name of the window nib file; as a consequence, a default NSWindowController instance is created for the document, with the document as the nib file's owner. If a document has multiple windows or if an instance of a custom NSWindowController subclass is to be used, the NSDocument subclass must override `makeWindowControllers` to create these objects.

Printing and page layout

Normally, a document-based application can change the information it uses to define how document data is printed (an NSPrintInfo object). Subclasses can override `shouldChangePrintInfo:` to disallow this change. If an application is to print document data, subclasses of NSDocument must override `printShowingPrintPanel:`.

Backup files

When it saves a document, NSDocument creates a backup of the old file before it writes data to the new one (backup files have the same name as the new file, but with a tilde just before the extension). Normally, if the write operation is successful, it deletes the backup file. Subclasses can override `keepBackupFile` to return `YES`, and thus retain the most recent backup file.

Menu items

NSDocument implements validateMenuItem: to manage the enabled state of the Revert and Save As menu items. If you want to validate other menu items, you can override this method, but be sure to invoke super's implementation. For more information on menu item validation, see the description of the NSMenuValidation informal protocol.

Initializers

The initializers of NSDocument are another issue for subclassers. The init method is the designated initializer, and it is invoked by the other initializer initWithContentsOfFile:ofType:. The init method is directly invoked when a new document is created; the initWithContentsOfFile:ofType: method is directly invoked when a document is opened. Therefore, if you have any initializations that apply only to documents that are opened, you should override initWithContentsOfFile:ofType:; if you have general initializations, you should, of course, override init. In both cases, be sure to invoke super's implementation as the first thing.

Implement the NSDocument Subclass

Now you will override a handful of NSDocument's methods to support reading and writing RTF data:

1. Open MyDocument.h and add the following instance variable. This variable will hold a reference to the raw RTF data loaded from a file:

   ```
   NSData *dataFromFile;
   ```

2. Open the subclass implementation file MyDocument.m.

3. Override the dealloc method to clean up dataFromFile:

   ```
   - (void)dealloc {
       [dataFromFile release];
       [super dealloc];
   }
   ```

4. Implement the dataRepresentationOfType: method so that the object will be able to save its contents. This method simply selects all of the text in the text view and returns it as RTF data:

   ```
   - (NSData *)dataRepresentationOfType:(NSString *)aType {
       return [textView RTFFromRange:
               NSMakeRange(0, [[textView string] length])];
   }
   ```

5. Add a method that will load data from a file into the interface's text view object. In order to support both opening a file from disk and reverting to a previously saved state, this method selects all of the text in the text view (if any) and replaces it with the incoming data:

```
- (void)loadtextViewWithData:(NSData *)data {
    [textView replaceCharactersInRange:
            NSMakeRange(0, [[textView string] length])
            withRTF:data];
}
```

6. Implement the `loadDataRepresentation` method. This method needs to handle loading data for two different cases. In the first case, the object is being reverted to a previously saved state. In this situation, a text view object already exists, so it can be directly loaded with the incoming data. However, when a file is being opened, `loadDataRepresentation` will be called before the nib file for the document has been loaded. To handle this case, the RTF data is retained and a reference to it is kept in an instance variable. When the document controller loads the nib file for the document, it will invoke the document object's `windowControllerDidLoadNib` method, at which time the data will be loaded into the text view and released:

```
- (BOOL)loadDataRepresentation:(NSData *)data ofType:(NSString *)aType {
    if (textView) {
        [self loadtextViewWithData:data];
    } else {
        dataFromFile = [data retain];
    }

    return YES;
}
```

7. Finally, implement the `windowControllerDidLoadNib` method. This method checks to see if there is any data waiting to be loaded from a file. If so, it loads the data into the text view object and releases the reference. This method also turns on support for undo in the text view object. Because NSTextView implements undo, you don't have to write any code to support multiple undo/redo. As a byproduct of enabling undo, the document will keep track of modifications automatically, so it knows whether the user needs to be prompted to save the document when the window is closed:

```
- (void)windowControllerDidLoadNib:(NSWindowController *)aController {
    [super windowControllerDidLoadNib:aController];

    if (dataFromFile) {
        [self loadtextViewWithData:dataFromFile];
        [dataFromFile release];
        dataFromFile = nil;
    }
```

```
        [textView setAllowsUndo:YES];
    }
```

OK, you're done. Build the application and try it out. Create a new document, type in some text, and save it. Try the undo/redo function. Try opening an RTF document created by another application. Try printing a document. Amazingly, you've accomplished all of this in fewer than 20 lines of code.

12

To Do: Basics

In Chapter 11, *Cocoa's Multiple-Document Architecture*, you learned how to create a very simple multidocument application. In this chapter you'll use Cocoa's multi-document architecture to create a document-based application called To Do—a fairly simple personal information manager.

This chapter guides you through the steps needed to create the basic framework of the To Do application. You'll define the data model and create the document interface, which includes a custom calendar view. When you finish the final version of To Do in Chapter 13, *To Do: Extended*, the application will allow users to go to specific dates on the calendar and enter a list appointments or tasks for a particular day. In its final form, it will look like Figure 12-1.

Each To Do document captures the daily "must-do" items for a particular purpose. For instance, one could have a To Do list for work and another one for home.

The Design of To Do

The To Do application far surpasses the Travel Advisor application from Chapter 10, *Travel Advisor Tutorial*, in terms of complexity. The To Do application has three nib files and seven custom classes. Figure 12-2 shows the interrelationships among instances of some of those classes and the nib files that they load.

The objects in this diagram should be familiar, fitting as they do into the Model-View-Controller paradigm. The ToDoItem class provides the model objects for the application; instances of this class encapsulate the data associated with the items appearing in documents. The view objects are contained in the three nib files; `MainMenu.nib`, `ToDoDocument.nib`, and `ToDoInfoWindow.nib`. And then there's the controller object—actually, there is more than one controller object. In addition to the default controllers provided by Cocoa's multiple-document architecture, there is the ToDoDocument object that coordinates the document UI and data model, and there is an Info window controller that displays the Info window and communicates with To Do document objects.

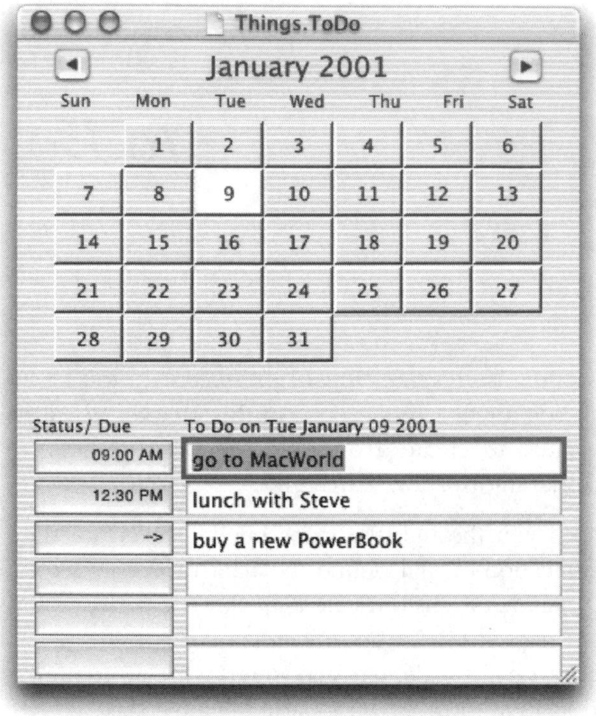

Figure 12-1. To Do application

To Do's Multidocument Design

Two types of controller objects are at the heart of multidocument application design. They claim different areas of responsibility within an application. To Do uses the default application controller to manage events that affect the application as a whole. Each ToDoDocument object is a document controller and manages a single document, including all the ToDoItems that belong to the document.

The File menu, which Interface Builder includes by default on the menu bar, contains the commands that multidocument applications typically need. When users choose New from the File menu, the application controller allocates and initializes an instance of the ToDoDocument class. When the ToDoDocument instance is initialized, the window controller loads the ToDoDocument.nib file. When the user has finished entering items into the document and chooses Save from the File menu, a

Save sheet appears and the user saves the document in the file system under an assigned name. Later the user can open the document using the Open menu command, which causes the Open dialog box to be displayed.

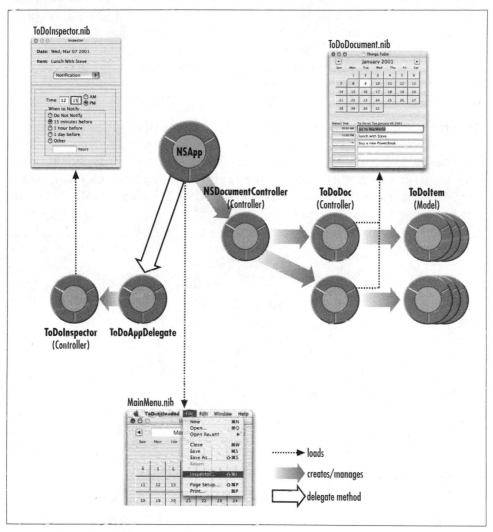

Figure 12-2. To Do design overview

The controller objects of To Do respond to a variety of delegation messages—primarily from windows and the application object—to maintain object state. One example of such an event is when the user closes a document window; another is when data is entered into a document. Often when these events happen, one controller sends a message or notification to the other controller to keep it informed.

How To Do Stores and Accesses Its Data

The data elements of a To Do document are ToDoItems. When a user enters an item in a document's list of activities, the ToDoDocument creates a ToDoItem and places that object into a mutable array (NSMutableArray); the ToDoItem occupies the same position in the array as the item in the list matrix's text field. This positional correspondence of objects in the array and items in the matrix is an essential part of the design. For instance, when users delete the first entry in the document's list, the document removes the corresponding ToDoItem (at index 0) from the array.

The array of ToDoItems is associated with a particular day. Thus, the data for a document consists of a (mutable) dictionary with arrays of ToDoItems for values and dates for keys. When users select a day in the calendar, the application computes the date, which it then uses as the key to locate an array of ToDoItems in the dictionary. Figure 12-3 illustrates the relationship between ToDoItems, the arrays of items, and the dictionary.

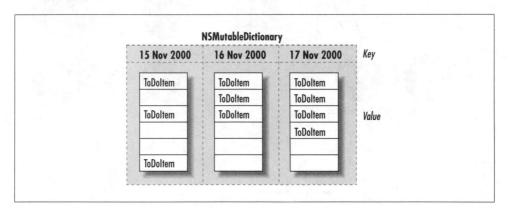

Figure 12-3. Data storage of ToDoItems

To Do's Custom Views

The discussion so far has touched on model objects and controller objects, but has said little about the second member of the Model-View-Controller triad: view objects. Unlike Travel Advisor, which uses only "off-the-shelf" views, To Do's final interface features objects from three custom Application Kit subclasses:

- **CalendarMatrix (subclass of NSMatrix).** A dynamic calendar that notifies its delegate about selected dates.

- **ToDoCell (subclass of NSButtonCell).** A tristate control with different images for each state. It also displays the times when items are due.

- **SelectionNotifyMatrix (subclass of NSMatrix).** A list of text fields that notifies observing objects when a selection occurs.

These three views are identified in Figure 12-4. You'll create only the CalendarMatrix class in this chapter. You'll build the others in Chapter 13.

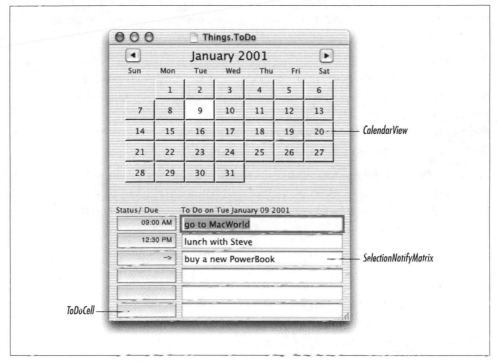

Figure 12-4. To Do's custom view objects

About Dates and Times in Cocoa

Because it's a scheduling application, To Do makes extensive use of dates and times. In Cocoa you represent dates and times as objects that inherit from NSDate. The major advantage of dates and times as objects is common to all objects that represent basic values: they yield functionality that, although commonly found in most operating systems, is not tied to the internals of any particular operating system.

NSDates hold dates and times as values of type NSTimeInterval and express these values as seconds. The NSTimeInterval type makes possible a wide and fine-grained range of date and time values, giving accuracy within milliseconds for dates 10,000 years apart.

NSDate and its subclasses compute time as seconds relative to an absolute refer-ence date (the first instant of January 1, 2001). NSDate converts all date and time representations to and from NSTimeInterval values that are relative to this refer-ence date.

NSDate provides methods for obtaining NSDate objects (including date, which returns the current date and time as an NSDate), comparing dates, computing rela-tive time values, and representing dates as strings.

The NSCalendarDate class, which inherits from NSDate, generates objects that rep-resent dates conforming to western calendrical systems. NSCalendarDate objects also adjust the representations of dates to reflect their associated time zones. Because of this, you can track an NSCalendarDate object across different time zones. You can also present date information from time-zone viewpoints other than the one for the current locale.

Each NSCalendarDate object also has a calendar format string bound to it. This for-mat string contains date-conversion specifiers that are very similar to those used in the standard C library function strftime. NSCalendarDate can interpret user-entered dates that conform to this format string.

NSCalendarDate has methods for creating NSCalendarDate objects from formatted strings and from component time values (such as minutes, hours, day of week, and the year). It also supplements NSDate with methods for accessing component time values and for representing dates in various formats, locales, and time zones.

Build the Application

In this section you'll create the basic infrastructure of the To Do application. First, you'll create an NSDocument subclass. Next, you'll implement the data model class for the application and set up the basic user interface for To Do documents. Finally you'll implement the set of methods the ToDoDocument class uses to accept, organize, display, and store entered data. When you're finished with this chapter, the application will allow you to click a day on the calendar and enter a list of to-do items. In Chapter 13 and Chapter 14, *To Do: Finishing Touches*, you'll expand on the work you do here to make To Do a full-fledged Mac OS X application.

Create the Project

Create a new Project Builder project named To Do using the Cocoa Document-based Application template as a project starting point.

Every Cocoa application project created with Project Builder has the same main function (in the file main.m). When users double-click an application or document icon in the Finder, main (the entry point) is called first; main, in turn, calls NSApplicationMain—and that's all it does.

The NSApplicationMain function does what's necessary to get a Cocoa application up and running—it responds to events, coordinates the activity of its objects, and so on. This function starts the network of objects in the application sending messages to one another. Specifically, NSApplicationMain:

- Gets the application's attributes, which are stored in the application wrapper as a property list. From this property list, it gets the names of the main nib file and the principal class (for applications, this is NSApplication or a custom subclass of NSApplication).

- Gets the Class object for NSApplication and invokes its sharedApplication class method, creating an instance of NSApplication, which is stored in the global variable, NSApp. Creating the NSApplication object connects the application to the window system and the Core Graphics server.

- Loads the main nib file, specifying NSApp as the owner. Loading unarchives and recreates application objects and restores the connections between objects.

- Runs the application by starting the main event loop. Each time through the loop, the application object gets the next available event and dispatches it to the most appropriate object in the application. The loop continues until the application object receives a stop: or terminate: message, after which the application is released and the program exits.

You can add your own code to main to customize application startup or termination behavior.

Rename the NSDocument Subclass

Before adding anything new to the project, go ahead and complete these steps to properly rename the NSDocument subclass for this application:

1. From Project Builder, select MyDocument.nib, choose Rename from the Project menu, and change the nib filename to **ToDoDocument.nib**.

2. Rename MyDocument.h to **ToDoDocument.h**, and MyDocument.m to **ToDoDocument.m**.

3. Use batch find/replace to change the name of the document subclass MyDocument to ToDoDocument:

   a. Open the Find tab and make sure that Textual is chosen in the pop-up menu.

   b. Type **MyDocument** in the Find field and click Find.

   c. Verify that all of the hits are in the files ToDoDocument.h and ToDoDocument.m. If there are other files, select the two that you want from the list.

   d. Type **ToDoDocument** in the Replace field and click Replace.

4. Double-click ToDoDocument.nib to open it in Interface Builder.

5. In the Classes pane of the nib file window, double-click MyDocument and rename it **ToDoDocument**.

6. In the Instances pane of the nib file window, select File's Owner and use the Info window to verify that its Class is ToDoDocument.

7. In Project Builder, select the Targets pane, click on To Do (if it's not already selected), and then select the Application Settings pane.

8. Click the Expert button to display a property list editor.

9. Open the CFBundleDocumentTypes array and then the 0 dictionary.

10. Find the property called NSDocumentClass, double-click on the value (MyDocument), and change it to ToDoDocument.

Now that the initial project infrastructure is in place, you can start working on the user interface.

Create the Model Class (ToDoItem)

The ToDoItem class provides the model objects for the To Do application. Its instance variables hold the data that define the elements of an item on a To Do list: tasks that should be done or appointments that have to be kept. Its methods allow access to this data. In addition, it provides functions that perform helpful calculations with that data. ToDoItem thus encapsulates both data and behavior that goes beyond accessing data.

Since ToDoItem is a model class, it has no user interface duties, so the expedient course is to create the class without using Interface Builder. We first add the class to the project; Project Builder helps by generating template source code files.

1. Choose New File from the File menu.

2. Select Objective-C Class template in the Assistant.

3. Name the new file **ToDoItem.m** (ToDoItem.h will be created automatically).

4. Click Finish to create the files and add them to the project.

Remember, build the project frequently to catch errors quickly, to get a sense of how the application is developing, and (just as important) to give yourself a break from coding.

Declare the instance variables

As you've done before with Travel Advisor, start by declaring instance variables and methods in the header file. Add the instance variables and protocols from Example 12-1 to ToDoItem.h. Table 12-1 further defines the variables.

Example 12-1. ToDoItem Instance Variable Declarations

```
@interface ToDoItem : NSObject <NSCoding>
{
    NSCalendarDate *day;
    NSString *itemName;
    NSString *notes;
    NSTimer *timer;
    long secsUntilDue;
    long secsUntilNotify;
    ToDoItemStatus status;
}
```

Table 12-1. Instance Variables for ToDoItem

Variable	What It Holds
day	The day of the to-do item (a date resolved to 12:00 A.M.).
itemName	The name of the to-do item (the contents of a document text field).
notes	The contents of the Info window's Notes display; this could be any information related to the to-do item, such as an agenda to discuss at a meeting.
timer	A timer for notification messages.
secsUntilDue	The time the item comes due (represented as seconds since midnight on the due date).
secsUntilNotify	The time at which a reminder notification is to be sent (represented as seconds before the due time).
status	Either INCOMPLETE, COMPLETE, or DEFER_TO_NEXT_DAY.

Declare methods

Add the method declarations from Example 12-2 to `ToDoItem.h`. They should all be familiar to you after having worked through the tutorials in previous chapters.

Example 12-2. ToDoItem Method Declarations

```
- (id)initWithName:(NSString *)aName andDate:(NSCalendarDate *)aDate;
- (void)dealloc;

- (id)initWithCoder:(NSCoder *)coder;
- (void)encodeWithCoder:(NSCoder *)coder;

- (void)setDay:(NSCalendarDate *)newDay;
- (NSCalendarDate *)day;
- (void)setItemName:(NSString *)newName;
- (NSString *)itemName;
- (void)setNotes:(NSString *)newNotes;
- (NSString *)notes;
- (void)setTimer:(NSTimer *)newTimer;
- (NSTimer *)timer;
- (void)setStatus:(ToDoItemStatus)newStatus;
- (ToDoItemStatus)status;
- (void)setSecsUntilDue:(long)secs;
- (long)secsUntilDue;
- (void)setSecsUntilNotify:(long)secs;
- (long)secsUntilNotify;
```

Define constants

These constants are values for the `status` instance variable:

```
typedef enum ToDoItemStatus
{
    INCOMPLETE=0,
    COMPLETE,
    DEFER_TO_NEXT_DAY
} ToDoItemStatus;
```

These constants are for convenience and clarity in the methods that deal with temporal values:

```
enum {
    SECS_IN_MINUTE = 60,
    SECS_IN_HOUR = (SECS_IN_MINUTE * 60),
    SECS_IN_DAY = (SECS_IN_HOUR * 24),
    SECS_IN_WEEK = (SECS_IN_DAY * 7)
};
```

Declare time-conversion functions

These functions provide computational services to clients of this class, converting time in seconds to hours and minutes (as required by the user interface) and back again to seconds (as stored by ToDoItem):

```
long ConvertTimeToSeconds(int hour, int minute, BOOL pm);
BOOL ConvertSecondsToTime(long secs, int *hour, int *minute);
```

Implement accessor methods

You should have no trouble implementing accessor methods for this class. One exception is the setTimer: method. It is slightly different from the other set accessor methods in that you must remember to send invalidate to timer to disable the timer before it is autoreleased. Timers (instances of NSTimer) are always associated with a run loop (an instance of NSRunLoop). You'll learn more about run loops later.

Implement a description method

The description method assists you and other developers in debugging the To Do application. When you enter the po (print object) command in GDB with a ToDoItem as the argument, this description method is invoked and essential debugging information is printed:

```
- (NSString *)description
{
    NSString *desc = [NSString stringWithFormat:
        @"%@\n\tName:%@\n \
        \tDate: %@\n \
        \tNotes: %@\n \
        \tCompleted: %d\n \
        \tSecs Until Due: %d\n \
        \tSecs Until Notify: %d\n",
        [super description],
        [self itemName],
        [self day],
        [self notes],
        (([self status] == COMPLETE) ? @"Yes":@"No"),
        [self secsUntilDue],
        [self secsUntilNotify]];

    return desc;
}
```

Implement init and dealloc

Understanding the implementations for ToDoItem's initWithName:andDate: and dealloc methods shouldn't present any problems. The iniWithName: method simply allows you to create, initialize, and set the name and date properties for a new

ToDoItem all in one step. The `dealloc` method, as always, sends `release` to any objects referenced by ToDoItem's instance variables.

Add the code from Example 12-3 to `ToDoItem.m`.

Example 12-3. Implementation of ToDoItem's init and dealloc Methods

```
- (id)initWithName:(NSString *)aName
     andDate:(NSCalendarDate *)aDate
{
    if ( self = [super init] ) {
        if ( !aName ) {
            [self release];
            return nil;
        }
        [self setItemName:aName];

        if ( aDate )
            [self setDay:aDate];
        else {
            NSCalendarDate *now = [NSCalendarDate date];
            [self setDay:[NSCalendarDate dateWithYear:[now yearOfCommonEra]
                    month:[now monthOfYear]
                    day:[now dayOfMonth]
                    hour:0 minute:0 second:0
                    timeZone:[NSTimeZone localTimeZone]]];
        }

        [self setStatus:INCOMPLETE];
        [self setNotes:@""];
    }

    return self;
}

- (void)dealloc
{
    [itemName release];
    [day release];
    [notes release];
    [timer invalidate];
    [timer release];

    [super dealloc];
}
```

Implement archiving and unarchiving

When you implement encodeWithCoder: and initWithCoder:, keep the following points in mind:

- Encode and decode instance variables in the same order.

- Copy or retain the object instance variables after you decode them.

- You don't need to archive the timer instance variable since timers are recreated and reset when a document is opened.

Recall that encoding and decoding object types is slightly different than doing so for standard types. Use the following as examples:

```
[coder encodeValueOfObjCType:@encode(long) at:&secsUntilDue];
[coder decodeValueOfObjCType:@encode(long) at:&secsUntilDue];
```

Implement time conversion

The final step in creating the ToDoItem class is implementing the functions that furnish "value-added" behavior. These functions go at the end of ToDoItem.m, immediately after the class implementation (i.e., after the @end statement). Implement ToDoItem's time-conversion functions:

```
long ConvertTimeToSeconds(int hour, int minute, BOOL pm )
{
    if (hour == 12)
        hour = 0;
    if (pm)
        hour += 12;

    return ((hour * SECS_IN_HOUR) + (minute * SECS_IN_MINUTE));
}

BOOL ConvertSecondsToTime(long secs, int *hour, int *minute)
{
    BOOL pm = NO;

    *hour = secs / SECS_IN_HOUR;
    if (*hour > 11) {
        *hour -= 12;
        pm = YES;
    }
    if (*hour == 0)
        *hour = 12;

    *minute = ((secs % SECS_IN_HOUR) / SECS_IN_MINUTE);

    return pm;
}
```

The ConvertSecondsToTime function uses indirection as a means for returning multiple values and directly returns a Boolean to indicate A.M. or P.M.

Now is a good time to compile and make sure you fix any typing errors.

Implement the Calendar view

The calendar on To Do's interface shown in Figure 12-5 is an instance of a custom subclass of NSMatrix. The CalendarMatrix dynamically updates itself as users select new months, notifies a delegate when users select a day, and indicates both today's date and the currently selected day by setting button-cell attributes.

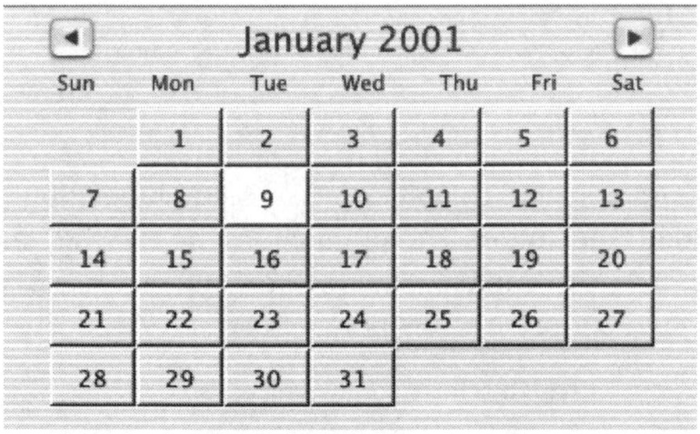

Figure 12-5. Calendar View

Creating a subclass of a class that is farther down the inheritance tree poses more of a challenge for a developer than does a simple subclass of NSObject. A class such as NSMatrix is more specialized than NSObject and carries with it more baggage: It inherits from NSResponder, NSView, and NSControl, all fairly complex Application Kit classes. And since CalendarMatrix inherits from NSView, it appears on the user interface; it is an example of a view object in the Model-View-Controller paradigm, and as such it is highly reusable.

Matrix as superclass

When you select a specialized superclass as the basis for your subclass, it is important to consider what your requirements are and to understand what the superclass has to offer. To Do's dynamic calendar should:

* Arrange numbers (days) sequentially in rows and columns
* Respond to and communicate selections of days

- Understand dates

- Enable navigation between months

If you have started to peruse the reference documentation on Application Kit classes and looked at the section on NSMatrix, you'll have read this:

> "NSMatrix is a class used for creating groups of NSCells that work together in various ways. It includes methods for arranging NSCells in rows and columns. An NSMatrix adds to NSControl's target/action paradigm by allowing a separate target and action for each of its NSCells in addition to the matrix's own target and action."

So NSMatrix has an inherent capability for the first of the requirements listed earlier and for part of the second (responding to selections). Our CalendarMatrix subclass thus does not need to alter anything in its superclass. It just needs to supplement NSMatrix with additional data and behavior so it can understand dates (and update itself appropriately), navigate between months, and notify a delegate that a selection was made.

Compose the interface

In this section you'll create the CalendarMatrix subclass and lay out the calendar view objects in Interface Builder.

1. Open `ToDoDocument.nib` in Interface Builder.

2. In the Classes pane, subclass NSMatrix to create a CalendarMatrix class.

3. Add the outlets and actions as shown in Figure 12-6. Notice that outlets and actions defined by the superclass appear grayed out.

When you created subclasses of NSObject in the Currency Converter and Travel Advisor, the next step was to instantiate the subclass. Because CalendarMatrix is a view (that is, it inherits from NSView), the procedure for generating an instance is different. You must put a custom NSView object on the user interface that will become a CalendarMatrix object at runtime. Do not create instances in Interface Builder for CalendarMatrix or ToDoDocument.

1. Open the nib file's main window if it is not already open.

2. Delete the text field Your Document Contents.

3. Turn off resizing for the document window.

4. Resize the window, using the example as a guide. If you want, you can use the Info window to make the document window exactly 374 × 482, which matches the completed example application available for download from the Apple and O'Reilly web sites.

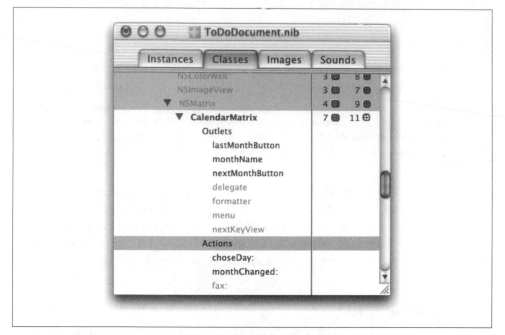

Figure 12-6. ToDoDocument outlets and actions

5. Drag a CustomView from the More Views palette onto the window.

6. Resize and position the CustomView. Notice that Interface Builder helps you with the layout by providing snap-to guides based on Aqua layout guidelines. The example in Figure 12-7 shows the recommended layout, but you're free to choose any size and placement you wish.

7. With the CustomView selected in the window, open the Attributes display of the Info window and set the CustomView's class to CalendarMatrix. The CustomView object is a "proxy" object that represents any custom NSView on the interface. You assign a class to the CustomView by selecting a class listed in the Info window. The custom class to be associated with the custom view proxy object must be defined in the nib file.

8. Finally, Control-drag from the CustomView object to the File's Owner instance and set the CalendarMatrix's delegate outlet. This establishes the ToDoDocument as a delegate of the Calendar Matrix.

9. Save the nib file.

Now put the controls and fields associated with CalendarMatrix on the window.

1. Drag a Rounded Bevel Button button onto the interface and use the Info window to select the icon position with no text label, as shown in Figure 12-8.

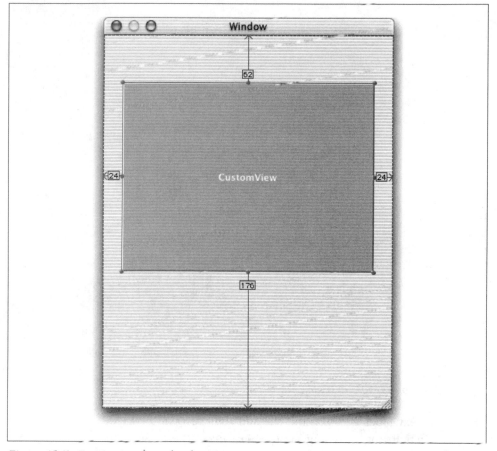

Figure 12-7. Positioning the calendar view

2. Open a Finder window and navigate to the folder where you downloaded the completed example for this chapter. If you don't want to use the provided art files, you can create your own art for the left and right arrow buttons instead.

3. Locate the source, click on `LeftArrow.tiff`, and drop it into the Images pane of the `ToDoDocument.nib` window. Insert the file into the Project Builder project when asked.

4. Click on `LeftArrow.tiff` and drop it over the button.

5. Resize the button to fit the arrow.

6. Repeat the same procedure using `RightArrow.tiff` to create a right-facing arrow.

7. Type the days of the week as individual labels, arrange them as a row, and then center the labels over the custom view. (This latter task will likely take some trial and error.) The window should look like Figure 12-9.

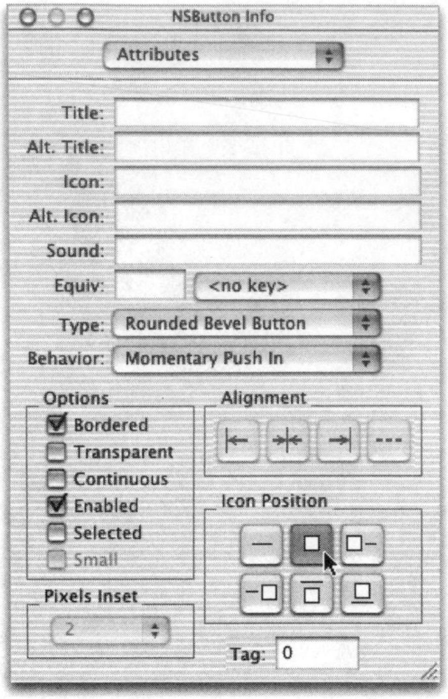

Figure 12-8. Rounded Bevel Button attributes

8. Add a text label between the left and right arrows to display the month and
   year. Initialize it by typing **September 9999** (the longest possible string). Set
   the text to Luucida Grande 18 points, center it, and then delete the text. Make
   sure the label is not editable or selectable.

9. Use the information in the Table 12-2 to connect CalendarMatrix to its satellite
   objects:

Table 12-2. CalendarMatrix Connections

Name	Connection	Type
monthName	From CalendarMatrix to the label field above it	Outlet
prevMonthButton	From CalendarMatrix to the left-pointing arrow	Outlet
nextMonthButton	From CalendarMatrix to the right-pointing arrow	Outlet
monthChanged	From both arrows to CalendarMatrix action	Action

Figure 12-9. Calendar view layout

10. Save ToDoDocument.nib.

11. Select CalendarMatrix in the Classes display and create files for it.

You might have noticed that there's an action message—choseDay:—left unconnected. Because it is impossible in Interface Builder to connect an object with
itself, you need to make this connection programmatically.

Add declarations to the header file

In Project Builder, modify CalendarMatrix.h as shown in Example 12-4. Existing
declarations created by Interface Builder are indicated by ellipses.

Example 12-4. CalendarMatrix Interface Additions

```
@interface CalendarMatrix : NSMatrix
{
    @private
    IBOutlet NSButton *lastMonthButton;
    IBOutlet NSTextField *monthName;
    IBOutlet NSButton *nextMonthButton;
```

Example 12-4. CalendarMatrix Interface Additions (continued)

```
    NSCalendarDate *selectedDay;
    short startOffset;
}
    /* ... */
- (id)initWithFrame:(NSRect)frameRect;
- (void)setSelectedDay:(NSCalendarDate *)newDay;
- (NSCalendarDate *)selectedDay;
@end

@interface NSObject(CalendarMatrixDelegate)
 - (void)calendarMatrix:(CalendarMatrix *)sender
        didChangeToDate:(NSDate *)date;
@end
```

There are a few interesting things to note about these declarations:

- The `@private` keyword tells the compiler that the instance variables to follow should not be directly accessible by other objects. This ensures that other objects in the network will use accessor methods to interact with CalendarMatrix.

- The cells in a CalendarMatrix are sequentially assigned a tag number, left to right, top to bottom. The instance variable `startOffset` contains the tag number of the cell on which the first day of the month falls.

- `CalendarMatrixDelegate` is a category on NSObject that declares the methods to be implemented by the delegate. This technique creates what is called an informal protocol, which is commonly used for delegation methods.

Declare CalendarMatrix's private methods

Private methods are methods "internal" to CalendarMatrix that will never be directly invoked by another object. Because you don't want other objects invoking these methods, you don't want to publish their existence to the outside world by putting them in the class's header file. Private methods can be declared either in a separate (private) header file or in the implementation file for the class. Since there are only a small number of private methods for this class, you will use the latter method.

1. Open `CalendarMatrix.m`.

2. Add the following code between the `#import` and `@implementation` statements:

   ```
   @interface CalendarMatrix (PrivateMethods)
   - (void)refreshCalendar;
   - (void)highlightTodayIfVisible;
   @end
   ```

This code declares a `PrivateMethods` category on CalendarMatrix. This declaration technique lets the compiler know about the methods, but keeps the outside world from seeing them.

Implement initWithFrame: and dealloc

In Chapter 8, *Event Handling*, you saw that you can override NSView's `initWithFrame:` method to perform custom initialization for your own NSView subclass. CalendarMatrix is a subclass of NSMatrix, which is in turn a subclass of NSControl, which inherits from NSView, so the same procedure applies here.

Add the implementation for `initWithFrame:` given in Example 12-5 to `CalendarMatrix.m`

Example 12-5. Implementation of CalendarMatrix's initWithFrame: Method

```
- (id)initWithFrame:(NSRect)frameRect
{
    int i, j;
    int count = 0;
    id cell = [[NSButtonCell alloc] initTextCell:@""];
    NSCalendarDate *now = [NSCalendarDate date];

    [cell setShowsStateBy:NSOnOffButton];

    [super initWithFrame:frameRect
            mode:NSRadioModeMatrix
            prototype:cell
            numberOfRows:6
            numberOfColumns:7];

    // set cell tags
    for (i=0; i<6; i++) {
        for (j=0; j<7; j++) {
            [[self cellAtRow:i column:j] setTag:count++];
        }
    }

    [cell release];

    selectedDay = [[NSCalendarDate dateWithYear:[now yearOfCommonEra]
            month:[now monthOfYear]
            day:[now dayOfMonth]
            hour:0 minute:0 second:0
            timeZone:[NSTimeZone localTimeZone]] retain];

    return self;
}
```

Some notes on the implementation:

- The class method date declared by NSDate returns the current date (today) as an NSCalendarDate. (NSCalendarDate is a subclass of NSDate.)

- The message to super (NSMatrix) sets the dimensions of the matrix, identifies the type of cell using a prototype (an NSButtonCell), and specifies the general behavior of the matrix (radio mode), which means that only one button can be selected at any time.

- The for loop sets the tag number of each cell sequentially left to right and down. Tags are the mechanism by which CalendarMatrix sets and retrieves the day numbers of cells.

- The selectedDay instance variable is initialized using an NSCalendarDate class method. This method returns an NSCalendarDay set to midnight of the current day, using the year, month, and day elements of the current date. The localTimeZone message obtains an NSTimeZone object with a suitable offset from Greenwich Mean Time.

Now that you've seen the initialization code, you should have no problem implementing dealloc for CalendarMatrix.

Implement awakeFromNib

The awakeFromNib method performs additional initializations (some of which could just have easily been done in initWithFrame:). Most importantly, it sets self as its own target object and specifies an action method for this target, choseDay:, something that couldn't be done in Interface Builder.

Add the code for awakeFromNib as given in Example 12-6.

Example 12-6. Implementation of CalendarMatrix's awakeFromNib Method

```
- (void)awakeFromNib
{
    [self setTarget:self];
    [self setAction:@selector(choseDay:)];
    [self setAutosizesCells:YES];
    [self refreshCalendar];
    [self choseDay:self];
}
```

Notes on the implementation:

- setAutosizesCells: causes the matrix to resize its cells on every redraw.

- refreshCalendar (which you'll write next) updates the calendar.

- `choseDay:` (also coming soon) is the action method invoked by a click on the CalendarMatrix. Invoking it here is a neat way to initialize the matrix's display; we're simply pretending that the user has clicked on the cell for today's date.

You are done with the initialization code for CalendarMatrix. Before you go on, implement accessor methods for the `selectedDay` instance variable.

Implement refreshCalendar

The `refreshCalendar` method is fairly long and complex—it is the workhorse of the class—so you'll approach it in sections.

To update the calendar, first initialize the static `gNumDaysInMonth[]` array and write the `isLeap` macro:

```
// "1" based array
containing the number of days in each month
static short gNumDaysInMonth[] =
    {0, 31, 28, 31, 30, 31, 30, 31, 31, 30, 31, 30, 31};

#define isLeap(year) (((year % 4) == 0 &&
((year % 100) != 0)) || (year % 400) == 0)
```

Begin the function definition and declare the local variables:

```
- (void)refreshCalendar
{
    NSCalendarDate *firstOfMonth, *selDate;
    int i, currentMonth, firstWeekd,
    unsigned int currentYear;
    short daysInMonth;
    id cell;
```

Before it can start writing day numbers to the calendar for a given month, CalendarMatrix must know what cell to start with and how many cells to fill with numbers. Begin the `refreshCalendar` method by calculating these values:

```
selDate = [self selectedDay];
currentMonth = [selDate monthOfYear];
currentYear = [selDate yearOfCommonEra];
```

Create an NSCalendarDate for the first day of the currently selected month and year (computed from the `selectedDay` instance variable):

```
firstOfMonth = [NSCalendarDate dateWithYear:currentYear
        month:currentMonth
        day:1 hour:0 minute:0 second:0
        timeZone:[NSTimeZone localTimeZone]];
```

Write the month and year (for example, February 2001) to the label above the calendar:

```
[monthName setStringValue:[firstOfMonth
       descriptionWithCalendarFormat:@"%B %Y"]];
```

Get from the gNumDaysInMonth static array the number of days for that month; if the month is February and it is a leap year, this number is adjusted:

```
/* correct Feb for leap year */
daysInMonth = gNumDaysInMonth[currentMonth];
if ((currentMonth == 2) && (isLeap(currentYear)))
    daysInMonth++;
```

Get the day of the week for the first day of the month and store this in the startOffset instance variable:

```
startOffset = [firstOfMonth dayOfWeek];
```

Write day numbers to the cells and set cell attributes:

```
dayLabel = 1; //start numbering days from the 1st

for (i=0; i < 42; i++) {
    cell = [self cellWithTag:i];
    if (i < startOffset || i >= (daysInMonth + startOffset)) {
        // Blank out unused cells in the matrix
        [cell setBordered:NO];
        [cell setEnabled:NO];
        [cell setTitle:@""];
        [cell setCellAttribute:NSCellHighlighted to:NO];
    } else {
        // Fill in valid days in the matrix
        [cell setBordered:YES];
        [cell setEnabled:YES];
        [cell setFont:[NSFont systemFontOfSize:12]];
        [cell setTitle:[NSString stringWithFormat:@"%d", dayLabel++]];
        [cell setCellAttribute:NSCellHighlighted to:NO];
    }
}
```

The for loop clears the leading and trailing cells that aren't part of the month's days and writes the day numbers of the month, starting at startOffset and continuing for daysInMonth. In the process it resets the font (since the selected day is in boldface) and other cell attributes. Because the current day is indicated by highlighting, it also turns off the highlighted attribute.

After the matrix of cells has been redrawn and correctly labeled with the day of the month, it is necessary to update the view to highlight the currently selected day (stored in the selectedDay instance variable). This may at first seem redundant because clicking on a cell highlights it, but in fact the step is necessary here to properly handle the "new month" case (when the user clicks the nextMonth and lastMonth buttons), as well as the "first run" case (when the application initially draws the calendar matrix).

When the month changes, the user has not had a chance to click on a cell, so the matrix does not know what day is current. The code in the monthChanged: action method handles this by setting selectedDay to the first day of the month, but this alone will not cause the cell corresponding to that day to be selected in the view. The selectCellWithTag: method selects the correct cell in the matrix view. By putting the selectCellWithTag: invocation here (instead of directly inside monthChanged:), we also handle the "first run" case:

```
[self selectCellWithTag:([selDate dayOfMonth] + startOffset - 1)];
```

The final step for the refreshCalendar method is to reset the Today cell attribute. The highlightTodayIfVisible method determines if the currently displayed month includes today's date, and if so highlights the cell corresponding to today:

```
    [self highlightTodayIfVisible];
}
```

Implement highlightTodayIfVisible

Add the implementation of highlightTodayIfVisible from Example 12-7 for this private "helper" method.

Example 12-7. Implementation of CalendarMatrix's highlightTodayIfVisible Method

```
- (void)highlightTodayIfVisible
{
    NSButtonCell *aCell;
    NSCalendarDate *now = [NSCalendarDate date];
    NSCalendarDate *selDate = [self selectedDay];

    if ((([selDate yearOfCommonEra] == [now yearOfCommonEra]) &&
        ([selDate monthOfYear] == [now monthOfYear]) &&
        ([selDate dayOfMonth] != [now dayOfMonth])))
    {
        aCell = [self cellWithTag:([now dayOfMonth] + startOffset - 1)];
        [aCell setHighlightsBy:NSMomentaryChangeButton];
        [aCell setCellAttribute:NSCellHighlighted to:YES];
    }
}
```

Implement the *choseDay:* action method

Example 12-8 specifies the behavior that occurs when users select a day on the calendar.

Example 12-8. Implementation of CalendarMatrix's choseDay: Method

```
- (IBAction)choseDay:(id)sender
{
    NSCalendarDate *selDate, *prevSelDate;
    unsigned int selDay;

    prevSelDate = [self selectedDay];

    selDay = [[[self selectedCell] tag] - startOffset + 1;
    selDate = [NSCalendarDate dateWithYear:[prevSelDate yearOfCommonEra]
            month:[prevSelDate monthOfYear]
            day:selDay
            hour:0
            minute:0
            second:0
            timeZone:[NSTimeZone localTimeZone]];

    [self setSelectedDay:selDate];
    [self highlightTodayIfVisible];

 if ([[self delegate] respondsToSelector:
        @selector(calendarMatrix:didChangeToDate:)])
    {
    [[self delegate] calendarMatrix:self didChangeToDate:selDate];
    }
}
```

This method is invoked when users click a day on the calendar. First, it gets the tag number of the selected cell and subtracts the offset from it (plus one to adjust for zero-based indexing) to find the number of the selected day. Next, it derives an NSCalendarDate that represents the selected date. Finally, it sets the selected-Day instance variable to the new date, highlights today's date if it's visible, and sends the calendarMatrix:didChangeToDate: message to the delegate.

Implement the *monthChanged:* action method

Example 12-9 specifies the behavior that occurs when users select a new month. The arrow buttons above CalendarMatrix send it the monthChanged: message when they are clicked. This method causes the calendar to move forward or backward a month.

Example 12-9. Implementation of CalendarMatrix's monthChanged: Method

```
- (IBAction)monthChanged:sender
{
    NSCalendarDate *thisDate = [self selectedDay];
    int currentYear = [thisDate yearOfCommonEra];
    unsigned int currentMonth = [thisDate monthOfYear];

    if (sender == nextMonthButton) {
        if (currentMonth == 12) {
            currentMonth = 1;
            currentYear++;
        } else {
            currentMonth++;
        }
    } else {
        if (currentMonth == 1) {
            currentMonth = 12;
            currentYear--;
        } else {
            currentMonth--;
        }
    }
    [self setSelectedDay:[NSCalendarDate dateWithYear:currentYear
            month:currentMonth
            day:1 hour:0 minute:0 second:0
            timeZone:[NSTimeZone localTimeZone]]];

    [self refreshCalendar];
    [self choseDay:self];
}
```

The monthChanged: method first determines which button is sending the message, then it increments or decrements the month accordingly. If it goes past the end or beginning of the year, it increments or decrements the year and adjusts the month. Next, it resets the selectedDay instance variable with the new month (and perhaps year) and invokes refreshCalendar to display the new month. Finally, it invokes the choseDay: method to properly update the view.

Build and test

Congratulations! You are finished with CalendarMatrix. You can compile the application now and test the behavior you've implemented so far. When you click the arrow buttons, CalendarMatrix will display the next or previous month. The days of the month will be properly highlighted in the window and the current day will be highlighted. You can also create new To Do documents and close them.

Complete the Document Interface

Before configuring the remaining user interface items for a To Do document, add the declarations from Example 12-10 to `ToDoDocument.h`. The outlets you're adding to the header file correspond to the interface objects you'll add to the document window in Interface Builder. The other instance variables and method declarations pave the way for the more advanced implementation of ToDoDocument, which you will complete during the rest of the tutorial.

Example 12-10. ToDoDocument Instance Variable and Method Declarations

```
#import "ToDoItem.h"
#import "CalendarMatrix.h"

@interface ToDoDocument : NSDocument {
    @private
    IBOutlet CalendarMatrix *calendar;
    IBOutlet NSTextField *dayLabel;
    IBOutlet NSMatrix *itemList;
    IBOutlet NSMatrix *statusList;
    NSMutableDictionary *activeDays;
    NSMutableArray *currentItems;
    ToDoItem *selectedItem;
    BOOL selectedItemEdited;
}

- (IBAction)itemStatusClicked:(id)sender;

- (ToDoItem *)selectedItem;

- (void)calendarMatrix:(CalendarMatrix *)matrix
    didChangeToDate:(NSDate *)date;
@end
```

Open `ToDoDocument.nib` and drag `ToDoDocument.h` from Project Builder into Interface Builder's `ToDoDocument.nib` window. This allows IB to read the new outlet and action declarations. Now the only work remaining to complete the application's document interface is adding the matrices of text fields and their labels, as shown in Figure 12-10. Remember, you create a matrix by Option-dragging a handle of a suitable object.

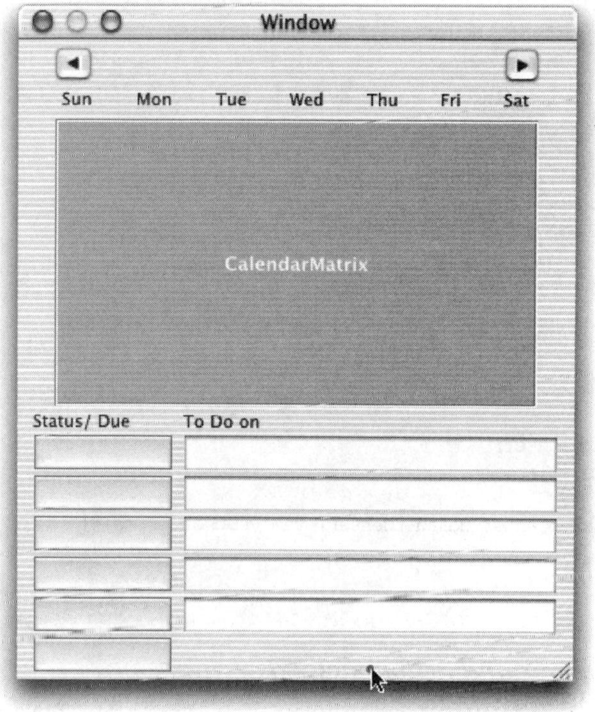

Figure 12-10. Creating a text field matrix

Connect the outlets and actions of ToDoDocument as described in Table 12-3.

Table 12-3. Outlets and Actions for a ToDoDocument

Name	Connection	Type
calendar	From File's Owner to the CalendarMatrix object	Outlet
dayLabel	From File's Owner to label To Do On	Outlet
itemList	From File's Owner to matrix of long text fields	Outlet
statusList	From File's Owner to matrix of short text fields	Outlet
itemStatusClicked	From matrix of short text fields to File's Owner	Action

Implement init and dealloc

The following `init` and `dealloc` implementations are standard and require no detailed discussion. Add the code from Example 12-11 to `ToDoDocument.m`.

Example 12-11. Implementation of ToDoDocument's init and dealloc Methods

```
- (id)init
{
    /* Make sure [super init] is successful before trying to set ivars */
    if (self = [super init]) {
        activeDays = nil;
        currentItems = nil;
        selectedItem = nil;
        selectedItemEdited = NO;
    }

    return self;
}

- (void)dealloc
{
    [activeDays release];
    [currentItems release];

    [[NSNotificationCenter defaultCenter] removeObserver:self];

    [super dealloc];
}
```

Implement accessor and action methods

Add an implementation for the `selectedItem` accessor method. All it needs to do is return the contents of the `selectedItem` instance variable. Later in the tutorial you'll write the code that sets `selectedItem` when the user clicks a ToDo item on the user interface.

Add an empty (stub) implementation for the `itemStatusClicked:` action method. A stub is an empty method declaration that keeps the compiler from complaining that the class doesn't implement all the methods that it declares in its header file. Later in the tutorial you'll fill in the stub with an implementation that does something useful.

Implement ToDoDocument's delegate methods

As you'll remember, CalendarMatrix declared two methods to allow delegates to hook into its behavior. Its delegate for this application is ToDoDocument. Implement a first version of the `calendarMatrix:didChangeToDate:` method:

```
- (void)calendarMatrix:(CalendarMatrix *)matrix
    didChangeToDate:(NSDate *)date
{
    [dayLabel setStringValue:[date descriptionWithCalendarFormat:
        @"To Do on %a %B %d %Y" timeZone:[NSTimeZone localTimeZone]
        locale:nil]];
}
```

The calendar sends `calendarMatrix:didChangeToDate:` when users click a new day of the month. In the the section "Update the CalendarMatrix delegate method," you'll implement a more complex version of this method, but for now the method simply changes the `dayLabel` on the interface to match the day clicked by the user.

Build and test

Now is a good time to check your work. At this point you should be able to click on a day in the Calendar Matrix and see the `dayLabel` change.

Manage To Do's Data and Coordinate Its Display

If you recall the discussion on To Do's design earlier in this chapter, you'll remember that the application's real data consists of instances of the model class, ToDoItem. To Do stores these objects in arrays and stores the arrays in a dictionary; it uses dates as the keys for accessing specific arrays. (Both the dictionary and its arrays are mutable, of course.) You might also recall that this design depends on a positional correspondence between the text fields of the document interface and the "slots" of the arrays.

This section takes you through the implementation of the process the ToDoDocument class uses to accept, organize, display, and store entered data. It also shows how the display and manipulation of data are driven by the selections made in the CalendarMatrix object.

Declare ToDoDocument's private methods

The more advanced implementation of ToDoDocument that you'll create in this portion of the tutorial uses several private "helper" methods to do its work. Since other objects in the application don't need to know about these methods, declare them privately in the class's implementation file. The methods themselves will be discussed in detail when it's time to add their implementations later in this section.

Add the code from Example 12-12 after the `#import` statements at the top of `ToDoDocument.m`.

Example 12-12. Declaration of ToDoDocument's Private Methods

```
@interface ToDoDocument (PrivateMethods)
- (void)setCurrentItems:(NSMutableArray *)newItems;
- (void)updateLists;
- (void)saveDocItems;
- (void)selectItemAtRow:(int)row;
- (void)initDataModelWithDictionary:(NSMutableDictionary *)dict;
@end
```

Modify *windowControllerDidLoadNib:*

As you've seen before, this method is called for the document object when its nib file has been loaded, so it functions much as awakeFromNib does for other objects. Change the default implementation so it looks like Example 12-13.

Example 12-13. Implementation of ToDoDocument's windowControllerDidLoadNib Method

```
- (void)windowControllerDidLoadNib:(NSWindowController *)aController
{
    [super windowControllerDidLoadNib:aController];

    // No undo manager implemented for To Do Documents
    [self setHasUndoManager:NO];

    // Make the document the delegate of the UI's To Do item list
    [itemList setDelegate:self];

    // Init data model
    [self initDataModelWithDictionary:nil];
}
```

The contents here are self-explanatory. After the message to super, the method configures the document object so it knows there is no active undo manager. Next it declares itself to be the delegate of the item list. Then it initializes the internal data model passing nil to force the object to create default initial data structures. Finally, the method makes the document window key and orders it frontmost.

Implement *initDataModelWithDictionary:*

The initDataModelWithDictionary: method is invoked by windowControllerDid-LoadNib: when ToDoDocument.nib has been loaded. It provides a way to manage the activeDays dictionary that is the central data structure for all To Do document objects. This method acts in many ways as a set accessor method and is like other such methods, except in how it handles a nil argument: In this case, nil signifies that the dictionary does not exist, and so it must be created. Add the code in Example 12-14 to ToDoDocument.m.

Example 12-14. ToDoDocument's initDataModelWithDictionary: Method

```
- (void)initDataModelWithDictionary:(NSMutableDictionary *)dict
{
    NSDate *date;

    [activeDays autorelease];

    if (dict)
        activeDays = [dict retain];
    else
        activeDays = [[NSMutableDictionary alloc] init];
```

Example 12-14. ToDoDocument's initDataModelWithDictionary: Method (continued)

```
        date = [calendar selectedDay];
        [self setCurrentItems:[activeDays objectForKey:date]];
}
```

The reasons for initializing a To Do document's data model inside this method will become clear when we deal with loading document data from disk in Chapter 13.

Implement the currentItems accessor methods

This method also acts as a set accessor method. Not only does setCurrentItems: create the array if nil is passed, but it "initializes" it with empty string objects. It does this because NSMutableArray's methods cannot tolerate nil within the bounds of the array. Add Example 12-15 to ToDoDocument.m.

Example 12-15. Implementation of ToDoDocument's setCurrentItems: Method

```
- (void)setCurrentItems:(NSMutableArray *)newItems
{
    int numRows, numCols;

    [currentItems autorelease];

    if (newItems)
        currentItems = [newItems mutableCopy];
    else {
        [itemList getNumberOfRows:&numRows columns:&numCols];
        currentItems = [[NSMutableArray alloc]
        initWithCapacity:numRows];
        while (numRows--)
            [currentItems addObject:@""];
    }
}
```

Implement updateLists:

The updateLists: method in Example 12-16 updates the document interface using the current items array. It is called by other ToDoDocument methods (as well as by other objects in the application) to update the user interface when modifications have been made to an item in the array.

Example 12-16. Implementation of ToDoDocument's updateLists Method

```
- (void)updateLists
{
    int i, numRows;
    ToDoItem *thisItem;
    NSDate *due;

    numRows = [[itemList cells] count];
```

Example 12-16. Implementation of ToDoDocument's updateLists Method (continued)

```
// For each row that has a valid To Do item
//   update its name, due time, and status.
for (i = 0; i < numRows; i++) {
    thisItem = [currentItems objectAtIndex:i];
    if ([thisItem isKindOfClass:[ToDoItem class]])
    {
        if ( [thisItem secsUntilDue] ) {
            due = [[thisItem day]
                    addTimeInterval: [thisItem secsUntilDue]];
        } else
            due = nil;

        [[itemList cellAtRow:i column:0]
                setStringValue:[thisItem itemName]];
        // [[statusList cellAtRow:i column:0] setTimeDue:due];
        // [[statusList cellAtRow:i column:0]
        //          setTriState:[thisItem status]];
    } else  {
        [[itemList cellAtRow:i column:0] setStringValue:@""];
        [[statusList cellAtRow:i column:0] setTitle:@""];
        [[statusList cellAtRow:i column:0] setImage:nil];
    }
  }
}
```

The updateLists method writes the names of the items (ToDoItems) in the currentItems array to the text fields of itemList. It also updates the visual appearance of the cells in the matrix (statusList) next to itemList. These cells are instances of a custom subclass of NSButtonCell that you will create in Chapter 13. For now, just type all the code in Example 12-16; later, when you create the custom cell class (ToDoCell) you can refer back to this example.

Basically, this method cycles through the array of items, doing the following:

* If an object in the array is a ToDoItem, it writes the item name to the text field pegged to the array slot and updates the button cell next to the field.

* If an object isn't a ToDoItem, it blanks the corresponding text field and cell.

Notice that in this version of the method two lines are commented out. This is to allow for building and testing the data model before the application is completely finished. The two methods referenced—setTimeDue: and setTriState:—haven't been implemented yet. When you implement them in Chapter 13, you'll uncomment these lines.

Implement saveDocItems:

This method inspects the currentItems array and, if it contains at least one ToDoItem, puts the array in the activeDays dictionary with a key corresponding to the date. This method is invoked whenever the currently selected day changes so that any items created for that day are saved. Add Example 12-17 to ToDoDocument.m.

Example 12-17. Implementation of ToDoDocument's saveDocItems Method

```
- (void)saveDocItems
{
    ToDoItem *anItem;
    int i, cnt = [currentItems count];

    // save day's current items (array) to document dictionary
    for (i=0; i<cnt; i++) {
        if ( (anItem = [currentItems objectAtIndex:i]) &&
            ([anItem isKindOfClass:[ToDoItem class]]))
        {
            [activeDays setObject:currentItems forKey:[anItem day]];
            break;
        }
    }
}
```

Implement selectItemAtRow:

This is a convenience method used to programmatically select a given To Do item by row number. The method is invoked in response to a notification that you'll learn about in Chapter 13:

```
- (void)selectItemAtRow:(int)row
{
    [itemList selectCellAtRow:row column:0];
}
```

Implement controlTextDidBeginEditing:

A control sends controlTextDidBeginEditing: to its delegate when the user types into a text field. We use this notification to keep track of the current item's state. When the insertion point leaves the text field, the control sends controlTextDidEndEditing:, at which point we must respond to whatever the user has typed:

```
- (void)controlTextDidBeginEditing:(NSNotification *)notif
{
    selectedItemEdited = YES;
}
```

Implement controlTextDidEndEditing:

This method is where most of the work of maintaining the document's data model occurs. To understand what it does, imagine yourself using the application. What are the user events that cause a ToDoItem to be added to the currentItems array? To Do allows entry of items "on the fly" and thus does not require the user to click a button to add a ToDoItem to the array. Specifically, items are added when users type something and then do one of the following:

- Press the Tab key.

- Press the Enter key.

- Click outside the text field.

The `controlTextDidEndEditing:` notifcation makes these scenarios possible. The matrix of editable text fields (`itemList`) invokes this method when the cursor leaves a text field. As items are entered in the interface, this method adds ToDoItems to internal storage and deletes or modifies them, as appropriate. Add Example 12-18 to `ToDoDocument.m`.

Example 12-18. Implementation of ToDoDocument's controlTextDidEndEditing: Method

```
- (void)controlTextDidEndEditing:(NSNotification *)notif
{
    id newItem;
    int row = [itemList selectedRow];
    NSString *newName = [[itemList selectedCell] stringValue];
    NSString *prevNameAtIndex;

    if (selectedItemEdited == NO)
        return;

    if ([[currentItems objectAtIndex:row] isKindOfClass:[ToDoItem class]]) {
        prevNameAtIndex = [[currentItems objectAtIndex:row] name];

        if ([newName isEqualToString:@""]) {
            [currentItems replaceObjectAtIndex:row withObject:@""];
        } else if (![prevNameAtIndex isEqualToString:newName])
        {
            [[currentItems objectAtIndex:row] setItemName:newName];
        }
    } else if (![newName isEqualToString:@""])
    {
        newItem = [[ToDoItem alloc] initWithName:newName
                andDate:[calendar selectedDay]];
        [currentItems replaceObjectAtIndex:row withObject:newItem];
        [newItem release];
    }

    selectedItem = [currentItems objectAtIndex:row];

    if (![selectedItem isKindOfClass:[ToDoItem class]])
        selectedItem = nil;

    [self updateLists];
```

Example 12-18. Implementation of ToDoDocument's controlTextDidEndEditing:
Method (continued)

```
    selectedItemEdited = NO;

    [self updateChangeCount:NSChangeDone];
}
```

A control sends `controlTextDidEndEditing:` to its delegate when the insertion point leaves a text field. In addition to creating new ToDoItems, this implementation of `controlTextDidEndEditing:` removes ToDoItems from arrays and modifies item text. What it does is appropriate to what the user does. If the item hasn't been edited, the code returns because there's no reason to proceed.

If the user deletes the text of an existing item, the code removes the ToDoItem that positionally corresponds to the row of that deleted text. It changes the name of an item if the text entered in a field doesn't match the name of the corresponding item in the `currentItems` array. If either of the two previous conditions don't apply and text has been entered, it creates a new ToDoItem and inserts it in the `currentItems` array. Finally, it updates the list of items in the document interface, resets the editing state, and marks the document as modified using NSDocument's `updateChangeCount:` method.

Update the CalendarMatrix delegate method

Update CalendarMatrix's delegate method from Example 12-19 with complete implementations so the application can respond to user actions in the calendar.

Example 12-19. Implementing ToDoDocument's calendarMatrix:didChangeToDate: Method

```
- (void)calendarMatrix:(CalendarMatrix *)matrix
    didChangeToDate:(NSDate *)date
{
    [self saveDocItems];
    [self setCurrentItems:[activeDays objectForKey:date]];

    [dayLabel setStringValue:[date descriptionWithCalendarFormat:
            @"To Do on %a %B %d %Y" timeZone:[NSTimeZone defaultTimeZone]
            locale:nil]];

    [self updateLists];
    [self selectItemAtRow:0];
}
```

The calendar sends `calendarMatrix:didChangeToDate:` when users click a new day of the month. This implementation saves the current items to the `activeDays` dictionary. It then sets the current items to be those corresponding to the selected date (if there are no items for that date, the `objectForKey:` message returns `nil` and the `currentItems` array is initialized with empty strings). Finally it updates the matrix with the new data and selects the first To Do item in the list.

Build and test

Compile the application and test the data model. Put breakpoints on key methods in the `ToDoDocument.m` and check to make sure that the delegation and notification methods are invoked properly. You should be able to add and remove items from the list of To Do items.

Now that the basic application framework is in place, you're ready to add the advanced features that will make To Do fully functional. In the next chapter you'll create an Info window for To Do that will let you inspect and configure a ToDoItem's properties, including the due date and alarm, completion status, and descriptive notes.

13

To Do: Extended

In Chapter 11, *Cocoa's Multiple-Document Architecture*, you learned the basics of Cocoa's multiple-document architecture, and in Chapter 12, *To Do: Basics*, you used the architecture to build the core functionality of the To Do application. In this chapter you will add features and functionality to the To Do application. These features include:

- A custom button for each item that displays the item's due time, which users can also click to change the item's status

- An Info window that you can use to inspect and modify the properties of a ToDo item

- Timers that allow the application to notify you with an alert before an item is due

- The ability to save To Do documents to disk

Finally, in Chapter 14, *To Do: Finishing Touches*, you'll add polish with features such as application and document icons, as well as document typing that will allow users to automatically launch the application by double-clicking a To Do document in the Finder.

Create and Manage an Info Window

An Info window contains a set of fields and controls that enables users to examine and set an object's attributes. Because objects often have many attributes and because you want to make it easy for users to set those attributes, Info windows usually have more than one display; users typically access these multiple displays using a pop-up menu. These displays allow users to:

- Specify the times those items are due

- Request that they be notified at a specified interval before the due time

- Associate notes with items

- Mark items as complete or deferred

- Reschedule uncompleted items

The To Do application has an Info window that allows users to inspect and set the attributes of the currently selected ToDoItem. The Info window has its own controller: InfoWindowController. While showing you how to create the Info window and InfoWindowController, this section focuses on the following tasks:

- Managing displays according to user selections

- Getting the current ToDoItem

- Updating the currently selected display

- Updating the current ToDoItem as users make changes to it

Customize the Application's Menu

Before you begin the process of building the Info window, add a menu item to the the application's main menu that will invoke the Info window when selected:

1. Open `MainMenu.nib`.

2. Place an additional separator line in the File menu between the Revert and Page Setup items.

3. Create a new menu command between these separators with a name of Show Info . . . .

4. Give this command the key equivalent Command-Shift-I.

Create and Configure an Application Delegate

The To Do Info window is both global and dynamic. In other words, there is only one Info window for all ToDoDocuments, and it is invoked from the application's File menu. This presents a tricky design problem because the menu item that the user selects to display the Info window is in one nib file (`MainMenu.nib`), while the Info window itself—which you'll create in the next section—is in another (`ToDoInfoWindow.nib`). To make this work, you must have an object in `MainMenu.nib` that can become the target of the Show Info . . . menu item's action method.

In this section you'll create a simple class called ToDoAppDelegate that can create a shared Info window and display it. This design has the added advantage of lazily loading the Info window. "Lazy" loading means that the Info window's controller object will not be created nor its nib file loaded until the Show Info... item is actually invoked from the File menu––thus conserving system resources until they are required.

If you would like to experiment with a simple application that demonstrates this design pattern, take a moment and examine the example application called TestInfoWindow.

Follow these steps to create the ToDoAppDelegate:

1. In the Classes pane of the `MainMenu.nib` window, create a subclass of NSObject called ToDoAppDelegate.

2. Add an action called `showInfo:`.

3. Create an instance of ToDoAppDelegate.

4. Connect the Show Info... menu item to ToDoAppDelegate, and select the `showInfo:` action.

5. Make ToDoAppDelegate a delegate of File's Owner (which at runtime will be NSApp).

6. Create the files for ToDoAppDelegate and add them to the project.

7. Open `ToDoAppDelegate.m` and add an import statement for `InfoWindowController.h`. The files for the InfoWindowController class don't exist yet, but you'll create them in the next section, so you may as well add the necessary code while you're here.

8. Fill in the action method definition as shown in the following code. This class method invocation causes the InfoWindowController class to create a shared instance of the Info window controller (if one hasn't already been created) and tells it to display itself:

```
- (IBAction)showInfo:(id)sender {
    [[InfoWindowController sharedInfoWindowController]
            showWindow:sender];
}
```

Create a nib File for To Do's Info Window

In this section you'll create the user interface for the Info window. The window has three different panes that allow you to access different sets of ToDoItem attributes. In the finished Info window, you can select which of the three panes is visible using a standard pop-up menu. Using the three panels, you can:

- Create a descriptive text note associated with an item (Figure 13-1)

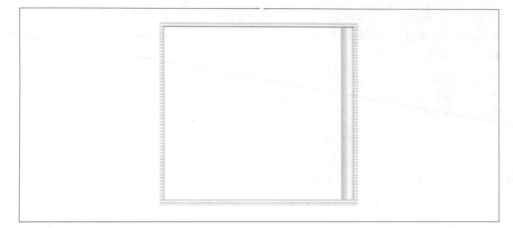

Figure 13-1. Notes pane of the Info window

- Mark an item as complete or reschedule it for another time (Figure 13-2)

Figure 13-2. Rescheduling pane of the Info window

- Set a due date and time for an item along with a notification alarm that will warn you that an item's due date is approaching (Figure 13-3)

Here are the steps for creating the window and its constituent panes:

1. In Interface Builder, choose New from the File menu.

2. Select Empty from the list of starting points to create a new nib file.

3. Save the nib file as `ToDoInfoWindow.nib` and insert it into the project.

4. Drag an NSPanel object from the Windows palette into the Instances pane of the `ToDoInfoWindow.nib` window.

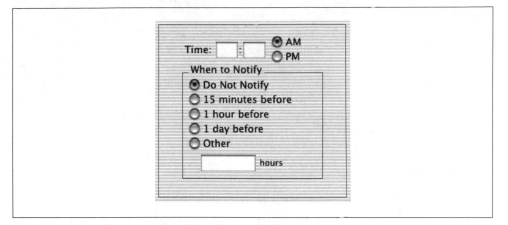

Figure 13-3. Notification pane of the Info window

5. Rename the panel instance **Info Window**.

6. Make the title of the panel **Info Window**.

7. Make the panel a Utility window.

8. Put labels, text fields, and a pop-up button on the panel as shown in Figure 13-4. The text fields should be borderless and should not be editable or scrollable, nor should they display their backgrounds.

9. Double-click the pop up to display in a floating window the three default items (Item1, Item2, Item3). Rename them **Notification**, **Reschedule**, and **Notes**, respectively. (Double-click the title of an item to select it.)

10. Assign the tags 0, 1, and 2 to the pop-up button cells.

11. Create a separator line just below the pop-up button.

12. Put an empty box object in the lower part of the panel. Turn off the box's Title attribute and resize the object so it fits just inside the lower part of the panel. Turn off the border after resizing.

13. Save the nib file.

You might be wondering about the empty box object in the lower part of the panel. This box by itself may not seem a promising thing for displaying object attributes, but it is critical to the workings of the Info window. A box that you drag from the Views palette contains one subview, called the Content view. NSBox's Content view fits entirely within the bounds of the box. NSBox provides methods for obtaining and changing the Content view of boxes. You'll use these methods to change what the Info window displays.

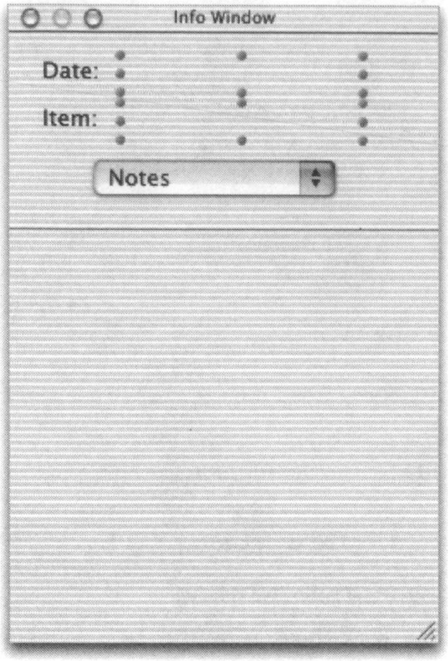

Figure 13-4. Info window

Create an Offscreen Panel

Create an offscreen panel holding the Info window's displays:

1. Drag a panel object from the Windows palette into the Instances pane of ToDoInfoWindow.nib.

2. Resize the panel, using Figure 13-5 as a guide.

3. Put the labels, text fields, scroll view, switch, and radio-button matrices on the panel, as shown in Figure 13-5.

4. Create the When to Reschedule and When to Notify groupings (boxes).

5. Create three other groupings for the three displays: Notes, Reschedule, and Notification.

6. Make the resulting outer boxes the same size as the dummy view in the Info window.

You may see now where the Info window gets its displays and how it puts them in place. When the Info window is first opened (and ToDoInfoWindow.nib is loaded), the Info window controller, InfoWindowController, replaces the Content view of the Info window's empty box (dummyView) with the Content view of the Notification box in the offscreen panel. Then every time the user chooses a new pop-up button in the Info window, InfoWindowController replaces the currently displayed Content view with the Content view of the associated offscreen box.

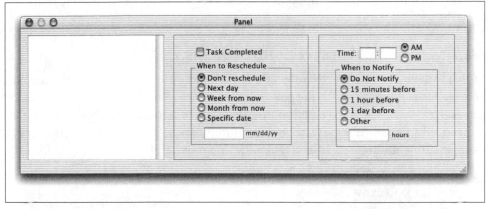

Figure 13-5. Info window panels

If you didn't look at it earlier, you might want to experiment with the example application TestInfoWindow that comes with the example files for this book. This very simple application implements a shared Info window with two views that you can swap using a pop-up button. The Info window itself doesn't do anything, but from looking at the code you'll be able to more clearly see how this design pattern works.

Apply Formatters

In this section you'll apply formatters to some of the Info window's text fields so that the data will display in a more visually appealing format. The formatters also act as a range-checking mechanism for the time fields, preventing users from entering invalid values for hours and minutes.

1. Drag a number-formatter object from the DataViews palette and drop it on the hours field of the Notification display (the first field after Time).

2. Select Integer Format.

3. In the Info window's Formatter display, set the field to have a minimum value of 1 and a maximum value of 12.

4. Apply a number formatter to the Minutes field (the second field after Time) and select Integer Format.

5. Set the field to have a minimum value of 0 and a maximum value of 59.

6. Drag a date-formatter object from the DataViews palette onto the date field in the Rescheduling display (the mm/dd/yy field).

7. In the Info window's Formatter display, select the %m/%d/%y format from the table.

Define the InfoWindowController Class

The InfoWindowController is responsible for loading the Info window's nib file and maintaining the state of the Info window's view. The Info window controller sets itself up to listen for notifications from other application objects so it can dynamically update the view when the current ToDo item or To Do document changes. Here are the steps for creating the controller class:

1. In Interface Builder, create the InfoWindowController class as a subclass of NSWindowController.

2. Add the outlets and actions shown in the lefthand column of Table 13-1 and Table 13-2. There's no need to create the window outlet because it already exists. It's listed in the table so you won't forget to connect it in step 4.

3. In the Instances pane of the ToDoInfoWindow.nib window, select File's Owner and use the File's Owner Info window to change its custom class to InfoWindowController.

4. Make the connections listed in the righthand column of Table 13-1 and Table 13-2 using File's Owner as the proxy for the InfoWindowController.

Table 13-1. InfoWindowController Outlets and Connections

Outlet	Connection to . . .
window	The Info window (draw the connection to the icon in the Instances panel or to the window's titlebar)
dummyView	The empty box object in the Info window
infoWindowViews	The offscreen window containing the swappable views (draw the connection to the icon in the Instances panel or to the window's titlebar)
notesView	The box in the offscreen window containing the text view
notifyView	The box in the offscreen window containing the fields and controls related to notification of impending items
reschedView	The box in the offscreen window containing the fields and controls related to rescheduling items
infoPopUp	The pop-up button on the Info window
infoDate	The uneditable text field next to the Date label
infoItem	The uneditable text field next to the Item label

Table 13-1. InfoWindowController Outlets and Connections (continued)

Outlet	Connection to . . .
infoNotes	The interior of the scrollable text view
infoNotifyHour	The text field next to the Time label
infoNotifyMinute	The second field after the Time label
infoNotifyAMPM	The matrix holding the A.M. and P.M. radio buttons
infoNotifyOtherHours	The text field in the When to Notify box
infoNotifySwitchMatrix	The matrix of radio buttons in the When to Notify box
infoSchedComplete	The Task Completed switch
infoSchedDate	The text field in the When to Reschedule box
infoSchedMatrix	The matrix of radio buttons in the When to Reschedule box

Table 13-2. InfoWindowController Actions and Connections

Action	Connection from . . .
swapInfoWindowView:	The pop-up button on the Info window
switchClicked:	The matrix of switches in the "When to Notify" box, the AM–PM matrix, the Task Completed switch, and the matrix of switches in the When to Reschedule switches

5. Connect each text field's delegate outlet to the InfoWindowController.

6. Close both windows and save `TodoInfoWindow.nib`.

7. Create source code files for InfoWindowController and add them to the project.

Type Outlets

In Chapter 6, *Essential Cocoa Paradigms*, you learned that it's good Cocoa programming practice to use statically typed outlets. This step is not absolutely necessary but will make debugging a lot easier, as the compiler will be able to do more strict type checking.

Spend a little time now to go through all of the outlets in `InfoWindowController.h` and change the type declarations from ID to the actual type of the interface object. If you're not sure of an interface object's class membership, open the nib file in Interface Builder, select the object in question, and bring up the Info window. The titlebar of the Info window will tell you the class of the interface object.

Add Declarations to *InfoWindowController.h*

In this section you'll add some of your own declarations to the header file created by Interface Builder. The enumerations at the top of Example 13-1 are used by the class to identify the various pop-up menu items and the radio buttons in the Notify pane, and the additional instance variable holds a reference to the current To Do document.

Go ahead and add the declarations from Example 13-1 to InfoWindowController.m (ellipses indicate existing declarations).

Example 13-1. Additions to InfoWindowController Interface

```
@class ToDoDocument;

enum { NOTIFY_TAG = 0, RESCHEDULE_TAG, NOTES_TAG };
enum { NotifyLengthNone = 0, NotifyLengthQuarter, NotifyLengthHour,
    NotifyLengthDay, NotifyLengthOther };

@interface InfoWindowController : NSObject
{
    @private
    /* ... */
    ToDoDocument *_inspectingDocument;
}
/* ... */
+ (id)sharedInfoWindowController;

@end
```

Implement Basic Methods

In this section you'll add the basic method implementations for the InfoWindow-Controller. These methods take care of creating the shared Info window instance, loading the nib file, and swapping the offscreen panel views into the Info window.

Import headers

In order for the InfoWindowController to display and modify ToDoItem data and to interact effectively with a ToDoDocument, it needs to know about the methods those classes implement. It gets this information from the class's public header files. Open InfoWindowController.m and import ToDoItem.h and ToDoDocument.h.

Add private declarations

Add the following helper method declarations to `InfoWindowController.m`:

```
static void clearButtonMatrix(id matrix);

@interface InfoWindowController (PrivateMethods)
- (void)updateInfoWindow;
- (void)setMainWindow:(NSWindow *)mainWindow;
@end
```

These declarations are helper functions that will be explained to you in detail later in the tutorial.

Implement the class method *sharedInfoWindowController*

This class method uses a static variable called `_sharedInfoWindowController` to keep a shared reference to the controller object. The method simply checks to see if an instance of the shared InfoWindowController already exists, and if not it creates one.

```
+ (id)sharedInfoWindowController
{
    static InfoWindowController *_sharedInfoWindowController = nil;

    if (!_sharedInfoWindowController) {
        _sharedInfoWindowController = [[InfoWindowController
                allocWithZone:[self zone]] init];
    }
    return _sharedInfoWindowController;
}
```

Implement *init*, *windowDidLoad*, and *dealloc*

Example 13-2 contains implementations for InfoWindowController's basic initialization and cleanup methods. You will add to these implementations later, but the initial versions will allow you to test the Info window before adding more complexity.

Example 13-2. Implementing InfoWindowController's init, windowDidLoad, and dealloc Methods

```
- (id)init
{
    self = [self initWithWindowNibName:@"ToDoInfoWindow"];
    if (self)
        [self setWindowFrameAutosaveName:@"Info"];

    return self;
}

- (void)windowDidLoad
```

Example 13-2. Implementing InfoWindowController's init, windowDidLoad, and
*   dealloc Methods (continued)*

```
{
    [super windowDidLoad];

    [notifyView retain];
    [notifyView removeFromSuperview];

    [reschedView retain];
    [reschedView removeFromSuperview];

    [notesView retain];
    [notesView removeFromSuperview];

    [infoWindowViews release];
    infoWindowViews = nil;

    [infoNotes setDelegate:self];

    [self swapInfoWindowView:self];
    [self setMainWindow:[NSApp mainWindow]];
    [self updateInfoWindow];

    [[NSNotificationCenter defaultCenter] addObserver:self
            selector:@selector(mainWindowChanged:)
            name:NSWindowDidBecomeMainNotification object:nil];
}

- (void)dealloc
{
    [notifyView release];
    [reschedView release];
    [notesView release];

    [[NSNotificationCenter defaultCenter] removeObserver:self];

    [super dealloc];
}
```

Note that `windowDidLoad` and `dealloc`, respectively, `retain` and `release` the views
contained in the nib file's offscreen window. This is necessary because swapping
the views in and out of the Info window changes the view objects' ownership. By
retaining them as soon as the nib file is loaded, the Info window controller is
guaranteed that the view objects won't be released while they are out of view.

After retaining the swappable views, the `windowDidLoad` method makes itself the
delegate for the Notes view. This way it can receive delegate methods that inform
the Info window about changes to the text in the Notes view. Next, the method
swaps in the default (Notify) view and sends itself the `setMainWindow:` message.
Finally, the method sets up the InfoWindowController to receive notifications

when the application's main window changes or is resigned. These notifications will give the controller an opportunity to update the Info window's view appropriately.

Add a Stub for the updateInfoWindow Method

A stub method is an empty, placeholder implementation that exists so other methods can refer to it. This keeps the compiler and runtime happy so you'll be able to compile and test the application in its current, partially completed state. Later in this chapter you'll provide a complete implementation that updates the Info window's interface to reflect changes that the user makes to the current ToDoItem in the main ToDoDocument window:

```
- (void)updateInfoWindow
{
}
```

Implement setMainWindow:

This method is used by the controller to keep track of the ToDoDocument that is currently being inspected by the user. In windowDidLoad, the Info window registered itself with the default notification center to receive a notification when the main window changes. This is the method that is invoked when the notification is received:

```
- (void)setMainWindow:(NSWindow *)mainWindow
{
    NSWindowController *controller = [mainWindow windowController];

    if ([[controller document] isKindOfClass:[ToDoDocument class]])
        _inspectingDocument = [controller document];
    else
        _inspectingDocument = nil;

    [self updateInfoWindow];
}
```

Implement mainWindowChanged:

This is the implementation for the helper method that was registered with the notification center to be called when an NSWindowDidBecomeMainNotification notification is posted:

```
- (void)mainWindowChanged:(NSNotification *)notification
{
    [self setMainWindow:[notification object]];
}
```

Implement swapInfoWindowView:

This method, shown in Example 13-3, changes Info window displays based on the user's selection in the pop-up menu.

Example 13-3. Implementing InfoWindowController's swapInfoWindowView:
Method

```
- (IBAction)swapInfoWindowView:(id)sender
{
    int selected;
    NSBox *newView;

    selected = [[infoPopUp selectedItem] tag];

    switch (selected) {
        case NOTIFY_TAG:
            newView = notifyView;
            break;
        case RESCHEDULE_TAG:
            newView = reschedView;
            break;
        case NOTES_TAG:
            newView = notesView;
            break;
    }

    if ([dummyView contentView] != newView) {
        [dummyView setContentView:newView];
        // more code to follow later...
    }
}
```

This method switches the current Info window display according to the pop-up button a user selects; it does this switching by replacing the dummyView's content view. Toward this end, the method:

- Gets the tag of the selected pop-up button and assigns the newView local variable to the offscreen box object corresponding to the tag

- Returns if the selected display is already in the Info window

Build and Test

Take a break from coding now and build the application. Experiment with the basic Info window operation. You should be able to invoke the Info window from the File menu and use the pop-up button to swap views in the lower part of the Info window.

Implement Advanced InfoWindowController Methods

In this section you'll complete the Info window by adding support for synchronizing the Info window's display with the currently selected ToDoItem.

For an Info window to function properly, it needs a way to modify the current ToDoItem in response to user actions in the Info window. The Info window also needs to keep track of modifications made to the current item in the frontmost ToDoDocument window.

The Info window solves the first problem by maintaining an internal reference to the current ToDoDocument in its _inspectingDocument instance variable. InfoWindowController updates this reference whenever it receives a notification from the system that the frontmost window has changed. This way, the Info window always displays the correct information. When the user clicks a control in the Info window, the InfoWindowController makes the corresponding change to the current ToDoItem and sends a message to the ToDoDocument that an item has been modified. This gives the document an opportunity to update its interface to reflect the change initiated in the Info window.

The Info window tracks changes made to the current ToDo item in the document window by listening for a notification. Later in this chapter you'll implement methods that track the current ToDo item and post a notification when the item is modified. The InfoWindowController listens for this notification and updates its interface appropriately.

Implement updateInfoWindow

This method updates the current Info window display when a new ToDoItem is selected in the frontmost To Do document window. The updateInfoWindow method is a long one, so we'll approach it in stages. This first part updates the common data elements (item name and date). If the current pane in the Info window is the Notification pane, the method updates that display.

Start by filling in the stub implementation with the first part of the method given in Example 13-4.

Example 13-4. Start of InfoWindowController's updateInfoWindow Method

```
- (void) pdateInfoWIndow
{
    int minute=0, hour=0, selected=0;
    long notifySecs, dueSecs;
    BOOL pmFlag;
    ToDoItem *selectedItem;
```

Example 13-4. Start of InfoWindowController's updateInfoWindow Method (continued)

```
    selected = [[infoPopUp selectedItem] tag];
    selectedItem = [_inspectingDocument selectedItem];

    if ([selectedItem isKindOfClass:[ToDoItem class]])
{
        [infoItem setStringValue:[selectedItem itemName]];
        [infoDate setStringValue:[[selectedItem day]
                descriptionWithCalendarFormat:@"%a, %b %d %Y"
                timeZone:[NSTimeZone localTimeZone] locale:nil]];

        switch (selected) {
            case NOTIFY_TAG:
                dueSecs = [selectedItem secsUntilDue];
                pmFlag = ConvertSecondsToTime(dueSecs, &hour, &minute);

                [[infoNotifyAMPM cellAtRow:0 column:0] setState:!pmFlag];
                [[infoNotifyAMPM cellAtRow:1 column:0] setState:pmFlag];
                [infoNotifyHour setIntValue:hour];
                [infoNotifyMinute setIntValue:minute];

                notifySecs = [selectedItem secsUntilNotify];

                clearButtonMatrix(infoNotifySwitchMatrix);

                switch(notifySecs) {
                    case 0:
                        [[infoNotifySwitchMatrix
                                cellAtRow:NotifyLengthNone column:0]
                                setState:NSOnState];
                        break;
                    case (SECS_IN_HOUR/4):
                        [[infoNotifySwitchMatrix
                                cellAtRow:NotifyLengthQuarter column:0]
                                setState:NSOnState];
                        break;
                    case (SECS_IN_HOUR):
                        [[infoNotifySwitchMatrix
                                cellAtRow:NotifyLengthHour column:0]
                                setState:NSOnState];
                        break;
                    case (SECS_IN_DAY):
                        [[infoNotifySwitchMatrix
                                cellAtRow:NotifyLengthDay column:0]
                                setState:NSOnState];
                        break;
                    default:  // other
                        [[infoNotifySwitchMatrix
                                cellAtRow:NotifyLengthOther column:0]
                                setState:NSOnState];
                        [infoNotifyOtherHours setIntValue:
                                (notifySecs/SECS_IN_HOUR)];
                        break;
```

Example 13-4. Start of InfoWindowController's updateInfoWindow Method (continued)

```
                        }
                    break;
                case RESCHEDULE_TAG:
                    // left as an exercise
                    break;
                case NOTES_TAG:
                    [infoNotes setString:[selectedItem notes]];
                    break;
            } //switch
```

The first part of the method shown in Example 13-4:

- Gets the tag assigned to the selected pop-up button.

- Tests the argument `selectedItem` to see if it is a ToDoItem. This test is important because if the `selectedItem` is `nil`, the method clears the display of existing data (next example).

- If selectedItem is a ToDoItem, `updateInfoWindow:` first updates the Item and Date fields.

- If the tag of the selected pop-up button is `NOTIFY_TAG`, it updates the associated Info window display. This task starts by converting the due time from seconds to hour, minute, and P.M. Boolean values and then setting the appropriate fields and button matrix with these values. Then it sets the appropriate switch in the When to Notify matrix. It calls `clearButtonMatrix` to turn all switches off and then, in a switch statement, sets the switch corresponding to the notification length (given in seconds).

Note that this tutorial omits the rescheduling logic of the To Do application, including the code in this method that would update the Reschedule display. Rescheduling of ToDoItems is reserved as an optional exercise for you at the end of this chapter.

Finish the implementation of `updateInfoWindow:` by resetting all displays if the argument is `nil`, as shown in Example 13-5.

Example 13-5. End of InfoWindowController's updateInfoWindow Method

```
} else { // selectedItem is not a ToDoItem
        [infoItem setStringValue:@""];
        [infoDate setStringValue:@""];
        [infoNotifyHour setStringValue:@""];
        [infoNotifyMinute setStringValue:@""];
        [[infoNotifyAMPM cellAtRow:0 column:0] setState:NSOnState];
        [[infoNotifyAMPM cellAtRow:1 column:0] setState:NSOffState];
        clearButtonMatrix(infoNotifySwitchMatrix);
        [[infoNotifySwitchMatrix cellAtRow:NotifyLengthNone column:0]
                setState:NSOnState];
        [infoNotifyOtherHours setStringValue:@""];
```

Example 13-5. End of InfoWindowController's updateInfoWindow Method (continued)

```
        [infoNotes setString:@""];
    }
}
```

As you've most likely noticed, the `updateInfoWindow` method calls the function `clearButtonMatrix`, which resets the states of all button cells in a switch matrix to NO.

Implement clearButtonMatrix

Add the code for the `clearButtonMatrix` utility function:

```
    void clearButtonMatrix(id matrix)
    {
        int i, rows, cols;
        [matrix getNumberOfRows:&rows columns:&cols];
        for(i=0; i<rows; i++)
            [[matrix cellAtRow:i column:0] setState:NO];
    }
```

The `getNumberOfRows:columns:` message returns, by indirection in the first argument, the number of cells in `matrix`.

Implement switchClicked:

This method, shown in Example 13-6, updates the current item with new values entered in the Info window.

Example 13-6. Implementation InfoWindowController's switchClicked: Method

```
- (IBAction)switchClicked:(id)sender
{
    long dueSecs = 0;
    int idx = 0;

    ToDoItem *theItem = [_inspectingDocument selectedItem];

    if (sender == infoNotifyAMPM) {
        if ([infoNotifyHour intValue]) {
            BOOL pmFlag = ([infoNotifyAMPM selectedRow]==1);
            dueSecs = ConvertTimeToSeconds([infoNotifyHour intValue],
                    [infoNotifyMinute intValue], pmFlag);
            [theItem setSecsUntilDue:dueSecs];
        }
    } else if (sender == infoNotifySwitchMatrix) {
        idx = [infoNotifySwitchMatrix selectedRow];
        switch(idx) {
            case NotifyLengthNone:
                [theItem setSecsUntilNotify:0];
                break;
```

Example 13-6. Implementation InfoWindowController's switchClicked: Method (continued)

```
        case NotifyLengthQuarter:
            [theItem setSecsUntilNotify:(SECS_IN_HOUR/4)];
            break;
        case NotifyLengthHour:
            [theItem setSecsUntilNotify:SECS_IN_HOUR];
            break;
        case NotifyLengthDay:
            [theItem setSecsUntilNotify:SECS_IN_DAY];
            break;
        case NotifyLengthOther:
            [theItem setSecsUntilNotify:
                    ([infoNotifyOtherHours intValue] * SECS_IN_HOUR)];
            break;
        default:
            NSLog(@"Error in selectedRow");
            break;
        }
    } else if (sender == infoSchedComplete) {
        [theItem setStatus:COMPLETE];
    } else if (sender == infoSchedMatrix) {
        // left as an exercise
    }

    [self updateInfoWindow];
    [_inspectingDocument selectedItemModified];
}
```

When users click any switch button on the Info window or when they click one of the AM–PM radio buttons, the switchClicked: method is invoked. This method works by evaluating the sender argument.

If sender is the radio-button matrix (AM–PM), the code gets the new time due by calling the utility function ConvertTimeToSeconds; which sets the current item to have this new value. If sender is the When to Notify matrix, it gets the index of the selected cell and uses a switch statement to set the current item's new secsUntil-Notify value. If sender is the Task Completed switch, it sets the status of the current item to COMPLETE. As before, implementation of the rescheduling block is left as a final exercise.

Finally, the method updates the Info window view and tells the current document that the selected (and inspected) item has been modified. This gives the ToDoDocument a chance to update its state based on the changes made in the Info window.

Since text fields are controls, they can send target/action messages when the user presses Return and, if the sendsActionOnEndEditing is set, upon losing first responder status. Therefore, you could also have switchClicked: respond when data is entered in the fields. To illustrate an alternative design, we will rely upon delegation messages for handling the text entries.

Implement notification methods

The `textDidEndEditing:` method shown at the top of Example 13-7 is invoked when the Info window's Notes view posts a notification that the user completed editing text. It resets the Notes attribute of the current ToDo item and sends a message to the current ToDoDocument advising it of the modification. The `controlTextDidEndEditing:` method, also shown in Example 13-7, updates the current ToDoItem if changes are made to the contents of any of the text fields in the Info pane.

Example 13-7. Implementation of InfoWindowController's Text Notification Methods

```
- (void)textDidEndEditing:(NSNotification *)notification
{
    if ([notification object] == infoNotes) {
        [[_inspectingDocument selectedItem] setNotes:[infoNotes string]];
        [_inspectingDocument selectedItemModified];
    }
}


- (void)controlTextDidEndEditing:(NSNotification *)notification
{
    long dueSecs = 0;
    ToDoItem *theItem = [_inspectingDocument selectedItem];

    if ([notification object] == infoNotifyHour ||
        [notification object] == infoNotifyMinute) {
        dueSecs = ConvertTimeToSeconds([infoNotifyHour intValue],
                [infoNotifyMinute intValue],
                [[infoNotifyAMPM cellAtRow:1 column:0] state]);
        [theItem setSecsUntilDue:dueSecs];
    } else if ([notification object] == infoNotifyOtherHours)
    {
        if ([infoNotifySwitchMatrix selectedRow] == NotifyLengthOther)
            [theItem setSecsUntilNotify:
                    ([infoNotifyOtherHours intValue] * SECS_IN_HOUR)];
        else
            return; // nothing changed
    } else if ([notification object] == infoSchedDate)
    {
        // left as an exercise
    }

    [_inspectingDocument selectedItemModified];
}
```

The `textDidEndEditing:` and `controlTextDidEndEditing:` notification messages are sent to the delegate (and all other observers) when the cursor leaves a text object or text field, respectively, after editing has occurred.

After editing takes place in the Notes text object, `textDidEndEditing:` is invoked, and it responds by resetting the Notes instance variable of the ToDoItem with the contents of the text object.

If the object behind the notification is the hour or minute field of the Notifications display, `controlTextDidEndEditing:` computes the new due time and then sets the current item to have this new value.

If the object behind the notification is the Other . . . hours text field in the When to Notify box, the method verifies that the Other switch is checked and, if it is, sets the ToDoItem with the new value. Finally, there is another empty rescheduling block of code that you can fill out in a later exercise.

At the end of both methods, the document is sent a `selectedItemModified` message.

It's a good idea to compile the application now to catch any typing (or cut/paste) errors you might have introduced. The only compiler warnings you should receive are notes that the ToDoDocument class does not respond to `selectedItemModified`. You'll implement this method later in this chapter.

Create SelectionNotifyMatrix

In the last section you implemented an Info window for the application and set up the infrastructure to coordinate changes to the current ToDo item. Now you want the Info window to synchronize its displays when the user selects a new ToDo item in a ToDoDocument by clicking or tabbing into a field. In this section you'll implement this functionality.

As you'll recall from Chapter 12, the list of ToDo items displayed in a ToDoDocument's window is an NSMatrix of text cells. To implement proper synchronization of the application's Info window with the current ToDo item, you'll create a subclass of NSMatrix that can detect changes in the current selection and post a notification for interested observers (e.g., the InfoWindowController).

This section provides a good example of how to override the behavior of an Application Kit class. You can often achieve the desired changes in object behavior by creating a subclass that adds only a small amount of code to its superclass. Such is the case with the subclass you'll create now: SelectionNotifyMatrix.

Create Files for SelectionNotifyMatrix

In Project Builder, create the interface and implementation files for the new class
and add them to the project. Add the following declarations to the header file:

```
#import <Cocoa/Cocoa.h>

extern NSString *RowSelectedNotification;

@interface SelectionNotifyMatrix : NSMatrix {
}
@end
```

Add the definition for the string to the implementation file:

```
@implementation SelectionNotifyMatrix

NSString *RowSelectedNotification = @"RowSelectedNotification";
/*...*/
```

RowSelectedNotification is a string constant identifying the notification that will
be posted when the currently selected row is changed.

Override mouseDown:

The Dot View application you created in Chapter 8, *Event Handling*, demonstrated
how you can subclass NSView and override its mouseUp: method to track mouse
clicks in the view. The same technique applies to subclassing NSMatrix. In this
section you'll override NSMatrix's mouseDown: to customize its event processing.

Add the implementation for mouseDown: to SelectionNotifyMatrix.m, as shown in
Example 13-8.

Example 13-8. Implementation of SelectionNotifyMatrix's mouseDown: Method

```
- (void)mouseDown:(NSEvent *)theEvent
{
    int row;
    [super mouseDown:theEvent];

    row = [self selectedRow];
    if (row != -1) {
        [[NSNotificationCenter defaultCenter]
                postNotificationName:RowSelectedNotification
                object:self
                userInfo:nil];
    }
}
```

The version of mouseDown: shown in Example 13-8 invokes NSMatrix's implementation of mouseDown: to allow the normal processing of this event, then gets the row of the cell clicked. If it's a valid row, the method posts the RowSelectedNotification to the default notification center. In the completed application, the Info window's Controller object receives the notification and updates the Info window's view with data from the newly selected ToDo item.

Override selectCellAtRow:column:

To handle the selection of new items using tabbing, you must override the selectCellAtRow:column: method. As with the preceding implementation of mouse-Down:, the only change is to add code that posts the RowSelectedNotification so the Info window will know about the new selection.

```
- (void)selectCellAtRow:(int)row column:(int)col;
{
    [super selectCellAtRow:row column:col];

    [[NSNotificationCenter defaultCenter]
            postNotificationName:RowSelectedNotification
            object:self
            userInfo:nil];
}
```

Reassign the Class of the itemList Matrix

Now that you've created the SelectionNotifyMatrix class, you must reassign the class membership of the object in the interface. You can do this easily in Interface Builder:

1. Open ToDoDocument.nib.

2. In Project Builder, click on SelectionNotifyMatrix.h and drag it into the nib file window.

3. Select the itemList matrix of text cells.

4. Choose SelectionNotifyMatrix in the Custom display of the Info window.

5. Save the nib file.

Respond to the Notification

Now that you have set up the infrastructure for tracking selections, you need to write the code that responds to the notification posted when the user clicks on a ToDoItem in the itemList:

1. At the top of `ToDoDocument.h` (after the `#import` statements), declare the `ToDoItemChangedNotification`:

   ```
   extern NSString *ToDoItemChangedNotification;
   ```

2. Open `ToDoDocument.m`.

3. Add the definition for the notification:

   ```
   NSString *ToDoItemChangedNotification =
       @"ToDoItemChangedNotification";
   ```

4. Add the following method implementation:

   ```
   - (void)rowSelected:(NSNotification *)notification
   {
       int row = [[notification object] selectedRow];

       selectedItem = [currentItems objectAtIndex:row];

       if (![selectedItem isKindOfClass:[ToDoItem class]])
           selectedItem = nil;

       [[NSNotificationCenter defaultCenter]
               postNotificationName:ToDoItemChangedNotification
               object:selectedItem
               userInfo:nil];
   }
   ```

5. Make ToDoDocument an observer of the `RowSelectedNotification` posted by the SelectionNotifyMatrix. This notification is posted when a user clicks on, or tabs into, a ToDo item. Add the code to ToDoDocument's `windowController-DidLoadNib:` method. Hint: `rowSelected:` is the method to use for the observer selector and two `addObserver:` calls should be made, one for `itemList` and one for `statusList`.

The `rowSelected:` method uses the row number obtained from the object passed by the notification to figure out which item to make current and posts a ToDoItemChanged notification to let the Info window know (if one exists) that the current item has changed.

While you're here in `ToDoDocument.m`, uncomment the two lines of code in the `updateLists` method so that the status list will be displayed properly.

Data Synchronization

Now it's time to add functionality to the ToDoDocument class to facilitate synchro-nizing data display with an Info window. The Info window must display informa-tion about the ToDoItem currently selected in the ToDoDocument and update its view if a new document is opened (or brought to the front). Also, the ToDoDocument must update its display when an item is modified in the Info window. In this section you'll make this communication work.

The `controlTextDidEndEditing:` method in `ToDoDocument.m` is where ToDoItems are added, removed, or modified, so you must let the Info window know when there's a change in the current ToDoItem. Modify the method to post a `ToDoItemChangedNotification`, passing in `selectedItem` as the object related to the notification.

1. Open `ToDoDocument.m`.

2. Import `InfoWindowController.h`. While you're here, import `SelectionNotifyMatrix.h` as well, to pick up the `RowSelectedNotification` declaration.

3. Add the following code to the `controlTextDidEndEditing:` method:

```
/* ... */
[self updateChangeCount:NSChangeDone];

[[NSNotificationCenter defaultCenter] postNotificationName:
        ToDoItemChangedNotification object:selectedItem
        userInfo:nil];
```

4. Open `InfoWindowController.m` and modify the `windowDidLoad` method to register the InfoWindowController as an observer of the ToDoItemChangedNotification:

```
[[NSNotificationCenter defaultCenter] addObserver:self
        selector:@selector(selectedItemChanged:)
        name:ToDoItemChangedNotification object:nil];
```

5. Add the definition of the `selectedItemChanged:` method to `InfoWindowController.m`:

```
- (void)selectedItemChanged:(NSNotification *)notification {
    [self updateInfoWindow];
}
```

Now you must also make ToDoDocument respond properly to the `selectedItemModified` message sent by the Info window when it makes changes to the current ToDoItem:

1. Open `ToDoDocument.h` and add a declaration for the method:

```
- (void)selectedItemModified;
```

2. Open `ToDoDocument.m` and add the implementation:

```
- (void)selectedItemModified
{
    if (selectedItem)
```

```
        [self setTimerForItem:selectedItem];
        [self updateLists];
        [self updateChangeCount:NSChangeDone];
    }
```

This method first updates the selected item's timer and then updates the view to reflect the changes made in the Info window and then mark the document as modified.

The use of notifications to communicate changes in one object to another object in an application is a good design strategy because it removes the need for the objects to have specific knowledge of one another. It also makes the application more extensible, because any number of objects can also become observers of the changes.

Create a Custom View to Display ToDoItem Status

For the To Do application, you'll implement a three-state button to indicate a ToDoItem's status. The button will show, with an image, three possible states: not done (no image), done (an *X*), and deferred (an *O*). These states correspond to the possible states of a ToDoItem.

The ToDoCell class, which you will implement in this section, generates cells that behave as three-state buttons. These buttons also display the time an item is due. Here's how you add the cell images to the project:

1. In Project Builder, create an Images group inside the Resources group.

2. Choose Add Files from the Project menu.

3. In the Add Images, select the file `DoneMark.tiff`.

4. If you want to create a self-contained project, choose the option to copy the files into the project directory.

5. Click OK.

6. Repeat the same steps for file `DeferredMark.tiff`, which is in the same location.

7. Now that you have an Images group, move `LeftArrow.tiff` and `RightArrow.tiff` into it.

Why Choose NSButtonCell as a Superclass?

The superclass of ToDoCell is NSButtonCell. In creating ToDoCell, you will add data and behavior to NSButtonCell and override some existing behavior. This choice prompts two questions:

- Why a button cell and not the button itself?
- Why this particular superclass?

NSCell defines state as an instance variable, so all cells inherit it. Cells, rather than controls, hold state information for reasons of efficiency—one control (a matrix) can manage a collection of cells, each cell with its own state setting. NSButton does provide methods for getting and setting state values, but it accesses the state value of the cell that it contains (usually NSButtonCell).

NSButtonCell is ToDoCell's superclass because button cells already have much of the behavior you want. By virtue of inheritance from NSActionCell, button cells can hold target and action information. Button cells also have the unique capability to display an image and text simultaneously. These are all aspects of behavior needed for ToDoCell.

When you think that you need a specialized subclass of a Cocoa class, you should first spend some time examining the header files and reference documentation on not only that class, but also its superclasses and any sibling classes.

Implement the ToDoCell Interface

In this section you'll create the class files for ToDoCell and provide declarations for the class interface.

1. In Project Builder, create the interface and implementation files for ToDoCell.
2. Make the superclass NSButtonCell.
3. Add the enum constants, instance variables, and method declarations shown in Example 13-9.

Example 13-9. ToDoCell Interface

```
typedef enum ToDoButtonState {NOT_DONE=0, DONE, DEFERRED} ToDoButtonState;

@interface ToDoCell : NSButtonCell
{
    ToDoButtonState triState;
    NSImage *doneImage, *deferredImage;
    NSDate *timeDue;
}
- (void)setTriState:(ToDoButtonState)newState;
- (ToDoButtonState)triState;
- (void)setTimeDue:(NSDate *)newTime;
```

Example 13-9. ToDoCell Interface (continued)

```
- (NSDate *)timeDue;
@end
```

The `triState` instance variable will be assigned ToDoButtonState constants as values. The NSImage variables hold the "O" and check mark images that represent completed and deferred (that is, rescheduled for the next day) status, respectively. The `timeDue` instance variable carries the time the item is due as an NSDate; for display, this object will be converted to a string.

Declare Private Methods

Add the following declaration at the top of `ToDoCell.m` to declare ToDoCell's private helper method:

```
@interface ToDoCell (PrivateMethods)
- (void)updateImage;
@end
```

Implement init and dealloc

ToDoCell's `init` method sets some superclass (NSButtonCell) attributes, such as button type, image and text position, font of text, and border.

1. Implement `init` as shown in Example 13-10.

2. Implement `dealloc`.

Example 13-10. Implementation of ToDoCell's init Method

```
- (id)init
{
    NSString *path;
    [super initTextCell:@""];

    triState = NOT_DONE;
    [self setType:NSToggleButton];
    [self setImagePosition:NSImageLeft];
    [self setBezelStyle:NSShadowlessSquareBezelStyle];
    [self setFont:[NSFont userFontOfSize:10]];
    [self setAlignment:NSRightTextAlignment];

    doneImage=[[NSImage imageNamed:@"DoneMark"] retain];

    deferredImage=[[NSImage imageNamed:@"DeferredMark"] retain];

    return self;
}
```

Implement Accessor Methods

Accessing state information is a dual-path task in ToDoCell. It involves not only setting and getting the new state instance variable, triState, but also properly handling the inherited instance variable by overriding the superclass accessor method for state.

1. Write the methods that get and set the triState instance variable:

```
- (void) setTriState: (ToDoButtonState) newState
{
    if (newState > DEFERRED)
        triState = NOT_DONE;
    else
        triState = newState;
    [self updateImage];
}
```

```
- (ToDoButtonState) triState { return triState; }
```

2. Override the superclass methods that get and set state:

```
- (void) setState: (int) val
{
}
```

```
- (int) state
{
    if (triState == DEFERRED)
        return (int) DONE;
    else
        return (int) triState;
}
```

In the supplied implementation, if the new value for triState is greater than the limit (DEFERRED), reset it to 0 (NOT_DONE); otherwise, assign the value. The reason behind this logic is that (as you'll soon learn) when users click a ToDoCell, setTriState: is invoked with an argument 1 more than the current value. This way users can cycle through the three states of ToDoCell.

setState: is overridden to be a null method. The reason for this override is that NSCell intervenes when a button is clicked, resetting state to 0 (NO). This override nullifies that effect.

Set the Cell Image

This portion of code handles the display of the cell's image by evaluating the tri-state argument and setting the cell's image appropriately (setImage: is an NSButtonCell method). Then it sends updateCell: to the Control view of the cell's control (a matrix) to force a redraw of the cell.

Implement the updateImage: method given in Example 13-11.

Example 13-11. Implementation of ToDoCell's updateImage Method

```
- (void)updateImage
{
    switch ([self triState]) {
        case NOT_DONE:
            [self setImage:nil];
            break;
        case DONE:
            [self setImage:doneImage];
            break;
        case DEFERRED:
            [self setImage:deferredImage];
            break;
    }

    [(NSControl *)[self controlView] updateCell:self];

}
```

Track Mouse Clicks

When you create your own cell subclass, you might want to override some methods that are intrinsic to the behavior of the cell. Mouse-tracking methods, inherited from NSCell, are among these. You can override these methods to incorporate specialized behavior when the mouse clicks the cell or drags over it. ToDoCell overrides these methods to increment the value of triState.

Override two NSCell mouse-tracking methods as shown in Example 13-12.

Example 13-12. Implementation of ToDoCell's Mouse-Tracking Methods

```
- (BOOL)startTrackingAt:(NSPoint)startPoint inView:
    (NSView *)controlView
{
    return YES;
}

- (void)stopTracking:(NSPoint)lastPoint at:(NSPoint)stopPoint
    inView:(NSView *)controlView mouseIsUp:(BOOL)flag
{
    if (flag == YES)
        [self setTriState:([self triState]+1)];
}
```

In this case, you override startTrackingAt:inView: to return YES, thus signaling to the control that the ToDoCell will track the mouse. Then you override stopTracking:at:inView:mouseIsUp: to evaluate the flag and make sure this is a mouse-up event; if it is, the method increments the triState instance variable.

The setTriState: method "wraps" the incremented value to 0 (NOT_DONE) if it is greater than 2 (DEFERRED).

Get and Set the Time Due

The setTimeDue: method is similar to other set accessor methods, except that it handles interpretation and display of the NSDate instance variable it stores. The timeDue accessor method is standard.

1. Implement setTimeDue: as shown:

```
- (void)setTimeDue:(NSDate *)newTime
{
    [timeDue autorelease];

    if (newTime) {
        timeDue = [newTime retain];
        [self setTitle:[timeDue descriptionWithCalendarFormat:
                @"%I:%M %p" timeZone:[NSTimeZone localTimeZone] locale:nil]];
    } else {

        timeDue = nil;
        [self setTitle:@"-->"];
    }
}
```

2. Implement timeDue to return the NSDate.

If newTime is a valid object, it uses decriptionWithCalendarFormat:time-Zone:locale:, an NSDate method, to interpret and format the date object before displaying the result with setTitle:. If newTime is nil, no due time has been specified, so the method sets the title to "→".

You've now completed all code required for ToDoCell. However, you must now install instances of this class in the To Do interface.

Create and Install the Custom Cells

In this section you'll modify ToDoDocument to create and install your custom cells in the matrix when a new document is created.

1. Open ToDoDocument.m.

2. Import ToDoCell.h.

3. Insert the following code in windowControllerDidLoadNib just after the [itemList setDelegate:self]; statement:

```
        int index;
        /*...*/
        index = [[statusList cells] count];
        while (index--) {
            ToDoCell *aCell = [[ToDoCell alloc] init];
            [aCell setTarget:self];
            [aCell setAction:@selector(itemStatusClicked:)];
            [statusList putCell:aCell atRow:index column:0];
            [aCell release];
        }
```

This block of code substitutes a ToDoCell for each cell in the left matrix (statusList) you created for the To Do interface. It creates a ToDoCell, sets its target and action message, then inserts it into the statusList by invoking NSMatrix's putCell:atRow:column: method.

Finally, you must implement the action message sent when the matrix of ToDoCells is clicked. (This response to mouse-down is intended for objects external to ToDoCell, while the mouse-tracking methods in ToDoCell.m maintains state internally.)

Respond to Mouse Clicks

The itemStatusClicked: method gets the ToDoCell that was clicked and the object in the corresponding text field. If that object is a ToDoItem, the method updates its status to reflect the state of the ToDoCell. It then marks the window as containing an edited document.

In ToDoDocument.m, complete the implementation for itemStatusClicked: as shown in Example 13-13.

Example 13-13. Implementation of ToDoDocument's itemStatusClicked: Method

```
- (IBAction)itemStatusClicked:(id)sender
{
    int row = [sender selectedRow];
    ToDoCell *cell = [sender cellAtRow:row column:0];
    id item;

    item = [currentItems objectAtIndex:row];
    if (item && [item isKindOfClass:[ToDoItem class]]) {
        [item setStatus:[cell triState]];

        [self setTimerForItem:item];
        [self updateLists];
        [self updateChangeCount:NSChangeDone];
```

Example 13-13. Implementation of ToDoDocument's itemStatusClicked: Method (continued)

```
        [[NSNotificationCenter defaultCenter]
            postNotificationName:ToDoItemChangedNotification
            object:item
            userInfo:nil];
    }
}
```

Set Up Timers

One of To Do's features is the capability for notifying users of items with impending due times. Users can specify various intervals before the due time for these notifications, which take the form of a message in an Alert window. In this section you will implement the notification feature of To Do. In the process you'll learn the basics of creating, setting, and responding to timers.

Here's how it works. Each ToDoItem with a When to Notify switch (other than Do Not Notify) selected in the Info window—and hence has a positive secsUntilNotify value—has a timer set for it. If a user cancels a notification by selecting Do Not Notify, the document controller invalidates the timer. When a timer fires, it invokes a method that displays the Alert window, selects the Do Not Notify switch, and sets secsUntilNotify to 0.

Implementing the timer feature takes place entirely in Project Builder.

Set a Timer for an Item

An item's timer must be reset whenever its day, due time, notify time, or status changes. The item's accessor methods could handle this, but there are times when several instance variables get set in sequence. It would be better not to reset the timer at each individual change in this case, so instead a separate update step, setTimerForItem:, is implemented in ToDoDocument.

All timer-related values for a document's selected ToDoItem can be set and modified by InfoWindowController. Following each modification, InfoWindowController sends the document a selectedItemModified message. As this method then calls setTimerForItem: with the selected item, nothing more is required for all changes made in the Info window.

ToDoDocument also modifies ToDoItems at several locations: When an item's status button is clicked, ToDoDocument's itemStatusClicked: method updates the item's status. This case has been implemented already. After an item's timer fires, its secsUntilNotify needs to be cleared and the timer turned off; you'll implement this functionality here in this section. And finally, when reading ToDoItems from a file, each item must have its timer set up after the item is initialized. You'll implement that in the section "Implement Archiving and Unarchiving (Save and Open)."

Implement setTimerForItem:

This method sets or invalidates a timer, depending on the ToDoItem's notification and status values. Here's how:

1. Open `ToDoDocument.h` and add a declaration for `setTimerForItem:`.

   - (void)setTimerForItem:(ToDoItem *)anItem

2. Open `ToDoDocument.m`.

3. Implement the `setTimerForItem:` method, which is shown in Example 13-14.

Example 13-14. Implementation of ToDoDocument's setTimerForItem: Method

```
- (void)setTimerForItem:(ToDoItem *)anItem
{
    NSDate *notifyDate;
    NSTimer *aTimer;

    if ([anItem secsUntilNotify] && [anItem status] == INCOMPLETE) {
        notifyDate = [[anItem day] addTimeInterval:
                ([anItem secsUntilDue] - [anItem secsUntilNotify])];
        aTimer = [NSTimer scheduledTimerWithTimeInterval:
                [notifyDate timeIntervalSinceNow]
                target:self
                selector:@selector(itemTimerFired:)
                userInfo:anItem
                repeats:NO];
        [anItem setTimer:aTimer];
    } else
        [anItem setTimer:nil];
}
```

First, this method tests the ToDoItem to see if it has a nonzero `secsUntilNotify` value and a status of `INCOMPLETE`. If it does, the method composes the time the notification should be sent. Then it creates a timer and schedules it to fire at the right time, directing it to invoke `itemTimerFired:` when it fires. It also sets the timer in the ToDoItem. If the `secsUntilNotify` variable is 0, it invalidates the item's timer.

Respond to Timers

When a ToDoItem's timer goes off, it invokes the `itemTimerFired:` method (remember, you designated this method when you scheduled the timer).

Implement itemTimerFired: from Example 13-15.

Example 13-15. Implementation of ToDoDocument's itemTimerFired: Method

```
- (void)itemTimerFired:(id)timer
{
    id anItem = [timer userInfo];
    NSDate *dueDate = [[anItem day] addTimeInterval:[anItem secsUntilDue]];

    NSBeep();
    NSRunAlertPanel(@"To Do", @"%@ on %@", nil, nil, nil,
            [anItem itemName],
            [dueDate descriptionWithCalendarFormat:@"%b %d, %Y at %I:%M %p"
            timeZone:[NSTimeZone defaultTimeZone] locale:nil]);

    [anItem setSecsUntilNotify:0];

    [self setTimerForItem:anItem];
    [self updateLists];

    [[NSNotificationCenter defaultCenter]
            postNotificationName:ToDoItemChangedNotification
            object:anItem
            userInfo:nil];
}
```

This method composes the due time (as an NSDate), beeps, and displays an Alert window specifying the name of a ToDoItem and the time it is due. It then sets the ToDoItem's secsUntilNotify instance variable to 0 to prevent further notifications. Finally, it updates the display and posts a notification that the item has changed.

Build and Test

Now is a good time to test the application. The only major feature yet to be implemented is saving and loading To Do documents to/from the file system. Go through the following sequence and observe To Do's behavior:

1. When you choose New from the Document menu, the application creates a new To Do document and selects the current day.

2. Enter a few items. Click a new day on the calendar and enter a few more items. Click the previous day and notice how the items you entered reappear.

3. Choose Show Info from the File menu. When the Info window appears, click an item and notice how the name and date of the item appear in the top part of the Info window. Enter due times for a couple of items and some associated notes. Note how the times, as you enter them, appear in the Status/Due column of the To Do document. Click among a few items again and note how the Notifications and Notes displays change.

4. Click a Status/Due button; the image toggles among the three states. Then with an item that has a due time, select a notification time that has already passed. The application immediately displays an Alert window with a notification message. When you dismiss this window, To Do sets the notification option to Do Not Notify.

Implement Archiving and Unarchiving (Save and Open)

Now that you have implemented and debugged all of To Do's major features, it's time to finish up by adding support for saving and opening documents to `ToDoDocument.m`.

Implement dataRepresentationOfType:

As you learned previously, this method is responsible for archiving the document's data and returning it in the form of an NSData instance. It's very simple:

```
- (NSData *)dataRepresentationOfType:(NSString *)aType
{
    [self saveDocItems];
    return [NSArchiver archivedDataWithRootObject:activeDays];
}
```

This method saves the current day's items to the `activeDays` dictionary and archives it.

Implement loadDataRepresentation:ofType:

This method checks to see if `calendar` exists before deciding how to proceed. If `calendar` does exist, it means that the nib file has already been loaded and the document controller is being asked to display the data (this is what happens when Revert is selected from the File menu). If `calendar` doesn't yet exist (meaning the nib file has not yet been loaded), the method saves a reference to the document data in the `dataFromFile` instance variable. When `windowControllerDidLoadNib` is called, that method checks to see if any data is pending, and if it is, that data is loaded into the document.

1. Add the instance variable `dataFromFile` to `ToDoDocument.h`. Statically type the variable as an NSData*.

2. Add the following method definition to `ToDoDocument.m`:

```
- (BOOL)loadDataRepresentation:(NSData *)data ofType:(NSString *)aType
{
    if (calendar)
```

```
        [self loadDocWithData:data];
    else
        dataFromFile = [data retain];

    return YES;
}
```

Modify *windowControllerDidLoadNib:*

Go to the `windowControllerDidLoadNib:` method and replace the line `[self initDataModelWithDictionary:nil];` with the following:

```
if (dataFromFile)
{
    [self loadDocWithData:dataFromFile];
    [dataFromFile release];
    dataFromFile = nil;
} else {
    // A new ToDoDocument is being created so there's no data to load.
    [self loadDocWithData:nil];
}
```

This code loads any pending data. If there is none, it just initializes the document with an empty dictionary.

Implement *loadDocWithData:*

Here's where the real work of unarchiving a To Do document is performed. Add the prototype for the method to ToDoDocument's list of private methods and a new instance variable `NSData *dataFromFile;`, then fill in the implementation as shown in Example 13-16.

Example 13-16. Implementation of ToDoDocument's loadDocWithData: Method

```
- (void)loadDocWithData:(NSData *)data
{
    NSEnumerator *dayEnum, *itemEnum;
    ToDoItem *anItem = nil;
    NSArray *itemArray;
    NSDate *itemDate, *now, *due;
    NSMutableDictionary *dict;
    NSTimeInterval elapsed;

    if (data) {
        dict = [NSUnarchiver unarchiveObjectWithData:data];

        [self initDataModelWithDictionary:dict];

        dayEnum = [activeDays keyEnumerator];
        now = [NSDate date];
        while ((itemDate - [dayEnum nextObject])) {
```

Example 13-16. Implementation of ToDoDocument's loadDocWithData: Method (continued)

```
            itemArray = [activeDays objectForKey:itemDate];
            itemEnum = [itemArray objectEnumerator];

            while ((anItem = [itemEnum nextObject]))
                if ([anItem isKindOfClass:[ToDoItem class]] &&
                    [anItem secsUntilNotify] &&
                    [anItem status] == INCOMPLETE)
                {
                    due = [[anItem day] addTimeInterval:
                            [anItem secsUntilDue]];
                    elapsed = [due timeIntervalSinceDate:now];
                    if (elapsed > 0)
                        [self setTimerForItem:anItem];
                    else {
                        NSBeep();
                        NSRunAlertPanel(@"To Do", @"%@ on %@ is past due!",
                            nil, nil, nil, [anItem itemName],
                        [due descriptionWithCalendarFormat:
                                @"%b %d, %Y at %I:%M %p"
                                timeZone:[NSTimeZone localTimeZone]
                                locale:nil]);

                        [anItem setSecsUntilNotify:0];
                    }
                }
        }
    } else
        [self initDataModelWithDictionary:nil];

    [self selectItemAtRow:0];
    [self updateLists];

    [dayLabel setStringValue:[[calendar selectedDay]
            descriptionWithCalendarFormat:@"To Do on %a %B %d %Y"
            timeZone:[NSTimeZone defaultTimeZone] locale:nil]];
}
```

This method unarchives the activeDays dictionary and uses it to initialize the controller's data model with the utility function you implemented earlier. Then it looks at all of the ToDo items in the document to see if they have a due date and alarm set. If the due date is in the future, the method creates a new timer and sets it to fire at the proper time. If the due date for an item has already passed, the method puts up an alert warning the user that an item has expired. Finally, the method selects the first ToDo item in the list for today, updates the view, and draws today's date in the document window.

Build and Test

At this point you should have a fully functional multidocument application. Try creating some items and saving the document. Open the document and verify that the timers are being properly recreated.

Optional exercises

You should be able now to supplement the To Do application with other features and behaviors. Try some of the following suggestions:

- **Indicate days with active ToDo items.** Modify the calendar so that days with active ToDo items appear visually different.

- **Implement application preferences.** Make a Preferences panel for the application. Follow what you've done for InfoWindowController, especially if the panel has multiple displays. Some ideas for Preferences include: how long to keep expired ToDoItems before logging and purging them (see the final item in this list), the default document to open upon launch; and the default rescheduling interval (see the next item). Store and retrieve specified preferences as user defaults; for more information, see the NSUserDefaults specification.

- **Implement rescheduling.** To Do's Info window has a Rescheduling display that does almost nothing now. Implement the capability for rescheduling items by the period specified.

- **Implement logging and purging.** After a certain period (set via Preferences), append expired ToDoItems (as formatted text) to a log and expunge the ToDoItems from the application.

14

To Do: Finishing Touches

In Chapter 12, *To Do: Basics*, you created the basic infrastructure of the To Do application, and in Chapter 13, *To Do: Extended*, you built on the basic framework to implement more advanced functionality. In this chapter, you'll polish up the To Do application and add some finishing touches. You'll:

- Configure final application settings in Project Builder

- Add an application icon

- Add document type information (and a document icon)

- Improve application performance using compiler optimizations

This chapter uses the To Do application as an example, but everything covered applies equally to all Cocoa applications (with the exception of the document type information, which is relevant only to multidocument applications).

Configure Application Settings

There are many application specific settings in Project Builder that allow you to control various aspects of an application's behavior. This section doesn't exhaustively cover every option (see Project Builder's online help for more information) but shows you what to do for the settings that are critical to correct application behavior.

Specify a Bundle Identifier

Bundle identifiers are the method Mac OS X uses to uniquely identify applications (and, in fact, any bundle). In one sense, a bundle identifier is very much like the creator code used by Mac OS 9 to identify applications. In Mac OS X, applications (including the Finder) use a framework called Launch Services to find out about registered apps, the documents and the URL schemes they open, and related information. Launch Services also provides APIs to open documents and launch apps. For example, when you double-click a document in the Finder (or click an alias in the Dock), Launch Services looks at the document's type and file extension, and—using a bundle identifier—locates the application to which the document belongs.

It is critical for Mac OS X applications to define a proper bundle identifier. Because this identifier must be unique, Apple has adopted the Java-style package naming convention. These names take the form of Internet domain names in reverse. For example, the Apple version of the ToDo application would use com.apple.ToDo as its bundle identifier. You should choose an appropriate identifier for your applications based on your personal or company domain name.

To specify a bundle identifier, click the Application Settings tab in the Target options area of Project Builder's main window, as shown in Figure 14-1. In the Basic Information area, enter the identifier string.

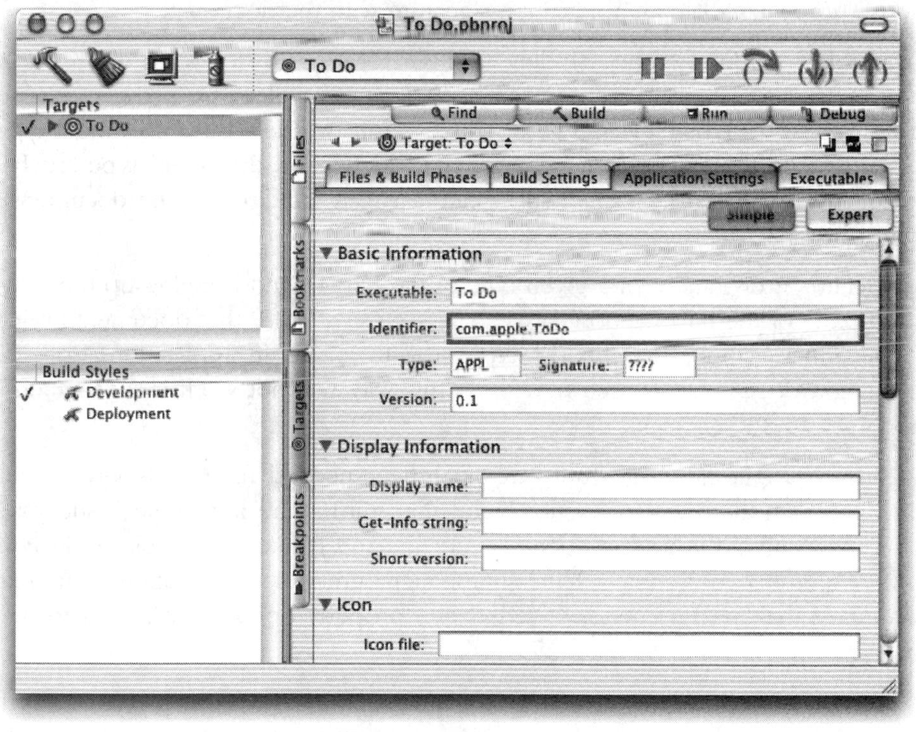

Figure 14-1. Project Builder's Application Settings pane

Specify an Application Signature

In addition to a bundle identifier, you can specify an *application signature* (also called a *creator code*) for your application. An application signature is a unique four-character code that Launch Services can use to identify the application that owns a given document. The signature itself is the same as Mac OS 9—a four-character OSType. As it applies to Classic applications and the Classic desktop database, the use is the same as in Mac OS 9. Launch Services gives precedent to the application signature when looking for an application with which to open a document.

If your application has an application signature and the document shares that creator, the document is said to be *strongly bound* to an application. Removing the document filename's extension (if it has one) will have no effect on the choice of application to open the document. As long as a document retains an application signature, that application will be called upon to handle the document. Of course, if you don't want the document to be strongly bound to your application, you can choose not to associate an application signature with the document.

In fact, the preferred launch-binding solution for X is to not write out a creator code with a document, which means the document will open in the user's preferred app for its type (selected in the Finder's Info window for a document type). This is usually the appropriate behavior for widely used document types such as images and text files. Users can still create a strong binding for the document in Finder if they wish, as shown in Figure 14-2.

By selecting a document of a given type in the Finder, and bringing up the Application pane of the Info window, a user can choose to have that document opened by the generic application for the type or with a specifc application. Note that changing a document's launch binding in this way will not work if a document is strongly bound to an application.

In general, application signatures are no longer needed for OS X–only applications, although there are some subsystems that still require it. One such subsystem is InternetConfig; if your app opens documents and is likely to be placed in InternetConfig, it is a good idea to have an app signature. Also, applications that create documents that need a creator code to open properly on OS 9 will want to write out a creator code.

A database of application signatures is maintained by Apple, and you can verify that the one you have chosen for your app is unique and then register it with Apple at *http://developer.apple.com/dev/cftype/register.html*.

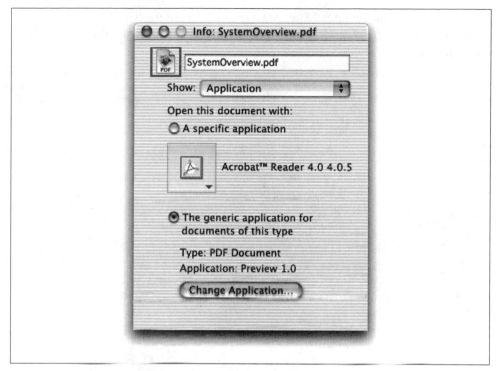

Figure 14-2. Changing the launch binding of a document in the Finder

Specify Display Information

The Display Name is the name that appears in the menu bar of the application. It should contain only one or two words and a maximum of 16 characters so it doesn't take up too much room in the menu bar. For this application, To Do is an appropriate name to use.

The Get-Info string is any information you want to appear in the Finder's Info window (see Figure 14-3). Generally it is the bundle's full name, version number, and copyright information, but it can be anything you want.

Short Version is the version number (for example, 1.0).

Add an Application Icon

The developer tools package on Mac OS X contains a very simple utility called Icon Composer that converts images into Mac OS X–style icon files. Using a standard graphics application, you can create art for your icon, save it as a 32-bit image in TIFF, PICT, or Photoshop format, then import it into Icon Composer. Once the image has been imported, Icon Composer can create icon masks for icon sizes that require one. Icon Composer saves files in the icns format used by Mac

OS X to store icon families. The Aqua Human Interface Guidelines document (*http://developer.apple.com/techpubs/macosx*) provides essential information about creating icons for Mac OS X.

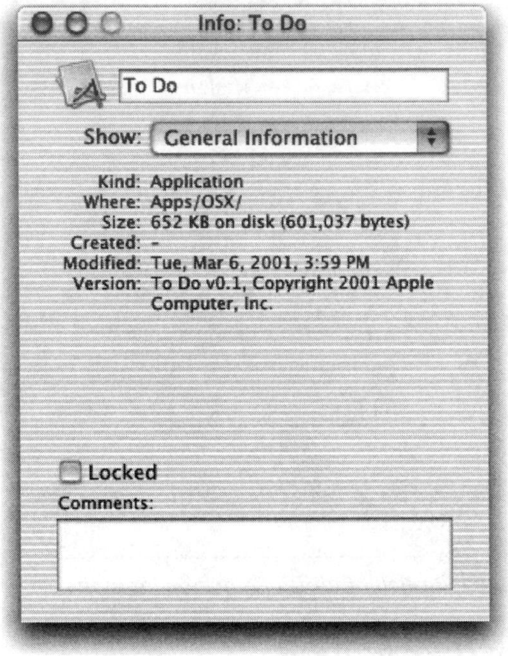

Figure 14-3. A Finder Info window showing To Do's Get-Info string

For those comfortable working with Adobe Photoshop, this section explains how to use that application to create source art for an icon in just a few seconds. If you aren't familiar with Photoshop, you can use the ToDo.tiff file included with the sample files, and skip the first four following steps:

1. Launch Photoshop and make a new a 128 × 128 pixel image with a transparent background.

2. Draw or copy/paste your art into the document.

3. Create a new image channel using the Channels tab. This new channel will function as an alpha mask. Paint the areas of the mask that you wish to be transparent in the Finder and in the Dock.

4. Save the file as a TIFF image. This is the recommended format for image files used in Cocoa.

5. Launch the Icon Composer application in `/Developer/Applications`.

6. Choose Import Image from the File menu. Icon Composer's Open dialog box features a pop-up menu that lets you specify what kind of icon to make from the imported image. You'll need a thumbnail icon at the very least, so select Thumbnail 32 Bit Data from the Import To pop up at the bottom of the dialog box and open the TIFF document.

7. Drag and drop the image from the Thumbnail row to the Huge, Large, and Small rows (see Figure 14-4). Icon Composer will automatically scale the image for each size. If your icon imagery doesn't scale well, you can create variations for each so users can clearly identify your application's icon no matter the icon size. the section "Add an Application Icon" shows the finished `ToDo.icns` file in Icon Composer's main window if you choose to create icons in all available sizes.

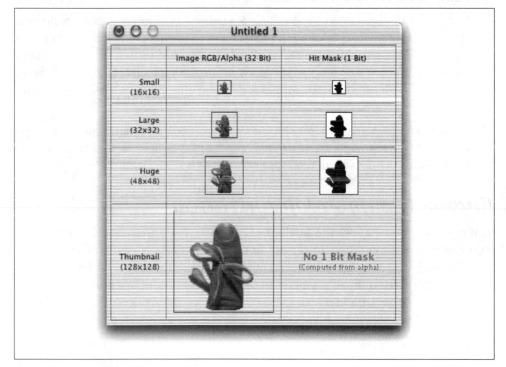

Figure 14-4. Completed To Do icon

8. Save the file from Icon Composer as `ToDoApp.icns`.

9. Add the icon file to the Project Builder project. It's a good idea to copy the file into the project directory so it will travel with the project.

10. In the Application Settings pane, type the name of the icon file in the text field labeled Icon.

11. Build the project. You should see the new icon in the Finder, and it should appear in the Dock when the app is launched.

Define a Document Type for To Do

You already learned about Document Types in Chapter 11, *Cocoa's Multiple-Document Architecture*, so setting up the To Do document type should be old hat:

1. In Project Builder, select the default document type in the Document Types listing. Change its name to **ToDoDocument**.

2. Leave the role set to Editor.

3. Make the document extension tdo.

4. In the section "Specify an Application Signature," you learned that application signatures can be associated with a document to create a "strongly bound document." You can add the To Do application signature to the To Do document type now if you wish; simply type **ToDo** in the OS types list. If you don't want to create a strongly bound application, leave this blank (delete the default entry "????").

5. To associate an icon with this document type, follow the same procedure you used in the previous section to create an application icon, and then specify the name of the document icon file.

Enable Compiler Optimization

In this section you'll apply the final bit of polish to the application by turning on compiler optimization. You can choose from several levels of optimization; in general, the higher the optimization level, the longer compilation will take to complete, and the more difficult it will be to debug the application. Choose Developer Tools Help in Project Builder's Help menu for more information about optimizing your application.

To enable optimization:

1. In Project Builder, select the Build Settings pane of the Target options display as shown in Figure 14-5.

2. Choose a deployment optimization level.

When you're ready to build final candidate versions of your application, select Deployment from the Build Styles pane. This will enable the optimization level that you selected.

If you wish, select an installation location. This is the folder where the application will be copied when the build is complete. This makes testing the finished app outside of Project Builder simple.

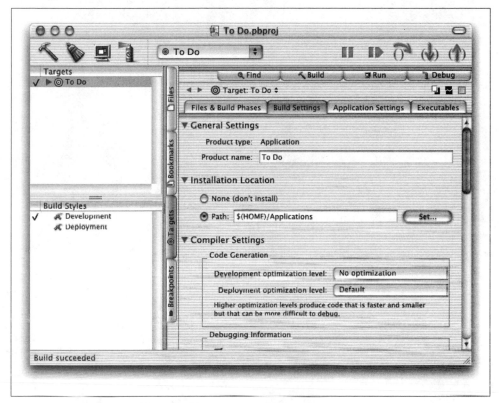

Figure 14-5. Project Builder's Build Settings window

IV

Reference

A

Drawing in Cocoa

Cocoa's Application Kit provides you with a wide array of ready-made user interface objects. However, most complex applications will require at least a few custom interface elements. In addition, many applications need to perform custom drawing in order to display data. This appendix explains the basics of Cocoa's imaging model and shows you how to create custom graphics.

In order to use the drawing facilities of Cocoa to their maximum potential, it is important to learn about Quartz, the imaging model underlying all graphics in Mac OS X. Quartz is based on Adobe's Portable Document Format (PDF), which is in turn based on the Adobe PostScript imaging model. A complete description of Quartz, PostScript, and PDF is beyond the scope of this appendix. Look to the many excellent third-party books that are available, such as the *PostScript Language Reference* from Adobe (known as the "Red Book") and the PDF 1.3 specification (*http://www.pdfzone.com/resources/pdfspec13.html*).

Coordinate Systems

The *screen coordinate system* is the basis for all other coordinate systems used for positioning, sizing, drawing, and event handling. You can think of the entire screen as occupying the upper-right quadrant of a two-dimensional coordinate grid as shown in Figure A-1. The other three quadrants, which are invisible to users, take negative values along their *x*-axis, their *y*-axis, or both axes. The screen's quadrant has its origin in the lower-left corner; the positive *x*-axis extends horizontally to the right and the positive *y*-axis extends vertically upward. A unit along either axis is expressed as a pixel.

Note that although Figure A-1 represents the screen coordinate system using the example of a single display device, the screen coordinate system is really a logical rectangular area that is determined by the union of all screen rectangles of all physical framebuffers attached to the computer. The origin lies at the lower-left corner of that unioned rectangle.

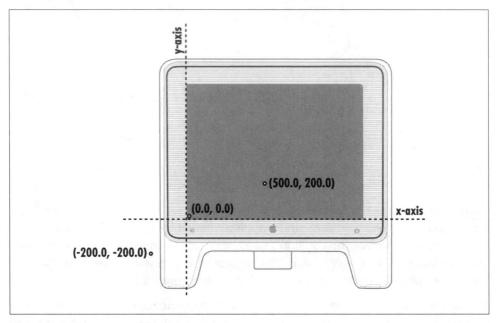

Figure A-1. Screen coordinate system

The screen coordinate system has just one function: to position windows on the screen. When your application creates a new window, it must specify the window's initial size and location in screen coordinates.

The reference coordinate system for a window (Figure A-2) is known as the *base coordinate system.* It differs from the screen coordinate system in only two ways:

- It applies only to a particular window; each window has its own base coordinate system.

- Its origin is at the lower-left corner of the window, rather than the lower-left corner of the screen. If the window moves, the origin and the entire coordinate system move with it.

For drawing, each NSView (detailed in Chapter 8, *Event Handling*, and the section "NSView," later in this chapter) uses a coordinate system transformed from the base coordinate system or from the coordinate system of its superview. This coordinate system also has its origin point at the lower-left corner of the NSView, making it more convenient for drawing operations. NSView has several methods for converting between base and local coordinate systems. When you draw, coordinates are expressed in the application's current coordinate system.

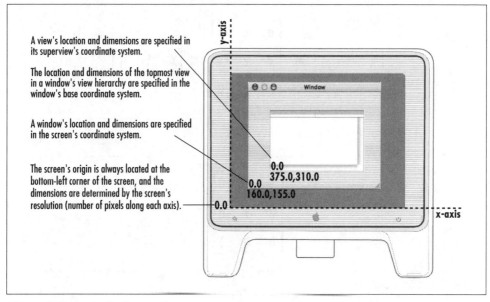

Figure A-2. A window's coordinate system

Before drawing into a particular NSView, focus has to be "locked" onto that view (using NSView's lockFocus method, which you'll learn more about later in this chapter). This causes NSView's coordinate system to become the current coordinate system; i.e., the one to which all drawing commands apply.

Transformation Matrices

A *transformation matrix* maps points from one coordinate space into another coordinate space. Cocoa and Quartz use transformation matrices to perform standard graphical display operations such as scaling, rotation, and translation.

The matrix used to accomplish two-dimensional transformations is described by a 3 × 3 matrix. Figure A-3 shows a sample 3 × 3 matrix. Note that u and v are always 0.0, and w is always 1.

The contents of a 3 × 3 matrix transform a point (x, y) into a point (x', y') by means of the following equations:

$$x' = ax + cy + t_x$$

$$y' = bx + dy + t_y$$

For example, the matrix shown in Figure A-4 performs no translation. It is referred to as the *identity matrix*.

Using the formulas discussed earlier, you can see that this matrix would generate a new point (x', y') that is the same as the old point (x, y):

$$\begin{bmatrix} X & Y & 1 \end{bmatrix} \times \begin{bmatrix} a & b & u \\ c & d & v \\ t_x & t_y & w \end{bmatrix} = \begin{bmatrix} X^1 & Y^1 & 1 \end{bmatrix}$$

Figure A-3. A point transformed by a 3 × 3 matrix

$$\begin{bmatrix} 1 & 0 & 0 \\ 0 & 1 & 0 \\ 0 & 0 & 1 \end{bmatrix}$$

Figure A-4. The identity matrix

$$x' = 1x + 0y + 0$$

$$y' = 0x + 1y + 0$$

$$x' = x \text{ and } y' = y$$

To move an image by a specified displacement, you can perform a translation operation. This operation modifies the x and y coordinates of each point by a specified amount. The matrix shown in Figure A-5 describes a translation operation.

$$\begin{bmatrix} 1 & 0 & 0 \\ 0 & 1 & 0 \\ t_x & t_y & 1 \end{bmatrix}$$

Figure A-5. A matrix that describes a translation operation

You can stretch or shrink an image by performing a scaling operation. This operation modifies the x and y coordinates by some scaling factor. The magnitude of the x and y factors governs whether the new images are larger or smaller than the original. In addition, by making the x factor negative, you can flip the image about the x-axis; similarly, you can flip the image horizontally, about the y-axis, by making the y factor negative. The matrix shown in Figure A-6 describes a scaling operation.

$$\begin{bmatrix} s_x & 0 & 0 \\ 0 & s_y & 0 \\ 0 & 0 & 1 \end{bmatrix}$$

Figure A-6. A matrix that describes a scaling operation

Finally, you can rotate an image by a specified angle by performing a rotation operation. You specify the magnitude and direction of the rotation by specifying factors for both x and y. The matrix shown in Figure A-7 rotates an image counter-clockwise by an angle, θ.

$$\begin{bmatrix} \cos(\theta) & \sin(\theta) & 0 \\ -\sin(\theta) & -\cos(\theta) & 0 \\ 0 & 0 & 1 \end{bmatrix}$$

Figure A-7. A matrix that describes a rotation operation

You can combine matrices that define different transformations into a single matrix. The resulting matrix retains the attributes of both transformations. For example, you can both scale and translate an image by defining a matrix similar to that shown in Figure A-8.

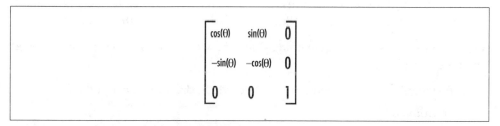

$$\begin{bmatrix} s_x & 0 & 0 \\ 0 & s_y & 0 \\ 0 & 0 & 1 \end{bmatrix} \times \begin{bmatrix} 1 & 0 & 0 \\ 0 & 1 & 0 \\ t_x & t_y & 1 \end{bmatrix} = \begin{bmatrix} s_x & 0 & 0 \\ 0 & s_y & 0 \\ t_x & t_y & 1 \end{bmatrix}$$

Figure A-8. A matrix that describes a scaling and translation operation

You combine two matrices by concatenating them. Mathematically, the two matrices are combined by matrix multiplication. Note that the order in which you concatenate matrices is important—matrix operations are not commutative.

Functions for working with transformation matrices can be found in the Application Kit's `NSAffineTransform.h` and Core Graphics's `CGAffineTransform.h`. Later in this chapter, the section "Draw with Quartz Primitives" contains an example of using a transformation matrix to scale an image.

NSView

All objects that inherit from NSView can render themselves on the screen. To be displayed, an NSView must be placed in an NSWindow. NSViews draw themselves by making calls to the Core Graphics (Quartz) programming interface.

Graphically, an NSView can be regarded as a framed canvas. The frame locates the NSView in its superview, defines its size, and clips drawing to its edges, while the canvas defines the NSView's own internal coordinate system and hosts the actual drawing. The frame can be moved around, resized, and rotated in the superview, so that the NSView's image moves with it. Similarly, the canvas can be shifted, stretched, and rotated, so that the drawn image moves within the frame.

NSView represents a context within which drawing can take place. This context has three components:

- A rectangular frame within a window to which drawing is clipped
- A coordinate system
- The current graphics state

NSView draws itself as an indirect result of receiving the `display` message (or a variant of `display`); this message is sent explicitly or through conditions that cause automatic display. The `display` message leads to the invocation of an NSView's `drawRect:` method and the `drawRect:` methods of all subviews of that NSView. The `drawRect:` method should contain all code needed to redraw the NSView completely.

An NSView object can be automatically displayed when:

- Users scroll it (assuming it supports scrolling)
- Users resize or expose the NSView's window
- The window receives a display message or is automatically updated
- An attribute changes for some Application Kit objects

Frame and bounds

NSView's frame specifies the location and dimensions of the NSView in terms of the coordinate system of the NSView's superview. It is a rectangle that encloses the NSView, as shown in Figure A-9.

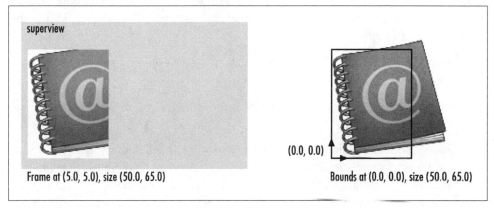

Figure A-9. Frame and Bounds

You can programmatically move, resize, and rotate the NSView within its super-view by reference to its frame (setFrameOrigin:, setFrameSize:, and so on).

To draw efficiently, the NSView must have its frame rectangle translated into its own coordinate system. This translated rectangle, suitable for drawing, is called the *bounds*. The bounds rectangle usually specifies exactly the same area as the frame rectangle, but it specifies that area in a different coordinate system. In the default coordinate system, an NSView's bounds is the same as its frame, except that the point locating the frame becomes the origin of the bounds ($x = 0.0, y = 0.0$). The *x*- and *y*-axes of the default coordinate system run parallel to the sides of the frame, so, for example, if you rotate the frame, the default coordinate system rotates with it. This relationship between frame and bounds has several implications important in drawing and compositing:

- Each NSView's coordinate system is a transformation of its superview's.

- Drawing instructions don't have to account for an NSView's location on the screen or its orientation.

- Changes in a superview's coordinate system are propagated to its subviews.

NSView allows you to flip coordinate systems (so the positive *y*-axis runs down-ward) and to otherwise alter coordinate systems.

Focus

Before a `display...` method invokes an NSView's `drawRect:`, it sets up Core Graphics with information about the view, including the graphics context it draws in, the coordinate system and clipping path it uses, and other graphics state information. The method used to do this is `lockFocus`. There is a companion method that undoes the effects of `lockFocus`, called `unlockFocus`. Focusing modifies the current graphics state by:

- Making the NSView's window the current graphics context

- Creating a clipping path around the NSView's frame

- Making the Core Graphics coordinate system match the NSView's coordinate system

All drawing code invoked by an NSView must be bracketed by invocations of these methods to produce proper results. If you define some methods that need to draw in a view without going through the `display...` methods, you must send `lockFocus` to the view that you're drawing in before sending commands to Core Graphics and send `unlockFocus` as soon as you are done.

Only one NSView can have focus at a time—if focus is already locked onto another NSView when `lockFocus` is invoked, it is put on a stack so focus can be restored to it the next time `unlockFocus` is called.

Note that every `lockFocus` must be balanced by exactly one `unlockFocus`.

Composite Images

The other technique NSViews use to render their appearance is *image compositing*. Compositing allows you to copy images as well as build a new image by overlaying images that were previously drawn. It's like a photographer printing a picture from two negatives, one placed on top of the other. Various compositing operators determine how the source and destination images merge. Three basic operators are depicted in Figure A-10.

NSImage allows you to copy images into your user interface. It uses various subclasses of NSImageRep to store the multiple representations of the same image—color, grayscale, TIFF, PDF, and so on—and chooses the representation appropriate for a given type of display. NSImage can read image data from a file in a bundle (including the application's main bundle), from the pasteboard, or from an NSData object. By compositing (with the SourceOver operator), NSViews can simply display an image within their frame. You usually composite an image using NSImage's `compositeToPoint:operation:` (or a related method). You can achieve interesting effects with compositing when the initial images are drawn with partially transparent paint.

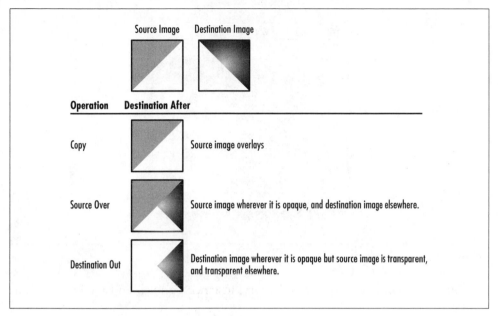

Figure A-10. Basic compositing operator

The CompositeLab application in /Developer/Examples/AppKit contains examples of how to do compositing in Cocoa.

Draw NSStrings

As a very simple introduction to drawing, in this section you'll create an application that renders a string into the upper-left corner of a custom NSView subclass:

1. Create a new Cocoa application project called Simple Draw.

2. Open the main nib file.

3. Create a subclass of NSView called MyView.

4. Create the files for MyView and add them to the project.

5. Make the application's window a bit smaller and drag a custom view from the More Views palette to the window, as shown in Figure A-11.

6. Select CustomView, bring up the Info window, and change the view's class to MyView.

Figure A-11. Adding a custom view object to the interface

7. Open MyView.h and add the following instance varibles and method declarations.

   These instance variables and setter methods allow the view to maintain a notion of the current string and the current font. Changing either will cause the view to redraw using the new object.

   ```
   @interface MyView: NSView
   {
       NSString *string;
       NSFont *font;
   }

   - (void)setString:(NSString *)value;
   - (void)setFont:(NSFont *)value;
   - (BOOL)isFlipped;

   @end
   ```

8. Open MyView.m and add the isFlipped method. This method flips the origin of the coordinate system to the upper-left corner of the view:

   ```
   - (BOOL)isFlipped
   {
       return YES;
   }
   ```

9. Override the `initWithFrame:` method to set the default string and font for the view:

```
- (id)initWithFrame:(NSRect)frame
{
    [super initWithFrame:frame];
    [self setString: @"Hello World"];
    [self setFont: [NSFont systemFontOfSize: 12]];
    return self;
}
```

10. Implement the `setString:` method:

```
- (void)setString:(NSString *)value
{
    [string autorelease];
    string = [value copy];
    [self setNeedsDisplay: YES];
}
```

11. Implement the `setFont:` method:

```
- (void)setFont:(NSFont *)value
{
    [font autorelease];
    font = [value retain];
    [self setNeedsDisplay: YES];
}
```

12. Implement the `drawRect:` method. The `drawAtPoint:` method renders the string in the view, starting one-quarter of the width of the view and 5 pixels down from the top of the view:

```
- (void)drawRect:(NSRect)rect
{
    NSRect myBounds = [self bounds];
    NSMutableDictionary *attrs = [NSMutableDictionary dictionary];

    [attrs setObject: font forKey: NSFontAttributeName];
    [string drawAtPoint:
            NSMakePoint((myBounds size.width/4.0), 5) withAttributes: attrs];
}
```

Notice that this example uses `[self bounds]` instead of `rect` to determine where to draw. The `rect` parameter that is passed into the `drawRect:` method is just the sub-area of the view that needs updating and could change from invocation to invocation—for example, if the view is being scrolled slowly inside a scroll view. The difference isn't noticeable if you just put the view into a window, but it's critical for code reuse. If you're not using `[self bounds]`, there will be big problems when the view is put into a scroll view or if it's involved in optimized drawing using `setNeedsDisplayInRect:`.

NSBezierPath

An NSBezierPath object allows you to create paths using PostScript-style commands. Paths consist of straight and curved line segments joined together. Paths can form recognizable shapes such as rectangles, ovals, arcs, and glyphs; they can also form complex polygons using either straight or curved line segments. A single path can be closed by connecting its two endpoints, or it can be left open.

An NSBezierPath object can contain multiple disconnected paths, whether they are closed or open. Each of these paths is referred to as a "subpath" of the NSBezierPath object. The subpaths of an NSBezierPath object must be manipulated as a group. The only way to manipulate subpaths individually is to create separate NSBezierPath objects for each.

For a given NSBezierPath object, you can stroke the path's outline or fill the region occupied by the path. You can also use the path as a clipping region for views or other regions. Using methods of NSBezierPath, you can also perform hit detection on the filled or stroked path. Hit detection is needed to implement interactive graphics, as in rubber banding and dragging operations.

Construct Paths

You can create an instance of NSBezierPath using either of the class methods `bezierPath` or `bezierPathWithRect:`. The `bezierPath` method initializes a new Bezier-path object with an empty path while the `bezierPathWithRect:` method creates a path with the specified rectangle. (You can also allocate memory for a new instance of NSBezierPath and use the default initializer, the `init` method, to initialize it to an empty path).

To add path information to an NSBezierPath object, you must invoke a sequence of path construction methods such as the `moveToPoint:`, `lineToPoint:`, and `curveToPoint:controlPoint1:controlPoint2:` methods. For example, to create a polygon path, send a `moveToPoint:` message, followed by a series of `lineToPoint:` messages, to the NSBezierPath object. When you are done adding points to the path and want to form a closed path, send a `closePath` message to connect the last point back to the starting point (see Figure A-12).

The order in which path construction methods are invoked is significant. Line segments connect only if they are defined consecutively. A path may be made up of one or more disconnected subpaths, which can themselves be either open or closed. The current point is the last point of the most recently added line segment.

Most construction methods implicitly use the current point as the starting point of the next segment. If you want to create a new subpath, you must explicitly invoke moveToPoint: first. For example, lineToPoint: adds a line segment from the current point to the specified point. Some methods may implicitly invoke moveToPoint:, thereby creating a new subpath automatically. See the method descriptions for more information.

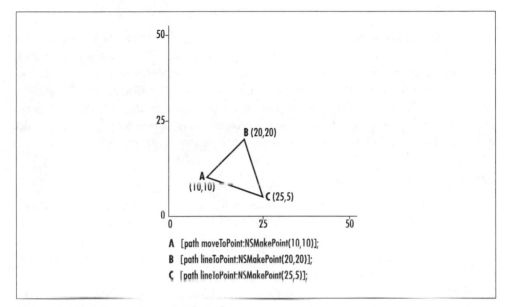

Figure A-12. Constructing a simple path

There are convenience methods for appending paths and common shapes to an existing path. The new path is usually discontiguous from the receiver's original path, although the appendBezierPathWithPoints:count: method creates a contiguous path from the specified points. Use the appendBezierPath... methods to append a path to an NSBezierPath object as in this example, which uses appendBezierPathWithOvalInRect: to create a circle:

```
NSRect aRect = NSMakeRect(0.0, 0.0, 50.0, 50.0);
aPath = [[NSBezierPath bezierPath] appendBezierPathWithOvalInRect:aRect];
```

Path Elements

No matter which construction methods you use, all paths are reduced to a sequence of data points and common element types corresponding to the methods moveToPoint:, lineToPoint:, curveToPoint:controlPoint1:controlPoint2:, and closePath.

These element types can be specified with the following constants from the enumerated type NSBezierPathElement:

- * `NSMoveToBezierPathElement`
- * `NSLineToBezierPathElement`
- * `NSCurveToBezierPathElement`
- * `NSCloseBezierPathElement`

Every element except `NSCloseBezierPathElement` has at least one data point associated with it. The only element that has more than one data point is `NSCurveTo-BezierPathElement` (which maintains additional control points to define the shape of the curve). NSBezierPath defines several methods for obtaining information about the path elements (and their associated points) directly, including `elementAtIndex:` and `elementTypeAtIndex:associatedPoints:`, among others. You could use these methods to break down a path and reconstruct it point by point.

Draw Paths

You typically render NSBezierPath objects inside an NSView's `drawRect:` method. At the time the `drawRect:` method is invoked, the focus is locked on the view and all drawing operations are clipped to that view. Therefore, most of the time you will want to construct paths whose points are specified in the view's coordinate system. You could also construct a path using an arbitrary coordinate system and transform the path to a view's coordinate system using an NSAffineTransform object. An NSAffineTransform object can translate, scale, and rotate paths (see the NSAffineTransform class specification in the online Cocoa documentation for details).

Before filling or stroking an NSBezierPath object, you should set the graphics attributes to use for the path. You can use the `set . . .` methods of NSBezierPath to set such attributes as the line cap style, line join style, line width, miter limit, curve flatness, and halftone phase. Other attributes must be set using the appropriate objects. For example, you set the color in the current graphics context by sending `set` to an NSColor object.

You can use either the `stroke` or `fill` method to render a path. The `stroke` method draws a line along the receiver's path using the color, line width, cap and join styles, and the curve flatness drawing attributes in the current graphics context. The `fill` method renders the path by painting the region enclosed by the path and uses the color and curve flatness attributes. The `fill` method performs a close operation (invoke `closePath`) if the path is not already closed. (A subpath is closed if the ending point is connected to the starting point; otherwise, the subpath is opened).

As a convenience, some class methods are provided for drawing immediate shapes without the creation of an NSBezierPath object. For example, you can use the `fillRect:` and `strokeRect:` class methods to draw a filled rectangle or outline of a rectangle, and use the `strokeLineFromPoint:toPoint:` class method to draw a line segment.

Draw with NSBezierPath

In this section you'll modify the Simple Draw application you created in the section "Draw NSStrings," to draw some simple shapes in the view using NSBezier-Path.

Draw Lines and Rectangles

You'll begin your exploration of NSBezierPath by extending Simple Draw's `drawRect:` method so that it will:

- Fill the view with an opaque white background

- Bisect the view with a pair of light gray crosshairs

- Draw a thin black border around the view

Here's how it works:

Open `MyView.m` and extend the `drawRect:` implementation as follows:

```
- (void)drawRect:(NSRect)rect
{
    NSRect myBounds = [self bounds];
    NSMutableDictionary *attrs = [NSMutableDictionary dictionary];

    // Paint a white background.
    [[NSColor whiteColor] set];
    [NSBezierPath fillRect:myBounds];

    // Draw some crosshairs on the view.
    [[NSColor lightGrayColor] set];

    [NSBezierPath strokeLineFromPoint:
            NSMakePoint(0,(myBounds.size.height/2.0))
            toPoint:NSMakePoint(myBounds.size.width, (myBounds.size.height/2.0))];

    [NSBezierPath strokeLineFromPoint:
            NSMakePoint((myBounds.size.width/2.0), 0)
            toPoint:NSMakePoint((myBounds.size.width/2.0), myBounds.size.height)];

    // Draw a black border around the view.
    [[NSColor blackColor] set];
    [NSBezierPath strokeRect:myBounds];
```

```
        // Render a string.
        [attrs setObject: font forKey: NSFontAttributeName];
        [string drawAtPoint:
                NSMakePoint((myBounds.size.width/4.0), 5) withAttributes: attrs];
    }
```

The new version of the drawRect: method starts by creating an NSColor object initialized to the color white and then sends it the set method. set changes the current color for the graphics context so all subsequent drawing is rendered using the specified color. Then, drawRect: uses the NSBezierPath class method fillRect: to fill MyView with white. Next, drawRect: changes the current color to light gray and draws two lines that split the view into quarters. After drawing the crosshairs, the method draws a black border around the view using the using NSBezierPath's strokeRect: method. Finally, drawRect: renders the string as before.

Build and run the application. You should see something like the results shown in Figure A-13.

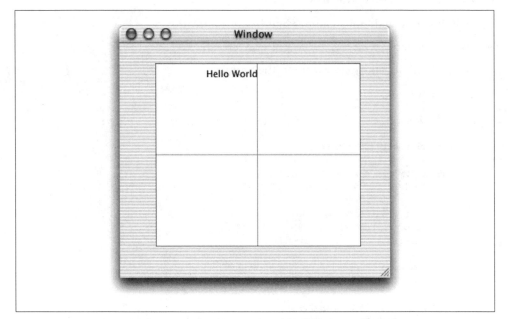

Figure A-13. MyView with opaque background and bisecting crosshairs

Draw Complex Shapes

In this section you'll extend the class even further so that it draws an arrow and circle with a plus sign in it. This part of the example uses an interesting technique wherein you create a model using NSBezierPath and then render the model into the view using transformation matrices. You can think of this process as being analogous to a rubber stamp: the model is the shape on the stamp, but the stamp is movable, stretchable, and rotatable using the transformation matrices, and the paper is the view.

Here how it works:

1. Open `MyView.h` and add instance variable declarations for the arrow and circle:

   ```
   NSBezierPath *arrowPath;
   NSBezierPath *circlePath;
   ```

2. Add declarations for `awakeFromNib` and `isOpaque`:

   ```
   - (void)awakeFromNib;
   - (BOOL)isOpaque;
   ```

3. Add declarations for the accessor methods for the models:

   ```
   - (NSBezierPath *)arrowPath;
   - (void)setArrowPath: (NSBezierPath *)newPath;

   - (NSBezierPath *)circlePath;
   - (void)setCirclePath: (NSBezierPath *)newPath;
   ```

4. Add declarations for the methods that create and draw the models:

   ```
   - (NSBezierPath *)createArrowPath;
   - (NSBezierPath *)createCirclePath;

   - (void)drawArrow;
   - (void)drawCircle;
   ```

5. Open `MyView.m` and add the implementations `isOpaque` and `awakeFromNib`. The `awakeFromNib` method invokes the methods to create the arrow and circle models for the class. `isOpaque` is a performance hint for the drawing subsystem.

   ```
   - (void)awakeFromNib
   {
       [self setArrowPath: [self createArrowPath]];
       [self setCirclePath: [self createCirclePath]];
   }

   - (BOOL)isOpaque
   {
       return YES;
   }
   ```

6. Modify `drawRect:` so that it calls the draw methods to render the arrow and circle. Add these to the end of the method implementation:

   ```
   /* ... */
       [self drawArrow];
       [self drawCircle];
   ```

7. Implement the accessor methods for the models:

```
- (NSBezierPath *)arrowPath
{
    return arrowPath;
}

- (void)setArrowPath:(NSBezierPath *)newPath
{
    [newPath retain];
    [arrowPath release];
    arrowPath = newPath;
}

- (NSBezierPath *)circlePath
{
    return circlePath;
}

- (void)setCirclePath:(NSBezierPath *)newPath
{
    [newPath retain];
    [circlePath release];
    circlePath = newPath;
}
```

8. Now, here's where it starts to get interesting.

Add the implementation for `createArrowPath` as shown in Example A-1. This is where the work of creating the NSBezierPath model for the arrow happens. The comments in the example explain the process.

Example A-1. Implementation for the createArrowPath Method

```
- (NSBezierPath *)createArrowPath
{
    // An NSPoint that is reused to create the arrow model.
    NSPoint point;

    // The ratio of arrowhead to arrow length
    float headLengthRatio = 0.30;

    // The ratio between the base midpoint and the actual point.
    // at which the arrowhead baselines meet.
    float headBaseRatio = 0.70;

    // The half-angle width of the arrowhead in radians.
    float arrowHeadWidth = 0.3;

    // The Bezier path used to draw the arrow.
    NSBezierPath *model = [NSBezierPath bezierPath];

    // Start the drawing process by moving to the origin at (0,0).
    point.x = 0;
```

Example A-1. Implementation for the createArrowPath Method (continued)

```
    point.y = 0;
    [model moveToPoint:point];

    // Draw a line to the middle point of the base of the arrowhead.
    point.x = 1 - (headLengthRatio*headBaseRatio);
    [model lineToPoint:point];

    // Draw line to the upper base point of the arrowhead.
    point.x = 1 - headLengthRatio;
    point.y = headLengthRatio* tan(arrowHeadWidth);
    [model lineToPoint:point];

    // Draw line to the tip of the arrowhead.
    point.x = 1;
    point.y = 0;
    [model lineToPoint:point];

    // Draw line to the lower base point of the arrowhead.
    point.x = 1 - headLengthRatio;
    point.y = -(headLengthRatio* tan(arrowHeadWidth));
    [model lineToPoint:point];

    // Draw line to the middle point of the base of the arrowhead.
    point.x = 1 - (headLengthRatio*headBaseRatio);
    point.y = 0;
    [model lineToPoint:point];

    // Finish drawing.
    [model closePath];

    return model;
}
```

9. Now implement the method that creates the circle model, as shown in Example A-2. The process is very similar to the previous step that creates the arrow model.

Example A-2. Implementation for the createCirclePath Method

```
- (NSBezierPath *)createCirclePath
{
    // An NSPoint that is reused to create the arrow model.
    NSPoint point;

    NSBezierPath *model = [NSBezierPath bezierPath];

    // Create simple circle with its center at (0,0).
    point.x = 0;
    point.y = 0;
    [model appendBezierPathWithArcWithCenter:point
            radius:1.0 startAngle:0 endAngle:360];
```

Example A-2. Implementation for the createCirclePath Method (continued)

```
    // Draw a plus sign.
    // Start with a horizontal line.
    point.x = .5;
    point.y = 0;
    [model moveToPoint:point];

    point.x = -.5;
    [model lineToPoint:point];

    // Draw the vertical line.
    point.x = 0;
    point.y = .5;
    [model moveToPoint:point];

    point.y = -.5;
    [model lineToPoint:point];

    return model;
}
```

10. Now add the implementation for the method that actually draws the arrow model into the view, as shown in Example A-3. This is where the transformation matricies are used to modify the arrow model before it is rendered into the view.

Example A-3. Implementation for the drawArrow Method

```
- (void)drawArrow
{
    // A reference to the model that will be drawn.
    NSBezierPath *arrowToDraw;

    // Transformation matrices to modify the arrow model.

    NSAffineTransform *scaleMatrix;
    NSAffineTransform *rotationMatrix;
    NSAffineTransform *translationMatrix;

    // This matrix will hold the combined transformations above.
    NSAffineTransform *arrowTransformMatrix;

    // Point onscreen (offset from NSView origin) to start drawing.
    NSPoint screenLocation = NSMakePoint(100, 100);

    // The colors to use for the arrow's outline and fill.
    NSColor *arrowStrokeColor = [NSColor blueColor];
    NSColor *arrowFillColor = [NSColor greenColor];

    // The size of the arrow to draw relative to the model. Change this
    // to draw bigger or smaller arrows.
    float scaleFactor = 100.0;
```

Example A-3. Implementation for the drawArrow Method (continued)

```
    // Create and configure the scaling matrix.
    scaleMatrix = [NSAffineTransform transform];
    [scaleMatrix scaleBy: scaleFactor];

    // Create and configure the rotation matrix.
    rotationMatrix = [NSAffineTransform transform];
    [rotationMatrix rotateByDegrees:45];

    // Create and configure the translation matrix.
    translationMatrix = [NSAffineTransform transform];
    [translationMatrix translateXBy: screenLocation.x
            yBy: screenLocation.y];

    // Combine scaling, rotation, and translation into
    // one matrix operation.
    arrowTransformMatrix = [NSAffineTransform transform];
    [arrowTransformMatrix appendTransform:scaleMatrix];
    [arrowTransformMatrix appendTransform:rotationMatrix];
    [arrowTransformMatrix appendTransform:translationMatrix];

    // Use the combined transformations to modify the model for drawing.
    arrowToDraw = [arrowTransformMatrix transformBezierPath: [self arrowPath]];

    // Draw the arrow outline.
    [arrowStrokeColor set];
    [arrowToDraw setLineWidth:2.0];
    [arrowToDraw stroke];

    // Fill in the arrow.
    [arrowFillColor set];
    [arrowToDraw fill];
}
```

11. Finally, add the implementation for the `drawCircle` method, as shown in Example A-4.

Example A-4. Implementation for the drawCircle Method

```
- (void)drawCircle
{
    // The local copy of the circle that will be drawn.
    NSBezierPath *circleToDraw;

    // Transformation matricies to use.
    NSAffineTransform *translationMatrix;
    NSAffineTransform *scaleMatrix;

    // Draw circle at this location.
    NSPoint screenLocation = NSMakePoint(50, 50);
```

Example A-4. Implementation for the drawCircle Method (continued)

```
    // Colors for the circle outline and fill.
    NSColor *circleStrokeColor = [NSColor blackColor];
    NSColor *circleFillColor = [NSColor redColor];

    // The size of the circle.
    float circleRadius = 10.0;

    // Create and configure the translation matrix.
    translationMatrix = [NSAffineTransform transform];
    [translationMatrix translateXBy: screenLocation.x
            yBy: screenLocation.y];

    // Create and configure the scaling matrix.
    scaleMatrix = [NSAffineTransform transform];
    [scaleMatrix scaleBy: circleRadius];

    // Combine the scaling and translation operations.
    [scaleMatrix appendTransform:translationMatrix];

    // Transform the circle path for drawing.
    circleToDraw = [scaleMatrix transformBezierPath:[self circlePath]];

    // Fill the circle.
    [circleFillColor set];
    [circleToDraw fill];

    // Stroke (outline) the circle.
    [circleStrokeColor set];
    [circleToDraw setLineWidth:2.0];
    [circleToDraw stroke];
}
```

Now build and test the program. You should see something like the output shown in Figure A-14.

Draw with Quartz Primitives

In general, you should be able to use the classes and functions in Cocoa for your application's drawing needs. If you find there is some functionality that you require that isn't provided by Cocoa, you can use the Core Graphics APIs directly. For the most part, the Cocoa drawing functions and objects have very little overhead compared with the overhead of the actual screen drawing operations. If, as a result of performance measurements, you find that the overhead is significant, this may also be reason to use the Core Graphics APIs.

Note that the Cocoa functions and objects will interact with the Cocoa display machinery more smoothly than with the Core Graphics calls. For instance, changing the current transformation matrix using Core Graphics may cause Cocoa objects in that context to be rendered incorrectly (rotated text, for instance, when drawn by the text subsystem). If you change the current transformation matrix using NSView, everything will work as expected.

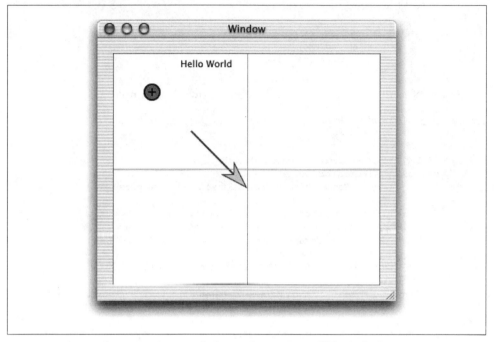

Figure A-14. Simple Draw output with shapes drawn using NSBezierPath

This section shows you how to modify the Simple Draw application from the previous sections to use Core Graphics drawing primitives in an NSView. The new version of the program will draw a multicolored spiral pattern in the upper-right-hand corner of MyView.

1. In Project Builder, open the Simple Draw project if it is not already open.

2. Select the Add Frameworks command in the Project menu and add the Core Services framework to the Simple Draw project. The Core Services framework is an umbrella framework that includes the Core Graphics framework. You need to link against the Core Graphics framework to use its drawing primitives.

3. Open MyView.m and import the Application Services header:

   ```
   #import <ApplicationServices/ApplicationServices.h>
   ```

4. Add the following local variables to the top of the drawRect: method. These variables will be used, respectively, as loop indices and angles, and to hold the Core Graphics context reference necessary to do Core Graphics drawing:

```
- (void)drawRect:(NSRect)rect {
    int i, j;
    float a0, a1;
    CGContextRef context;
    NSRect myBounds = [self bounds];
    /*...*/
```

5. At the bottom of drawRect:, add the code shown in Example A-5.

Example A-5. A drawRect: Implementation That Uses Quartz Primitives

```
/*...*/
// Get the Core Graphics context from MyView's window.
context = [[NSGraphicsContext
        graphicsContextWithWindow:[self window]] graphicsPort];

// Translate to the upper right corner of the view.
// Remember CG doesn't see the isFlipped setting so it's
// still using a coordinate system with the origin in the lower left.
CGContextTranslateCTM(context,
    NSMidX(myBounds) + 80.0, NSMidY(myBounds) + 80.0);

// Scale the transformation matrix to shrink the size of the drawing.
CGContextScaleCTM(context, 40.0, 40.0);

// Draw a sequence of Bezier curves.
for (i = 0; i < 20; i++) {
    CGContextSetRGBFillColor(context, i/19.0, i/30.0, 0.0, 1.0);
    CGContextScaleCTM(context, 0.9, 0.9);
    CGContextMoveToPoint(context, 1.0, 0.0);
    for (j = 0; j < 12; j++) {
        a0 = 2 * M_PI * (j + 0.5) / 12;
        a1 = 2 * M_PI * (j + 1.0) / 12;
        CGContextAddCurveToPoint(context, 2*cos(a0), 2*sin(a0),
            2*cos(a0), 2*sin(a0), cos(a1), sin(a1));
    }

    CGContextClosePath(context);
    CGContextFillPath(context);
}
}
```

Once again, build and test the program. You should see something like the output shown in Figure A-15.

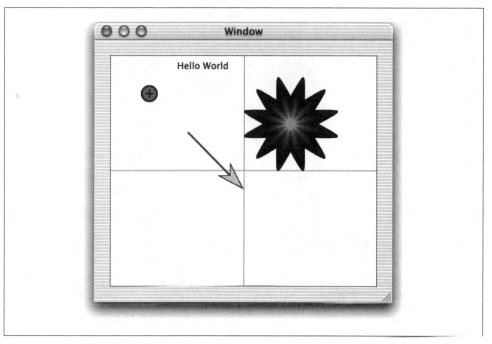

Figure A-15. The output of Simple Draw after adding Core Graphics calls

Spend a few minutes looking through the Core Graphics header files to familiarize yourself with what's availible in the API. You'll find the headers in the Core Graphics framework inside the Application Services framework in Project Builder's Groups and Files list. Some of the most interesting headers are:

- `CGGeometry.h`. This header defines the basic data types: CGPoint, CGSize, and CGRect, along with a set of functions for manipulating them.

- `CGContext.h`. This header contains the drawing operators.

- `CGAffineTransform.h`. This header contains functions for manipulating a transformation matrix.

You can learn a lot about drawing with Cocoa simply from spending some time modifying these examples. For more ideas to experiment with, look in Application Kit headers `NSView.h`, `NSBezierPath.h`, `NSGeometry.h`, `NSAffineTransform.h`, `NSFont.h`, `NSColor.h`, `NSGraphics.h`, and `NSImage.h`.

Index

Symbols

< > (angle brackets), protocol names in, 33
{} (braces) and delimiter checking, 43
[] (square brackets)
  message expressions, 22, 28, 36
    delimiter checking, 43
; (semicolon)
  terminating declarations with, 35
  terminating statements with, 36
: (colon), arguments in method declarations, 33
- (minus), preceding instance method declarations, 33, 35
+ (plus), preceding class method declarations, 33, 37
- minus, preceding instance method declarations, 37
// preprocessor directive, 29

Numbers

3 × 3 matrix, 325
3D graphics, using OpenGL, 5
@"" directive, 55

A

accessor methods
  implementing
    in Expenses application, 159, 162
    for selectedDay instance variable, 257
    selectedItem method, 264

setCurrentItems: method, 267
  for ToDoCell class, 301
  for ToDoItem class, 245
  in Travel Advisor tutorial, 202
initDataModelWithDictionary: method, acting as, 266
reference counting in, 94
setTimer: method, 245
action methods
  first responder, 225
  implementing, 89, 264
actions
  connecting
    CalendarMatrix class, 249
    text fields to, 190
    ToDoDocument class, 263
    user interface controls to, 86, 119
  defining
    for classes, 85, 116
    for TAController class, 192
activeDays dictionary, 308, 310
addRecord: method, 192
  connecting TAController via, 194
  implementing, 211
  testing implementation for extractFields: method, 206
  updating modified records, 210
Adobe Photoshop, creating source art for icons, 316
alert sheets, implementing, 142-144

We'd like to hear your suggestions for improving our indexes. Send email to *index@oreilly.com*.

About the Author

Learning Cocoa was created by the technical writers, engineers, support specialists, and other professionals at Apple Computer who are committed to making Mac OS X a superior platform for innovation, productivity, and enjoyment. These professionals have diligently collected, compiled, and edited the information in these books to ensure that it is a useful resource for Mac OS X developers.

Colophon

Our look is the result of reader comments, our own experimentation, and feedback from distribution channels. Distinctive covers complement our distinctive approach to technical topics, breathing personality and life into potentially dry subjects.

The animal on the cover of *Learning Cocoa* is an Irish setter. Bred as a sporting dog in the early 19th century, the Irish setter's agility and energy made it a prime companion for pheasant and quail hunters. By the 1890s, the dog's attractive, silky red coat and elegant build boosted its popularity as a show dog. For the past century, breeders have created a larger dog with a longer coat, with deep chestnut red or patches of red and white hair. The dog is also popular as a family dog. Described as loyal, gentle, energetic, and happy, the Irish setter gets along well with children. Some hospitals, nursing homes, and rehabilitation centers also adopt the Irish setter as a therapy dog.

Ann Schirmer was the production editor and proofreader for *Learning Cocoa*. Norma Emory was the copyeditor. Claire Cloutier, Jeffrey Holcomb, and Sarah Jane Shangraw provided quality control. Judy Hoer wrote the index. Interior composition was done by Claire Cloutier and Ann Schirmer. Emma Colby designed the cover of this book, based on a series design by Edie Freedman. The cover image is a 19th-century engraving from the Dover Pictorial Archive. Emma Colby produced the cover layout with QuarkXPress 4.1 using Adobe's ITC Garamond font.

Melanie Wang designed the interior layout based on a series design by Nancy Priest. Jason McIntosh converted *Learning Cocoa* into DocBook XML from Apple's native XML format and formatted the book with a program created by Norman Walsh, Lenny Muellner, and Erik Ray. The text and heading fonts are ITC Garamond Light and Garamond Book; the code font is Constant Willison. The illustrations that appear in the book were produced by Robert Romano and Jessamyn Read using Macromedia FreeHand 9 and Adobe Photoshop 6. This colophon was written by Ann Schirmer.

Whenever possible, our books use a durable and flexible lay-flat binding. If the page count exceeds this binding's limit, perfect binding is used.

How to stay in touch with O'Reilly

1. Visit Our Award-Winning Web Site

http://www.oreilly.com/

★"Top 100 Sites on the Web" —*PC Magazine*
★"Top 5% Web sites" —*Point Communications*
★"3-Star site" —*The McKinley Group*

Our web site contains a library of comprehensive product information (including book excerpts and tables of contents), downloadable software, background articles, interviews with technology leaders, links to relevant sites, book cover art, and more. File us in your Bookmarks or Hotlist!

2. Join Our Email Mailing Lists

New Product Releases

To receive automatic email with brief descriptions of all new O'Reilly products as they are released, send email to:
ora-news-subscribe@lists.oreilly.com
Put the following information in the first line of your message (*not* in the Subject field):
subscribe ora-news

O'Reilly Events

If you'd also like us to send information about trade show events, special promotions, and other O'Reilly events, send email to:
ora-news-subscribe@lists.oreilly.com
Put the following information in the first line of your message (*not* in the Subject field):
subscribe ora-events

3. Get Examples from Our Books via FTP

There are two ways to access an archive of example files from our books:

Regular FTP

- ftp to:
  ftp.oreilly.com
  (login: anonymous
  password: your email address)
- Point your web browser to:
  ftp://ftp.oreilly.com/

FTPMAIL

- Send an email message to:
  ftpmail@online.oreilly.com
  (Write "help" in the message body)

4. Contact Us via Email

order@oreilly.com
To place a book or software order online. Good for North American and international customers.

subscriptions@oreilly.com
To place an order for any of our newsletters or periodicals.

books@oreilly.com
General questions about any of our books.

software@oreilly.com
For general questions and product information about our software. Check out O'Reilly Software Online at **http://software.oreilly.com/** for software and technical support information. Registered O'Reilly software users send your questions to: **website-support@oreilly.com**

cs@oreilly.com
For answers to problems regarding your order or our products.

booktech@oreilly.com
For book content technical questions or corrections.

proposals@oreilly.com
To submit new book or software proposals to our editors and product managers.

international@oreilly.com
For information about our international distributors or translation queries. For a list of our distributors outside of North America check out:
http://www.oreilly.com/distributors.html

5. Work with Us

Check out our website for current employment opportunites:
http://jobs.oreilly.com/

O'Reilly & Associates, Inc.
101 Morris Street, Sebastopol, CA 95472 USA
TEL   707-829-0515 or 800-998-9938
          (6am to 5pm PST)
FAX   707-829-0104

O'REILLY®

International Distributors

UK, EUROPE, MIDDLE EAST AND AFRICA (EXCEPT FRANCE, GERMANY, AUSTRIA, SWITZERLAND, LUXEMBOURG, AND LIECHTENSTEIN)

INQUIRIES

O'Reilly UK Limited
4 Castle Street
Farnham
Surrey, GU9 7HS
United Kingdom
Telephone: 44-1252-711776
Fax: 44-1252-734211
Email: information@oreilly.co.uk

ORDERS

Wiley Distribution Services Ltd.
1 Oldlands Way
Bognor Regis
West Sussex PO22 9SA
United Kingdom
Telephone: 44-1243-843294
UK Freephone: 0800-243207
Fax: 44-1243-843302 (Europe/EU orders)
or 44-1243-843274 (Middle East/Africa)
Email: cs-books@wiley.co.uk

FRANCE

INQUIRIES & ORDERS

Éditions O'Reilly
18 rue Séguier
75006 Paris, France
Tel: 1-40-51-71-89
Fax: 1-40-51-72-26
Email: france@oreilly.fr

GERMANY, SWITZERLAND, AUSTRIA, LUXEMBOURG, AND LIECHTENSTEIN

INQUIRIES & ORDERS

O'Reilly Verlag
Balthasarstr. 81
D-50670 Köln, Germany
Telephone: 49-221-973160-91
Fax: 49-221-973160-8
Email: anfragen@oreilly.de (inquiries)
Email: order@oreilly.de (orders)

CANADA (FRENCH LANGUAGE BOOKS)

Les Éditions Flammarion ltée
375, Avenue Laurier Ouest
Montréal (Québec) H2V 2K3
Tel: 00-1-514-277-8807
Fax: 00-1-514-278-2085
Email: info@flammarion.qc.ca

HONG KONG

City Discount Subscription Service, Ltd.
Unit A, 6th Floor, Yan's Tower
27 Wong Chuk Hang Road
Aberdeen, Hong Kong
Tel: 852-2580-3539
Fax: 852-2580-6463
Email: citydis@ppn.com.hk

KOREA

Hanbit Media, Inc.
Chungmu Bldg. 210
Yonnam-dong 568-33
Mapo-gu
Seoul, Korea
Tel: 822-325-0397
Fax: 822-325-9697
Email: hant93@chollian.dacom.co.kr

PHILIPPINES

Global Publishing
G/F Benavides Garden
1186 Benavides Street
Manila, Philippines
Tel: 632-254-8949/632-252-2582
Fax: 632-734-5060/632-252-2733
Email: globalp@pacific.net.ph

TAIWAN

O'Reilly Taiwan
1st Floor, No. 21, Lane 295
Section 1, Fu-Shing South Road
Taipei, 106 Taiwan
Tel: 886-2-27099669
Fax: 886-2-27038802
Email: mori@oreilly.com

INDIA

Shroff Publishers & Distributors Pvt. Ltd.
12, "Roseland", 2nd Floor
180, Waterfield Road, Bandra (West)
Mumbai 400 050
Tel: 91-22-641-1800/643-9910
Fax: 91-22-643-2422
Email: spd@vsnl.com

CHINA

O'Reilly Beijing
SIGMA Building, Suite B809
No. 49 Zhichun Road
Haidian District
Beijing, China PR 100080
Tel: 86-10-8809-7475
Fax: 86-10-8809-7463
Email: beijing@oreilly.com

JAPAN

O'Reilly Japan, Inc.
Yotsuya Y's Building
7 Banch 6, Honshio-cho
Shinjuku-ku
Tokyo 160-0003 Japan
Tel: 81-3-3356-5227
Fax: 81-3-3356-5261
Email: japan@oreilly.com

SINGAPORE, INDONESIA, MALAYSIA AND THAILAND

TransQuest Publishers Pte Ltd
30 Old Toh Tuck Road #05-02
Sembawang Kimtrans Logistics Centre
Singapore 597654
Tel: 65-4623112
Fax: 65-4625761
Email: wendiw@transquest.com.sg

ALL OTHER ASIAN COUNTRIES

O'Reilly & Associates, Inc.
101 Morris Street
Sebastopol, CA 95472 USA
Tel: 707-829-0515
Fax: 707-829-0104
Email: order@oreilly.com

AUSTRALIA

Woodslane Pty., Ltd.
7/5 Vuko Place
Warriewood NSW 2102
Australia
Tel: 61-2-9970-5111
Fax: 61-2-9970-5002
Email: info@woodslane.com.au

NEW ZEALAND

Woodslane New Zealand, Ltd.
21 Cooks Street (P.O. Box 575)
Waganui, New Zealand
Tel: 64-6-347-6543
Fax: 64-6-345-4840
Email: info@woodslane.com.au

ARGENTINA

Distribuidora Cuspide
Suipacha 764
1008 Buenos Aires
Argentina
Phone: 5411-4322-8868
Fax: 5411-4322-3456
Email: libros@cuspide.com

O'REILLY®